THE
INVINCIBLES

THE INSIDE STORY OF
THE 1982 KANGAROOS
THE TEAM THAT CHANGED RUGBY FOREVER

MARK FLANAGAN

First published by Pitch Publishing, 2019

Pitch Publishing
A2 Yeoman Gate
Yeoman Way
Worthing
Sussex
BN13 3QZ
www.pitchpublishing.co.uk
info@pitchpublishing.co.uk

A CIP catalogue record is available for this book
from the British Library.

ISBN 978 1 78531 526 8

Typesetting and origination by Pitch Publishing
Printed and bound in India by Replika Press Pvt. Ltd.

Contents

Foreword

T HE 1982 Kangaroos were like nothing that had ever been seen before. Not only were they supremely skilful and athletic, but they seemed to have a command of time and space that defied the laws of physics. Through them, so it seemed, we caught a glimpse of what it would be like if an advanced civilisation from outer space ever landed on Earth.

The 1982 Kangaroos were not only the greatest rugby league team ever to play the game, they were also one of the greatest sports teams of all time.

Max Krilich and his men belong in the pantheon alongside Pele's 1970 Brazil, Dave Gallacher's 1905 All Blacks and America's 1992 Olympic basketball 'Dream Team'.

As Mark Flanagan points out in these pages, no one in Australia or Britain had any sense of what was about to happen when the tourists left Sydney. But, as the first matches of the tour unfolded, those who saw the Kangaroos play realised that something profound was happening. And that became apparent to everyone on the Saturday of October 1982 when the first Test was broadcast on the BBC.

Great Britain were humiliated, but by the end of the match no one really cared. We were watching players from another planet. Attack that seemed to be unstoppable. Defence that appeared impenetrable. Backs who played like forwards. Forwards who played like backs.

These were names that belonged to the ages. Eric Grothe ran with the ball as if he was auditioning for *Easy Rider*. Mal Meninga looked like the Colossus at Rhodes had come to life and decided to be a rugby league player. Peter Sterling appeared to know the precise position and intention of every player on the pitch before they themselves knew. Wayne Pearce seemed to have dropped in from the 21st century to show how the rugby league player of the future would play. And that is not even to mention such titans as Brett Kenny, Wally Lewis, Steve Rogers, Kerry Boustead and Ray Price.

The sheer breathtaking brilliance of the Kangaroos made the tour the most extraordinary sporting experience that British rugby league supporters had ever known. This was rugby league, but not as we knew it. This was the game how we had dreamed it could be, played at unrelenting pace and intensity by the most skilful athletes in the world.

They were the greatest team playing the greatest game of all. And rugby league still lives in their shadow today.

This book is their tribute.

Tony Collins

Introduction

THE prolific rugby league author and historian Robert Gate was in no doubt: 'Max Krilich's Kangaroos of 1982 were arguably the greatest international rugby combination either code has produced in any era. All the superlatives that were rained upon them barely did them justice. They were the true "nonpareils". Even allowing for the paucity of the opposition afforded them by Great Britain, those privileged to have witnessed the complete and utter annihilation of their antagonists were acutely aware that, as rugby teams go, Australia 1982 were as near to perfection as makes no difference.'

It is a view widely held by those lucky enough to have watched the Green and Golds light up the stagnating rugby league landscape of Britain in the autumn of that year. They blew through northern strongholds like a tornado, playing at a pace and with a purpose few had ever seen.

Including their games in France, Australia broke records galore, famously becoming the first international team to win all their tour matches (22), although perhaps more striking was the points difference. They piled up 1005 – it was the final season of three points for a try – and conceded just 120. In three Tests the beleaguered home side would cross the try line just once. Such statistics shook the rugby league establishment to its core.

Frank Stanton's Kangaroos were undeniably great. They redefined what was possible, a trait that unites the absolute standout sporting performers of the last 150 years. These include the likes of Don Bradman, Tiger Woods, Michael Jordan and Lionel Messi, the 1927 New York Yankees, Rinus Michels' Ajax side of the late 60s and early 70s and the Chicago Bulls basketball team who astonished on a weekly basis in the 90s.

Many seasoned watchers could see it coming, though. In 1979 the Great Britain tourists became the first for 40 years to be whitewashed in a three-Test series. Their defeats included a humiliating 35-0 rout in the opener at Lang Park in Brisbane, when Stanton's hugely successful stint in charge of the Kangaroos was gathering momentum. It is amazing to consider that for him, and Australia, the best was yet to come.

But many others saw the coming tsunami long before that. The last great high point for British rugby league was unquestionably the 1970 tour of Australia. Coached by John Whiteley and inspired by the likes of Cliff Watson, Malcolm Reilly and Roger Millward, the Lions roared back to win the series after being humbled in the first Test. The visiting Poms were lauded back home and down under for their excellence in both defence and attack. They were considered ahead of their time. During that trip, John, who would return to the GB hotseat in 1980, visited a primary school in New South Wales and watched dozens of 10- and 11-year-olds being put through their paces. One of the players who accompanied him was Leeds winger Alan Smith, who remembers the experience as one that proved sobering for 'Gentleman John'.

'John and I were watching them and it was serious stuff, even at that age,' said Smith. 'He just turned to me and said, "This lot will thrash us in ten years' time."'

Whiteley's extraordinarily prophetic, off-the-cuff comment was borne of a man so deeply ingrained in the sport and so sure of what was critical to success. He had led Hull to many honours. As an international he had been central during the Lions' golden age and between 1956 and 1962 Britain never lost an Ashes series. Whiteley was a fitness fanatic and in the 60s and 70s spent a lot of his spare time supporting the amateur game in his native Hull. He saw first-hand the decline of the game at grassroots level. During that same period in Australia, rugby league was booming at all levels. In the 70s it was spreading from its power bases in New South Wales and Queensland to all parts of the country. At schools' level the expansion was breathtaking.

At the top, the sport itself was also undergoing something of a revolution, led by coach Jack Gibson. While the authorities were getting tough with players to curb excessive on-field violence, Gibson, who led Eastern Suburbs (in 1974 and 1975) and Parramatta (from 1981 to 1983) to multiple Sydney Premiership titles, had studied the training methods of the top American football sides and incorporated much of what he saw into his coaching ethos.

Gibson built his incredible success on spending as much of his time focusing on defence as attack. He championed the benefits of detailed preparation, the importance of conditioning and training with heavy weights, and also the merits of coaches, rather than selectors, picking teams.

By the late 70s the fruit of all those labours was becoming evident down under and by 1982 British rugby league was wholly unprepared to meet this 'perfect storm'. On the eve of their flight to the UK, Australian loose forward Ray Price confided to an Australian journalist that he believed they would win every game.

In his book, Gibson wrote: 'Winning starts on Monday, not ten minutes before the game. It's confidence all week long, and it's confidence for the month before that and the year before that. People can't be motivated on a five-minute speech before they run out onto a football paddock. It's something you have to wake up with – knowing that your preparation was right. Having the confidence that, whatever comes up, you are ready.'

Stanton and the rest of the squad were ready. Britain's coach knew it too and there was little that even he, a great champion of the game, could do about the green and gold juggernaut.

Were they the greatest rugby league team of all time?

Well, that will be debated for ever and a day but undeniably their impact was felt for decades to come in both codes of the sport. Their feats also heralded a golden age for British rugby league in terms of a wider awareness outside of its northern heartlands, although the day-to-day reality for so many English clubs in the early 1980s was one of struggling to make ends meet. For years, so many at the top of the game failed to grasp what was required of them. The sport was professional in as much as players were paid to play. Otherwise it was largely old men in smoky committee rooms concerning themselves with petty politics.

The Invincibles brought into the sharpest possible focus everything that was wrong with the British game, especially on that astonishing October day in Hull when they won the first Test 40-4. We had so much ground to make up and the story of 1982 is as much about those who refused to give up on British rugby league and realised what was required, as it is as those brave souls who tackled the Invincibles on the pitch.

It was a dark hour for those in red, white and blue but ultimately what happened then proved to be the catalyst for so much of what we enjoy now.

And when push comes to shove, we can all sit back and rejoice in the brilliance of Stanton's team. If you appreciate all that makes watching rugby league good, then you have to stand up and applaud his side for that brilliance.

At times they took our breath away.

Chapter One

The Last Hurrah

ON 20 May 1970, a group of 28 men sat in Heathrow Airport as guests of the British Overseas Airways Corporation eating lunch ahead of their 4.15pm departure for Hong Kong (flight BA936). They had already flown down from Manchester, at the start of a long journey that would eventually lead to rugby league immortality.

Overseeing the 26-man Great Britain Lions squad were Leigh chairman Jack Harding (manager) and his 'assistant' John Whiteley, who would effectively act as coach, doctor, physio, kitman and press officer. Less than two days later the Lions played the first of 24 matches in Australia and New Zealand having touched down in the sub-tropical northern outpost of Darwin just 18 hours before the first kick-off.

Tired and jet-lagged they started with a 35-12 victory in front of just 3,000 rugby league fans from the Northern Territory. It would be the first of 22 wins on what has become widely regarded as the most successful Lions adventure ever. This is unsurprising, as they are likely to remain the last British rugby league team to beat the Kangaroos in a three-match series, famously coming from one down to beat Australia. They then whitewashed New Zealand 3-0.

The future of British rugby looked bright but those in the know knew differently. One of those men was Whiteley, a renowned thinker who cared passionately for the game. He led his squad in magnificent style but his experience of how rugby league was being managed both home and abroad led to a damning conclusion. On a visit to a rugby training session at a New South Wales primary school in 1970 he was astounded by the seriousness and skill levels on display. Turning to Leeds winger Alan Smith he uttered those prophetic words, 'This lot will thrash us in ten years' time.'

'It was frightening me how much more their game had advanced compared to the last time I had been there [1958],' recalled John, almost half a century later. 'I talked to a lot of people over there so got a pretty good sense of what was happening. Ironically Alan [Smith] was a forerunner in terms of he was always trying to find ways to get fitter. He was a very good athlete. Very committed. One of the easy professionals to be a part of. When you are a coach you deal with all walks of life and Alan was one of the 100 per centers.'

Ironically it was the golden age of British dominance, which John had been part of in the late 50s and early 60s, that provided the impetus for a major rethink of how rugby league should be coached in Australia and in everything else that followed thereafter.

Leading the way in that process was the man they called 'the Bradman of League'.

Dave Brown was one of the first superstars of Australian rugby league and earned that prestigious nickname due to his prolific try-scoring efforts with Eastern Suburbs in the 1930s. In the mid-60s he was part of the Australian Rugby League's National Coaching Panel, which included former stars such as Darrel Chapman, Keith Holman, Kevin Mosman, Alf Gallagher and Frank Johnson. Their job was to co-ordinate the country's coaching policy, and a collective decision was taken to forget about trying to copy the British model of producing rugby players and instead to build on what made Australian players different. By 1965 a modified coaching qualification was produced with the emphasis on encouraging skill and athleticism. The first person to pass the new course was a young school teacher called Peter Corcoran.

Having recently returned from a stint teaching in Brisbane, Corcoran not only passed but also received a mark of 100 per cent. So impressed were Messers Brown and co that they invited him onto the panel.

Corcoran said, 'I think it was a case that Dave Brown and the others believed for too long we had been looking at the English model and the way England played rugby league and it really hadn't produced the results that we wanted because our DNA, our culture if you like, wasn't totally au fait with the English attitudes. Also, of course, if you look at the background of the great England players, our players did not have that background.

'The panel, and I wholeheartedly agreed with them, wanted to bring a new look to Australian rugby league and one of the first things they wanted to do was improve coaching because obviously if you improve coaching, which is generally at the grassroots, then we automatically started to build that broad base well versed into how to play rugby league which could eventually rise to the apex of the pyramid and prove to be a tremendous influence on interstate and international football.

'I think what I brought to them [the panel] was you had to look holistically at coaching. Not just how to play the ball, how to kick the football, how to run with it ... there was a lot more to it. There was a lot more to proper coaching that would produce the result that we wanted for rugby league. I think at that time we still had that attitude "if you've played rugby league you could be a coach" and when you became a coach you simply again did what you had done throughout your whole career.'

Corcoran was a blue-sky thinker who had spent most of his twenties immersing himself in the study of coaching across a raft of sports and now, in his early-30s, he was about to start his own revolution.

'That [studying other sports] was part of my coaching career right back in the 50s. I had seen as a young teacher some of the useless ways people were being coached and with high expectations. I made it my endeavour to find, from wherever I could, those new ways. I joined the Coaches Association of Canada, I subscribed to a number of books on other sports but [which] were entirely on coaching.

'I was particularly interested in how we could programme the player mentally to realise there was more to it than just lace up your boots and just go out there and throw a ball around. In those days we had captain/coaches and a lot of players relied on him to take the lead. In my mind every player on the field was a leader. They had to be thinkers and if you are required to be a thinker you have to have knowledge to back that up, to give you the necessary number of options that would allow you, at any one stage, to take the action that was most appropriate rather than something that people had just been doing for ages.'

Corcoran also stressed the need to get scientific and also the importance of dealing with the person and not just the player. That belief was reinforced by spending time with a man regarded by most rugby league aficionados in Australia as 'the father of modern coaching'.

'One of the most important people I have ever met was Duncan Thompson up in Toowoomba. His approach was revolutionary and to my mind just what we wanted. He brought in what has commonly become known as "contract football". He promoted the feeling when you went out on the field and when you went to training, and, in fact, whenever you were together, [that] there was a binding contract which said, "I will look after you, I will watch your back. I will play my part and together we will have a good team."'

The new way of coaching coincided with a significant growth in schools' rugby league in the late 60s and early 70s. By 1970 there were 43,000 boys playing the game down under. The prestigious University Shield (U-18s) schools' competition in New South Wales was just one example of how the sport was taking hold. In 1969 the number of schools taking part was 118. Twelve months later that figure was 147.

In contrast, the introduction of the comprehensive school system in the UK in 1965 marked the start of a serious decline in schools playing rugby league. While the opposite was expected to happen, schools who had previously played rugby league switched instead to union so that they could organise fixtures against former grammar schools. In the 80s the numbers did start to rise again but that talent stream was reduced to a drip for a long time, which in turn affected amateur rugby league. That, together with a complete lack of long-term planning by the Rugby Football League (RFL), proved to be a recipe for disaster.

Corcoran added, 'The people that I worked with in those early days realised the tremendous significance of having people in a school background playing rugby league. School football was always strong but became a lot stronger in the late 60s and early 70s and from then on as well. But I think as far as the people I worked with were concerned we needed to get the attitude of our coaches and people in rugby league focused on the core skills and attitudes that were absolutely essential if you wanted to build on something to achieve success later on.

'That was the whole aim in those early days – to get people involved in courses to re-orientate the mindset towards rugby league not being a game of brawn – and I'm being a little bit careful there – but being a game of skill. Coupled with speed, it would become a powerful game that would get us the results we needed.'

The University Shield became a breeding ground for top players. It was split into 16 geographical regions with divisional winners playing knockout rugby. The final and the third and fourth place play-off took place at the Redfern Oval, the former home of the South Sydney Rabbitohs. The knockout matches attracted comprehensive TV coverage and would often be used as warm-up attractions ahead of more senior matches. On 4 July 1970 the last-16 tie between Tamworth and Riverstone schools was played at the Sydney Cricket Ground (SCG) and used as a taster for the third Ashes Test. Most pundits came away from the SCG that evening convinced that the Poms were set for a period of domination. However, the really significant match was actually the U-18s schools affair that preceded it. That fixture showcased the future while the Great Britain coach's ability to mould a brilliant team effectively acted as a giant sticking plaster on the game back home. The Lions of 1970 could play in any type of style, although, as it was the only Ashes tour played under the four-tackle rule, there were some frenetic, high-scoring encounters.

Captained by St Helens centre Frank Myler, the tourists scored 33 tries in winning their opening five matches ahead of the first Test at Lang Park, Brisbane on 6 June. However, in that game, their hopes of regaining the Ashes appeared to have taken a near fatal blow with the Kangaroos running out 37-15 victors. It was the first time since 1928 that the opening Test had been played in the Queensland stronghold and the match became synonymous with the brutal nature of the game at that time, producing what was perhaps the most famous headbutt in rugby league. Australian prop Jim Morgan unwisely tried to engage St Helens prop Cliff Watson, who later recalled: 'Jimmy came up and gave me a nudge on the nose with his head. So I thought, I'm not going to let him get away with that and hit him correctly and down he went.'

However, more importantly was the number of penalties being conceded by the visitors for 'technical offences', which gave the margin of victory a rather lop-sided look. After all, the home side had only outscored their opponents 5-3 in terms of tries. The Great Britain coach more recently conceded that it just took his young side a while to adjust to a different style of officiating.

'When you went to Australia the referees' interpretation was vastly different,' said John. 'I think that in the first game in Darwin the penalty count was 19-1. In the tour we had meetings with the referees and I think we brought one of them down to training to referee us. Obviously you are refereed by local referees and sometimes you don't think you are going to get a fair crack. I don't mean that nastily … the fervour of the crowd would sway decisions. Also, against those country sides you are that much faster and it sometimes looks like you are cheating. But in Brisbane we were beaten fair and square.'

The first Test defeat proved a wake-up call for the squad, a fact summed up in no uncertain terms by Millward, who laid bare the feeling within the GB camp in an article published in the Australian press.

'I think our poor first performance against you [Australia] in the first Test was due to the easy early matches we had. We made the big mistake of getting complacent. There we were riding along on the crest of a wave, getting easy victories, scoring tries like they were going out of style. Then … wham! You fooled us into thinking we were the greatest team of unbeatables ever. The truth is that before the first Test we didn't have any idea what Australia's potential was.'

John added, 'By the time we got to Brisbane a lot of the young lads were cock-a-hoop and thought they were seasoned internationals. But I was telling them "you have been sailing through calm waters so far and a storm is about to hit us", and we were hit by a storm that day. They came at us like something we had never experienced before ... strength and speed and ferocity. All the ingredients. We never really got into the game.

'On the Monday after the Brisbane Test we had a meeting at the training ground and discussed it in depth. How our attitude and mentality had been building up to that match. They [the Australian squad] all played in the Sydney Premiership and were playing in the highest standard comp in the world every week. We talked about it and realised we had quality players and were getting fitter. I knew we were quickly getting stronger, and built on that team spirit by building this strength through mindset, because we knew we had players who were capable of playing at that level. But it meant all of us being united. By the time that second Test came we were really firing. If that team had stuck together for two or three years they would have been invincible.'

While many pundits back home feared the worst, what was largely unknown was the huge effort being made to be physically up for the challenge. John had been given just enough time to get his young squad up to scratch. There were good early signs that they were buying into the coach's ethos.

'Every morning on that tour I went for a run before breakfast and when I got back one day Malcolm Reilly was leaning over the balustrades and he was asking about the run and he wanted to come with me the next morning. So, true to his word, the next day he joined me and when we got back half a dozen of them were waiting for us. By the end of the week everyone in the squad was running with me.'

The final warm-up encounter ahead of the second Test was against a formidable-looking New South Wales XIII – an unofficial 'fourth Test' – and the manner in which the tourists fought back from 15-2 down reflected their improved resolve and fitness. Only a brilliant tackle by Wests centre John Cootes denied the tourists a victory, the game finishing 17-17. It would be the last time they failed to win.

Seven days later came the second Test in Sydney where John made seven changes from the Brisbane mauling. Castleford full-back Derek Edwards replaced Bradford's Terry Price, Leeds winger Alan Smith was given a go in place of Hull's Clive Sullivan, and centre Syd Hynes took over from his Leeds team-mate Mick Shoebottom. At stand-off it was widely considered a huge gamble to allow Roger Millward to collect his third Lions cap as a replacement for Castleford legend Alan Hardisty. In the pack, young buck Dave Chisnall (Leigh) made way for experienced Castleford prop Dennis Hartley, Bradford hooker Tony Fisher got the nod ahead of Hull KR star Peter 'Flash' Flanagan and in the back row Featherstone's dynamic young second-rower Jimmy Thompson came in for Wigan's Dave Robinson.

'Jimmy Thompson was typical of what was happening,' recalls John. 'Jimmy was unknown, nobody had heard of him and he was a quiet and unassuming young man. Once he came into the fold he became a character of the side and improved beyond all recognition. His tackling was unbelievable. His courage … he was like a silent assassin.'

As a player John had been part of the outstanding 1958 Lions squad and used the team's historic status to motivate his players to keep pushing themselves.

'But all the players were contributing so well by that point … we were blowing teams away. It became a thing after each game: I would go into the changing room after and say … "Yes but you will never be as good as that 1958 team", and every time they would reply with:, "Whiteley … whack that!" It became a war cry.'

In Sydney, the Green and Golds, coached by the relatively-inexperienced Arthur Summons, were without talismanic captain and full-back Graeme Langlands, who had broken his thumb. Also missing through injury were pack leader Ron Lynch, prop Jim Morgan and hooker Elwyn Walters. Langlands in particular was going to be a big miss and many local pundits were also concerned that the new faces, particularly in the forwards, contributed to an overall sense that the side had lost a great deal of mobility and weight.

The changes contributed to a dramatic turnaround in fortunes as Millward claimed two brilliant tries in inspiring a 28-7 win, achieved despite Hynes being sent off midway through the second half for kicking out.

The Kangaroos had more injury problems for the decider with John Sattler now unavailable. The South Sydney stalwart had captained the side in Langlands' absence, which would mean a third skipper in as many matches. That honour went to St George stand-off Phil Hawthorne.

Meanwhile, John had a big decision to make at full-back with Edwards having picked up a rib injury and a type of whiplash against Riverina in the final warm-up clash before the Sydney showdown. With Ray Dutton out because of a dislocated shoulder the pundits expected Price to return to the position he had filled in the Brisbane opener, but centre Shoebottom was named in the No 1 position instead.

'Mick was a wonderfully versatile player,' said John. 'He was strong and was a big lad. You could play him anywhere. He filled in superbly.'

An interception try from John Atkinson, collecting a wild pass from Arthur Beetson, set the Lions on their way to victory. Even though they scored four more tries to Australia's one, the game was in the balance until the dying moments when Millward was the beneficiary of some excellent work from Dougie Laughton, who jinked past one and passed out of the tackle with perfect timing enabling the Hull KR stand-off to sprint onto the ball and score in the corner. For the first time in eight years Great Britain had won an Ashes series.

It was fitting that Roger 'the Dodger' should have the final say and ensure that justice was done. Even World Cup hero Bobby Charlton was rugby league-savvy enough to see that his fellow countrymen's dominance was not reflected in the final score (21-17).

'The scoreline looks ridiculous,' said Bobby. 'There was only one side in it as far as football was concerned and that was Britain.'

Manager Harding added, 'We beat the Australians and the referee and the touch-judges, who tried to give them all the penalty goal chances they could.'

The Leigh chairman was also delighted to report back to the RFL that the tour had made $150,000 with each player receiving a bonus of $2,001.10 (£984). In a sign of the times, more than half that amount came as a result of a TV commercial for Big Ben Pies.

It was a great moment for British sport and John puts their achievements alongside what the 1982 Invincibles would go on to achieve.

'We went to Australia and only lost one game. Everywhere we went we were commended on the discipline and in that third Test we were clapped off. Aussie fans don't normally clap off opposition sides.'

All of a sudden the British coach was a man in demand. According to former Wakefield player Brian Briggs, who was working for the Sydney club St George, John was offered an annual £4,000 to emigrate and join the St George coaching team, a claim that John later denied. However, Australia had already proved too tempting for the likes of Jim Mills and Tommy Bishop, who both missed out on a place in the Lions squad because they were playing down under.

'I did get an offer from a club called Dapto, who were a country club near Sydney,' recalls John. 'They wanted me to be in charge of all the county around Dapto, all the schools and things, but I had just gone into my own business and was doing well. I declined the offer. I never wanted to leave Hull.'

While the Lions coach was not going to emigrate he was happy to offer his hosts some advice. Speaking to *Big League* journalist Bill Mordey, he said, 'There is bags of potential in Australia and I feel you will be hard to beat in the World Cup. But Australia's style of play will have to be changed radically so that tries can be scored and the team don't rely on goal kicks. On muddy grounds back home goal kicks are no good and only try scoring will win matches. I think Australia's negative type of football enabled us to regain the Ashes. Once we organised our defence nothing was offered by Australia. A style change in Australia's play is desperately needed and if this is accomplished any side it fields will be hard to beat in the World Cup.'

Australia's answer in the short term was a good deal less sophisticated than that. The World Cup final at Headingley in November would become known as the 'Battle of Leeds', with the fixture, shown live on the BBC, making headlines for all the wrong reasons. Australia's victory would prove to be a very sad end to John's first stint as Great Britain coach. Ahead of the tournament he had told the players that he was going to resign at its conclusion.

Speaking on the subject nearly 50 years later it was obvious his treatment at the hands of the RFL still hurt.

'I had three kids and a mortgage and got a letter for the remuneration for the 13 weeks [of the tour] for £200. I had to borrow £400 off my dad because I came home and I didn't have a penny. The week before I went to Australia I got a letter from the RFL saying that Jack Harding was getting £250 and they didn't think it was fair I got the same as him. So they deducted me £50. When I got back every player got a £1000 bonus and I never got an extra penny or even one letter of thank you from that office.

'But I am clever and the World Cup was in England and I knew I would be the boss and the players loved me. Money couldn't buy that. Then we all meet on a Monday at Headingley and all the players sign a contract because sponsorship had come into the game. I am last to be seen. I am in debt from the tour and I have never been reimbursed and I'm coming back to my car and there is a knock on the window and it is Bill Fallowfield (RFL secretary) and he says: "I want a word with you, John."

'I walked back with him towards the offices and he put his hand on my shoulders and said to me, "I will give you £15."

'I didn't remember driving home. I was numb. I got home and Joan [his wife] thought I had had a crash. I felt ill. I told her I was finished in professional rugby league. I couldn't afford to do it. I used to go and watch all these players and never claim for expenses. No one ever mentioned expenses to me and never in my life did I claim a penny.'

On the Wednesday before the first game John told the players he was seeing out the World Cup and then finishing. His wage structure meant that for the tournament he would be paid the princely sum of £60. By that time he was running West Hull Working Men's Club so financially he was reasonably secure in the long term. He was also coaching Hull KR, having joined the Craven Park club a couple of weeks after returning from the New Zealand leg of the Lions tour).

Back in Australia the rugby league establishment were still coming to terms with the manner in which they had lost the Ashes, and coach Summons's parting shot, before he was replaced by Newtown's Harry Bath, was to suggest that the Kangaroos might not regain the Ashes for another decade.

'This is unquestionably the best side to come to Australia since 1962 and it may be the start of a cycle for England,' said Summons. 'With the young talent they have at their disposal and the quality of players still at home, England could dominate the series for the next ten years.' His view was echoed by many of the respected writers of the day, not least Allan Clarkson of the *Sydney Morning Herald*, who pointed to the ages of Britain's stars. Reilly, Millward, Atkinson, Thompson and Lowe were all 23 or younger.

World Cup winners they may have been but the manner in which the Kangaroos lost 24-2 to New Zealand the following June suggested that Summons could have been right – but for an extraordinary meeting of minds in Hawaii which helped to ensure instead that his prediction was way off the mark.

In December 1970, former Eastern Suburbs coach Jack Gibson was on holiday in Honolulu. But for him this was not a trip to enjoy beaches and warm Pacific temperatures. In town that week were all the coaches and general managers of America's National Football League (NFL), who met annually to discuss rule changes and other ways to improve top-level American football.

Gibson was hoping to gatecrash the party and pick some brains and fell on his feet with a chance meeting with San Francisco 49ers head coach Dick Nolan, who had just been named NFL coach of the year.

Chatting to former player and coach Roy Masters, Gibson explained his reasons for learning everything he could from the NFL: 'Their game is the same as ours. The only difference is the rules. They're looking for the same type of individual as we are: 6ft 6in, 17st and can run the 100 yards in 9.6 seconds. We're looking for people who can run the ball, catch and kick it. So are they. I went there because I was looking to learn something.'

It was in Hawaii that Gibson also took delight in learning of the value their game placed on the coaches themselves.

'I earned the right to be the sole selector. I spent years working with five and six selectors who didn't know which way the goalposts were pointing. I couldn't work to my potential until I got my way. If it wasn't working out they could have sacked me. More often than not you spent more time Tuesday night in selections than you would training the football team on two nights. Often [the meetings] would last one and a half hours – you'd be arguing your point, because in those days, selectors would have a lot to do with buying players and they'd sweetheart their own buys. They'd want them in the team … very seldom was it a true selection when you had to contend with five or six selectors.'

In 1967, his first full season coaching Easts, they won nine games in a row to make the play-offs and he was remunerated to the tune of $1,000. The following year they finished a place higher but he only received $800.

'I was thinking it was lucky I didn't run second or I might have got $600,' Gibson reportedly said. 'If I won the comp I might have just got a handshake. So I was very peeved about that and I just picked up my kit bag and left. I never told them why. If they didn't know why, well that was tough luck.'

Thereafter Gibson vowed that he would be the highest paid employee of any other club he coached; however, his lasting legacy was his commitment to defence and how his attention to detail gave him the edge over his opponents.

Speaking after he retired, he said, 'Now the modern coach is really conscious of his defence. In those days, selectors were only worried whether a player could run the ball. It didn't matter if he could tackle as long as he could advance it. But with our defence the boy who could run the football wasn't so successful because week after week we would jam our defence. We made that our number one priority. We gave recognition to players who went well in defence. I'd read out: "He made 17 tackles. He made three in a row." We drilled it in because in the old days, if you went to football training, there was no such thing as spending one minute on defence. They would spend one and a half hours running the football but on Sunday you are lucky to have the ball 50 per cent of the time. In reality, as training, the coach should spend 50 per cent of time on defence and 50 per cent on attack. That's what happens on game day.'

In 1971 Gibson took over St George and took them all the way to the Grand Final where the star-laden South Sydney Rabbitohs awaited. There would be no fairytale finish for the underdogs – they lost 16-10 – but Gibson had once again reminded everyone he was a coaching force to be reckoned with, although it is doubtful that even the man himself could imagine what he would achieve during the next decade.

That was the year that Malcolm Reilly joined Manly, and other top British performers – Cliff Watson, Phil Lowe and Dewsbury's star hooker Mike Stephenson – would soon join him in the Sydney Premiership.

And there was something of a shock introduction to training for the former Castleford loose forward.

'The natural advantages of a good climate and an abundance of good food became apparent in my early days in Australia after I made the big move,' said Reilly in his autobiography. 'I remember an informal training run in Manly which gave me quite a jolt on the subject of fitness. Manly coach Ron Willey arrived on the morning of the second day after my arrival to take me for a gallop. We had a run with Ken Arthurson (Manly club secretary) and some other guys around the front and around the harbour side of Manly. I was 23 at the time and considered myself fairly fit, having come from straight out of the English season.

'Some of the guys I was running with must have been in their late fifties or early sixties and I thought to myself, "I'm going to be waiting around for these old fellas." Anyhow we took off and they finished up waiting for me. I was one of those people who try very hard to compete but back then did not have the aerobic fitness level that they had. It really got me thinking. I mean, some of these blokes were 40 years older than me, yet they left me behind. And when we got there – I think the run was about five miles – we went through 15 minutes of callisthenics, sit-ups, push-ups and various other exercises. Then they said, "C'mon, we're going to run back now."

'I reckon my team-mates in Manly were 25 per cent fitter than me. People like Bobby Fulton were already training every day.'

While Reilly was gasping for breath many smaller clubs were holding theirs as the long-running battle for freedom of movement, forced by Balmain loose forward Dennis Tutty, came to a head at the end of the year. It reached a dramatic conclusion on 13 December 1971 when Australia's High Court upheld a previous judgement that essentially made the transfer system redundant and left players free to switch clubs once their contracts expired. For the likes of Newtown, who survived by selling their best players to the Sydney powerhouses, the decision would ultimately cost them their existence.

On the flip side, outfits like St George, who rebuilt their clubhouse at a cost of A$2m in 1970, had a plethora of revenue streams on a dizzying scale. While attendances were dropping, TV money and sponsorship were replacing gate receipts. On top of that, leading clubs held nightly shows, entertained hundreds of diners and welcomed punters into their own slot-machine arcades. This funded the drive towards professionalism as we know it today in the National Rugby League (NRL), and with Gibson and the other leading coaches in tune with the philosophies and ideas of Corcoran and his colleagues on the coaching panel, the Australian game was taking even bigger steps towards leaving its British counterpart behind.

Chapter Two

The Gap Widens

BRITAIN'S 1970 Ashes heroes returned home in late July ready to play their part in a brave new world.

The previous year a ground-breaking four-year TV deal with the BBC was agreed to show a range of live club and international rugby league matches until the end of the 1973/74 campaign. Five years after the Floodlit Trophy was first broadcast on BBC2, the RFL was prepared to 'risk' the potential fallout of supporters staying at home to watch instead of going to the grounds; it would be the start of a long-standing partnership between the two bodies. The Beeb was committed to paying a minimum of £110,000 per year for the exclusive rights to all professional matches, with each of the 30 clubs receiving an equal share.

In an era when just one live professional soccer game was televised each season – the Cup final – it was truly revolutionary stuff. On a Saturday afternoon, if you were a sports fan and you weren't either playing or watching, you were engrossed in *Grandstand*. A bit of racing and then ... boof ... rugby league at 3pm apart from when the Five Nations rocked up. Matches 80 minutes long were perfect for the TV producers because the referee would blow his whistle at Headingley or the Boulevard and it would be quickly back to Frank Bough just in time for the full-time soccer scores.

Concerns that attendances would be affected with all this televised rugby league were debated long and hard by the full council before they agreed to the deal. After all, the Football League waited until 1984 before agreeing to the TV broadcast of live soccer games because of similar worries.

Crowds across the four soccer divisions had been steadily falling for 30 years. The 70s and early 80s, in particular, was a time when millions of people stopped watching live sport.

But rugby league was prepared to embrace the TV experiment and there was a feeling the added exposure would help attract lucrative sponsorship. With that in mind a marketing expert called John Caine was employed, with the brief to maximise potential, although league secretary Bill Fallowfield was a not a fan. Manchester-based Caine had 'radical' ideas but became frustrated at the barriers erected by Fallowfield, and was reportedly dismayed at the deal done with John Player for a new league cup competition starting in 1971/72. Caine quickly realised the £20,000 per annum agreement constituted a massive underselling of the sport's true potential.

Caine compiled a blueprint which included abolishing the RFL Council in favour of a seven-man board that could make decisions more quickly. The situation rapidly developed into a nasty battle between Caine and Fallowfield, who even threatened to sue the marketeer for libel. Those forward-thinking chairmen who supported Caine at a meeting of the chairmen's association also largely helped pass a vote of confidence in Fallowfield three days later.

Caine said: 'I would like to know whether the vote [for Fallowfield] relates to the work done by the secretary over 26 years or was a method of buffering him against any possible criticism in our report.'

Fears over the impact of TV were heightened by dismal gates for the 1971 autumn series with New Zealand. A meagre aggregate of 13,351 spectators watched the Kiwis take it 2-1 with all three Tests screened live by the BBC.

Great Britain also went into the series opener without a coach and, after an 18-13 defeat at Salford on 25 September, the clamour for John Whiteley's return was picked up by the press. Ahead of the second Test at Castleford the RFL hierarchy turned itself into something of a laughing stock with its attempts to reinstate Whiteley. His 're-appointment' was leaked to the press to the bemusement of the man himself and on 30 September he made the following rather unusual statement: 'I have not yet received official notification of the appointment but when I am informed I shall turn down the job.'

In an embarrassing U-turn, Great Britain's chairman of selectors, Wilf Spaven, responded 24 hours later with the following: 'John gave me his decision last night and I understood that his mind was made up on this issue some time ago. It was not something he decided yesterday after the appointment was made.'

Certainly something needed to be done about the lack of bodies through the turnstiles. New Zealand clinched the series thanks to a 17-14 success in front of just 4,108 hardy souls at Wheldon Road. The Great Britain team was unrecognisable from the one that had blazed a trail in Sydney just 15 months earlier, although they did win the third Test 12-3. It would be the last international played under the four-tackle rule, introduced in 1967 and considered to have ended the often dour rugby that was prevalent under the unlimited tackle system.

RFL football committee chairman Jack Myerscough, the long-standing Leeds chairman, said: 'The proposed six-tackle rule should be given a trial, as this can only bring about faster and more positive football. But generally I feel that basically there is nothing wrong with the game as it is.

'What is wanted is for players, officials, referees and all connected with rugby league to realise that it is still the best and most exciting spectator sport in the world. Once this fact sinks in and everyone decides to play the game as it should be – fast, open and to the rules – then it won't take long for the missing fans to come flooding back in their thousands.'

The six-tackle rule came into force for the start of the 1972/73 campaign but before a ball was kicked the sport was rocked by extraordinary allegations made by Jack Harding. As Leigh chairman and successful GB manager, whatever he said carried weight, so his insistence that there was a 'backhander bug' in the game and his revelation that he had compiled a dossier of illegal dealings was dynamite.

This was something of a crusade for Harding. During his tenure as RFL chairman in 1966 he instigated random checking of club finances. His successful proposal meant that, twice a year, two teams were drawn out the hat and their books checked by League auditors. However, that arrangement was largely kept 'in house', unlike his own club's annual meeting where he said, 'I am not going to mention any names now but if these illegal approaches do not stop that dossier will be brought into the open. The people involved in it will be put out of the game – even if I must go with them. During the past 12 months we have had to suffer illegal approaches to our players. It is something which is ruining rugby league, a cancer in the game today. When you are signing a player these days the first question from them is invariably: "How much is there in it for me?"

'Although it is strictly against the rules it has become the usual thing. Some players not on the [transfer] list at a club are coming along with requests for large amounts of money to continue playing. We at Leigh have suffered much of this last season and we have kept our mouths shut. But no longer.'

Harding went on to allege that David Eckersley, who would soon leave for St Helens, had refused to play for the club, having had his head turned.

'It is obvious that the player has been "got at". A few weeks ago he couldn't wait to begin the new season with Leigh. Now he doesn't want to know.'

Another unhappy man was Jim Challinor, recently appointed as Great Britain coach to fill the long-standing void left by John Whiteley. The former Warrington stalwart was preparing for the 1972 World Cup, which started in France at the end of October. The lacklustre effort against New Zealand had dulled expectations among British fans, a fact which clearly riled Challinor.

'I am sick of hearing people bring the team down. We are apparently the backmarkers in this competition. If that is so I reckon we can surprise a few people. We have a happy blend of experience and youth and provided they click they are a team which can produce the shocks.'

Anyone who watched the Lions beat the Kangaroos 27-21 in Perpignan would not have been playing down their chances and events would prove Challinor right. A 10-10 draw after extra time against Australia in the deciding fixture in Lyon – Clive Sullivan's 80-yard try proving the highlight – meant that the destination of the trophy was decided on points scored. Britain's 53-19 thrashing of the Kiwis in Pau proved critical to the outcome of the trophy.

The only downside for the squad was the incredibly low-key return. Less than 100 relatives were waiting for them as they stepped off their plane at a rainy Castle Donnington. It is hard to imagine a World Cup winning team ever receiving a more understated 'welcome home'. But it was typical of the apathy towards the sport. In February 1973 the RFL held a crisis meeting to address the alarming drop in attendances for club matches. League secretary Fallowfield confirmed that gates were down 14.5 per cent compared to 1971/72. The figures were shocking across the board. That season, Wigan averaged just 4,427 spectators, Hull a pitiful 2,279 and Leeds 5,973. Warrington were the biggest crowd-pullers with 6,488. Ten years earlier 11 clubs including Wigan (14,863), St Helens (12,193), Wakefield (10,407) and Leeds (10,121) exceeded that figure.

The answer was to embrace the long-standing wish of many club chairmen and split the league in two. In a rare display of urgency clubs voted 19-11 in favour of a rapidly assembled motion at an historic meeting in Salford on 15 February. For it to pass a three-fifths majority was needed – they made it by one vote – and with the changes coming into place for the following season – 16 teams in Division One and 14 in Division Two – it is remarkable to consider the likes of struggling Doncaster (placed 27th out of 30 at the time of vote), Barrow (26th), Bradford (25th), Hull (24th) and Keighley (23rd) all effectively relegated themselves. Widnes (9th) were the highest-placed team to vote against it.

The play-offs were also scrapped so whoever finished top would be champions. The pay-off for those in the second division was that the 15 per cent levy on gate receipts would only be paid by top-flight clubs. First introduced in 1939/40 when the rate was just 5 per cent, the pooled money was originally used to pay for referees. Ten years later it was increased to 10 per cent and the funds used at the discretion of the executive committee. It became 15 per cent in 1956/57 and when two divisions were in operation between 1962 and 1964 all clubs paid it. Now the money would be used for first-team referees and a league-wide central insurance policy, with the rest distributed equally among all clubs at the end of the season.

While the RFL was finally showing evidence of some long-term thinking, it did not stretch to the national team, where Challinor was appointed for just the first Test of the autumn Ashes series, staged at Wembley on 3 November, 1973. There was speculation that the Saints coach's reluctance to confirm whether he was available to lead the Lions in Australia the following year was the reason for the decision, although no one at Chapeltown Road, the RFL's headquarters, would explain why.

On the pitch, the classy Phil Lowe led the way as the hosts took it 21-12 but the result was overshadowed by the poor attendance (9,874). Wembley was less than a tenth full and how the RFL must have rued acquiescing to the Australians' insistence that the fixture be played in London.

Kangaroos tour manager Charlie Gibson said: 'I was bitterly disappointed with the crowd. I'll be recommending that if another Test is ever planned for London then there should be no live TV coverage. If the match must be televised I would advise a recording later in the evening.'

Gates for warm-up matches had also been a huge cause for concern for the Australian management. Against Castleford just 2,424 turned up and it was not much better at Oldham (3,020), Wakefield (5,863) and Widnes (5,161). In 1959 the matches at Oldham and Wakefield had both attracted more than 17,000 people.

There was at least guaranteed to be a proper international match atmosphere at Headingley for the second Test, at which the tourists were minus player-coach Langlands and influential second-rower Terry Randall. Both damaged their hands in a club encounter at Leigh. For Great Britain the absence of the injured second-row stalwart George Nicholls would prove a huge headache. His replacement was Welsh star John Mantle (St Helens).

The wind howled in Leeds that November afternoon and Langlands' replacement, Graham Eadie, showed remarkable composure to kick five goals from five attempts in a 14-6 victory.

The decider would take place in Warrington on 1 December. In freezing temperatures, on a pitch more suited to ice skating, Australia defied the conditions to run in five tries, the last of which, by Elwyn Walters, went through seven pairs of hands. Many in the know realised that the game only took place because it was being shown live on the BBC.

'They would have beaten us on any pitch,' conceded Challinor. 'Our tackling was atrocious.'

The Lions coach would have the chance to take revenge the following summer but would have to do so without some of his stars. With Stephenson and Morgan having already joined Reilly in moving to an Australian club, the news that Lowe had signed a three-year contract with Manly was a hammer blow to his plans. A number of other top British players were being approached, notably Dougie Laughton, who chose Canterbury. The second-rower would spend just one season overseas but that would be enough to end Challinor's plan to make him captain.

Meanwhile at the RFL it was the end of an era. Fallowfield, who had been league secretary for 26 years, was stepping down at the end of the 1973/74 season. His replacement would be David Oxley, an Oxford-educated deputy head teacher from Hull. Despite his softly spoken, public-schoolboy manner he was from east Hull and was a dedicated Hull KR supporter. He was also a progressive thinker, open to making changes.

Laughton's replacement was Salford centre Chris Hesketh, who was one of six players from the soon-to-be league champions named by tour manager Reg Parker. The others were Paul Charlton, Colin Dixon, Keith Fielding, Kenny Gill and David Watkins. Parker led a seven-man selection panel, reportedly advised by the coach.

The first Test was at Brisbane on 15 June 1974 with the second and third Tests in Sydney (6 and 20 July). There would also be clashes with New Zealand on 27 July and 4 and 10 August.

Despite some hefty early victories against Queensland club sides Challinor wasted little time in asserting his authority by imposing a curfew and cutting down on social functions.

After beating Ipswich 36-8 in the fifth tour match just nine days before the first Test, Challinor said, 'They won't know what's hit them. We should have won by twice that margin. They obviously wanted to just coast through the game. I ripped into them at half-time. I was ashamed of their first-half performance. I'll make myself the most unpopular man in the team, but it (the curfew) has to be done. It will probably upset the breweries, but that can't be helped. The team is not playing well and I have not been happy with their form since we arrived here. We are going to work hard to iron out our problems.'

The hosts would take the honours in the first Test in Brisbane 12-6 but as the tour developed there were undoubted highlights. Featherstone scrum-half Steve Nash was proving something of a revelation, while recent rugby union convert John Gray's massively effective round-the-corner kicking style left seasoned rugby league watchers scratching their heads.

Gray said: 'In those three Tests they said how on earth did you kick a ball like that but for most people it is a lot easier to do it like that because that's how we were taught to kick a soccer ball.'

The Wigan player, who also was a handy fast bowler for Warwickshire, kicked four goals as the Lions tied up matters thanks to a 16-11 win at Sydney. Leeds centre Les Dyl made his debut on the wing while Millward was also forced out wide because of injuries.

'I believe in miracles now,' said Challinor as he surveyed the scene in the post-match dressing room. 'It was a game they had to win ... they did wonderfully well out there today.' There would be no fairy tale finish. Hopes of repeating the 1970 heroics were dashed as Langlands returned and inspired Australia to a 22-18 series-clinching win in front of a partisan 55,506-strong crowd at the SCG. The Kangaroos had roared back in the second half after tries from Dyl and Salford winger Maurice Richards had helped Challinor's men to a 16-10 half-time lead.

Great Britain had come so close and the future looked bright with the likes of the then 21-year-old Dyl making a big impression. However, the Leeds centre remembers being shocked at the standard of training and the facilities down under compared to what he was used to in Leeds.

'You would watch [Australian club sides] train and they never dropped the ball. It was unbelievable ... playing touch and pass or whatever. Go to training at Leeds ... the ball's all over the place. And our training facilities were dreadful. We used to practice on a small, knackered field behind one of the stands at Headingley.'

That year the Australian authorities, worried about declining gates, offered to help clubs with money to upgrade grounds, while on the pitch fans were being treated to great entertainment, especially from a revitalised Eastern Suburbs side, who now had Gibson as head coach. They finished top of the standings having failed to make the play-offs the previous year, and won the Grand Final against Canterbury 19-4. Their giant backs, Bill Mullins and Mark Harris, proved too much for their old rivals.

Gibson's new training methods had proved an instant success, although he was able to add one more strand to his coaching armoury thanks to one of the staff he inherited. The unheralded Gerry Seymour had taken it upon himself to keep all manner of in-game statistics and when Gibson got to grips with what he was doing he immediately realised it could make a difference.

Gibson said: 'One of the little things he [Seymour] used to keep was tackle counts. I really fell in love with that. I went along with that all the way. The main reason I did it wasn't so much for criticism but to give recognition to a defensive player. I might have read it in *Sports Illustrated* where in the American game it takes more talent, experience and a tougher individual to be a defensive player than a runner. A lot of their star players they put on defence. They thought that was more important because if you can stop a team from crossing your line you never get beat. I gave them as much publicity as I could as far as my joint was concerned.

'A lot of coaches were critics of it. All the dumb cliches came out about … "What is an important tackle? What about if he chases and all that?" They were saying they didn't need it. Before two seasons were out they had two tackle counters. The whole lot of them. In fact one coach even added "loom" to his statistic count. This applied to the player who moved up in defence on a player who may have been about to receive the ball. He loomed up, as it were, and whenever he did so was credited with one loom.'

Easts were even more dominant the following year, topping the table by ten points and then destroying St George 38-0 in the Grand Final. Captain Arthur Beetson scored one of eight tries as the nation watched the season finale in colour for the first time. It caused a sensation. Australia was hooked on live rugby league and everyone wanted to know Gibson's secrets.

However, nobody in the UK took much notice. Possibly the constant squabbling with the British Amateur Rugby League Association (BARLA) was proving too much of a distraction. BARLA had been founded in 1973 because many leading amateur administrators believed they were getting a raw deal, particularly when it came to how grants from the Sports Council were being used. They were also upset that rugby union players could not play amateur rugby league. As they were all amateurs they felt it should not matter. The net effect of what became a timeless, uneasy relationship was that the top juniors in the country were dragged in different directions with BARLA's national age-group sides in one corner and the schools/RFL in the other. In contrast, the systems in Australia and New Zealand for maximising the talent of their best kids were simple, straightforward and incredibly effective. Young stars of the future were carefully guided through the system, getting the best coaching money could buy.

The RFL also became embroiled in a battle instigated by smaller clubs who wanted a return to a single division. On 7 January 1976 the matter came to a head at a meeting of the full council. The main aim of the move was to help those less well off because playing the big boys meant a significant increase in gate receipts. Ahead of the debate, league secretary Oxley wrote a passionate plea for the two-division set-up to remain. He cited moves in union to create a competitive league pyramid.

Representatives from Barrow, Blackpool, Doncaster, Halifax and Huyton had met at Rochdale to plan their attack. They wanted a return to how things were in 1964/65 when 34 league fixtures were played and travelling was kept to a minimum because clubs only played others from the same county home and away. They also proposed making room for the extra league fixtures by abolishing county cup competitions.

In the end Oxley's arguments won the day although a new competition structure had been embraced by Alex Murphy, who had been tasked with steering England through the elongated 1975 World Cup format. The tournament was effectively a championship series. England, Wales, France, New Zealand and Australia would play each other home and away with the table-toppers taking the crown, although there would be a finale of sorts with the champions playing a rest-of-the-world side. Well, that was Plan A, anyway.

Murphy had laid down the law from the outset and wanted a fast start, with England playing their competition opener against France at Headingley on 16 March.

'I want a squad of men who are fit and able to take the strain of several hard matches strung together over a matter of days. We can't afford to take half-fit players because of injuries.'

Speaking after his new-look side had edged out France 11-9 in Perpignan in January, Murphy also outlined his desire to see regular weekly training sessions and players be examined regularly by physio Dennis Wright.

'I'd be worried if some of these lads played for me at club level,' said the England supremo. 'I'd never question their ability – just their fitness. We couldn't have had a better result in Perpignan. Certain weaknesses were highlighted and we must set them right. We didn't show good sense. The French set the example in the first half by kicking in the wind. But we didn't and I was disappointed international-class players couldn't read the game from the field.

'We want a team to play as a team. It may mean there won't be any stars in the side – but the team will be a working unit. There is no answer to skill and that will always be the match-winner. But we also need effort and teamwork. I am going to keep the squad together. If players don't want to know, I don't want to know them.'

Roger Millward was in full agreement: 'We need to keep the team together. We need to get to know each other.'

Murphy's desire to try out some new faces ahead of the World Cup meant England only retained Dyl, captain Millward, Salford's Mike Coulman, Gray and John Cunningham (Hull KR) for a hastily arranged extra warm-up clash with Wales at Salford on 25 February. With so many changes the home side struggled to assert their authority, particularly in the forwards, even when Welsh prop Jim Mills was sent off midway through the second half. The hosts led 10-3 at half-time but could only manage one more score thereafter via the boot of Gray, while the Welsh, with David Watkins outstripping Tommy Martyn to touch down three minutes after the restart, pushed hard for a shock win but were just denied 12-8.

Union convert Keith Fielding, Salford's flying winger, would be one of the great success stories for England throughout the course of the World Cup and he started in great style with two tries as Murphy's men won 20-2 against France at Headingley.

Team manager Bill Oxley then met with his three fellow selectors – Harry Womersley, Arthur Walker and Wilf Spaven – on 16 April to select a 20-man squad for the Australia/Kiwi-based leg of the competition when they would play three internationals in 19 days in June. Only one specialised hooker (Keith Bridges) was included; the four half-backs were all playing scrum-half for their clubs. 'We were given an assurance that Barry Philbin (Warrington) played regularly as a hooker in his days with Swinton and I believe he will be a worthy stand-in if necessary,' said Oxley.

Murphy gave the squad his seal of approval, adding: 'It was not an easy meeting. I did not have a vote but the selectors asked my advice and I gave it. They have done a grand job. I'm in complete agreement with the squad. It has strength in depth and they are the best 20 players in the country.'

The omission of Wakefield's star back-row forward Mick Morgan raised eyebrows. He was one of four players to appear in all three of England's internationals that year and had played for Yorkshire as a hooker.

But things did not go well, as a 12-7 defeat to Wales in Brisbane was followed by draws with New Zealand (17-17) and Australia (10-10), leaving the champions with a mountain to climb. The Kangaroos had won three and drawn one at the halfway stage so were firmly in the driving seat as the event restarted back in England at the end of September.

Murphy had been critical of the squad that headed down under and there was talk of Malcolm Reilly being recalled on his return to coach Castleford following his five-year spell with Manly. However, the star of the 1970 Ashes success had enough to wrestle with at Wheldon Road and he was not named in a 19-man squad unveiled by Oxley.

'The gap between Australian and English football had widened noticeably by the time I got back home in late 1975,' said Reilly. 'Coming back after five years with Manly, the difference in fitness levels in the two countries stood out a mile with the Aussies way ahead. I had been on holiday and hadn't played for two or three weeks, but I was as quick as the backs, even though I was a forward playing with a bung knee.

'I didn't realise how bad things were until I started chasing balls with them and it became glaringly evident. My level of fitness had automatically increased with the intensity and general fitness level of the game in Australia. I know if I had stayed in England, my fitness would have stayed at the British level. That's human nature; you do as much as you need to do.

'At Castleford I began the process of change. We used tractor tyres for tackling practice and a weights machine. I was very aware by then that the physical side of the game had to be addressed. Some players saw the way immediately – but you can't make all horses drink, even if you do lead them to water. Some of the players were going along only half-heartedly, reluctant to change their ways.'

England had to win all four home matches to be in with a chance of claiming the trophy and got off to a positive start at Wilderspool with a 22-16 defeat of the Welsh. Tries from Fielding and Leeds playmaker John Holmes helped put their team 12 points ahead after 17 minutes only for St Helens duo John Mantle and Kel Coslett to reply in kind and keep their side in it. That was until Widnes centre Eric Hughes settled matters with a try on his debut.

Murphy identified his captain as the main difference between the two teams. 'Roger Millward has again confirmed that he is the best scrum-half in the world.'

Worrying news came after Australia beat Wales 18-6 at the St Helens ground in Swansea. The official attendance was given as 13,766 but recently appointed RFL press officer David Howes believed the truer figure was nearer 20,000 and investigations were going to be made. Not for the first time international teams were concerned at the under-reporting of gates. In 1972 the Kiwis had complained of the same after a tour match in France. Their meeting with local team Albi officially attracted 952 people but Kiwi officials thought the figure closer to 3,500.

New Zealand's players would definitely have been more concerned to see a full-grown lion being paraded around Odsal when they ran out onto the pitch on 25 October. England's new mascot, Simba, was on loan from Flamingo Land zoo. One man roaring was stand-off Ken Gill as he inspired the home side to a 27-12 success, although Murphy was not particularly impressed. The low-key nature of the affair – there were only 5,507 in attendance – might have been down to Australia's win over Wales six days earlier which all but secured them the title (it would be confirmed in Perpignan when the Kangaroos thrashed France 41-2 on 26 October).

With the tough-tackling Jimmy Thompson back in the ranks England completed their pool matches with a 16-13 success over Australia. It left Murphy's side just one point behind the Kangaroos in the final reckoning and the England coach put the victory down to teamwork, although conceded his side had been lucky after the visitors somehow contrived to waste a glorious overlap opportunity in the dying stages.

'We showed that we do play football now and again. The crowd were right behind us – they were absolutely fantastic – and the lads responded magnificently. It was the best Test match I have ever seen. Australia are a better side than we played over there and they played against a better side. It was a tremendous game.'

Team manager Bill Oxley added: 'The Aussies haven't beaten us. They're just not good enough.'

The Kangaroos' failure to beat England in both their World Cup meetings led to a change in the competition finale. The winners' game against a Rest of the World XIII was scrapped in favour of another Anglo-Australia encounter. Finding a date proved tricky, though. With the Aussies returning home on 14 November the domestic county championship had to be rejigged to allow the encounter to take place at Headingley 48 hours before their departure.

England would have to tackle the champions without their coach, who wanted to step down 'for one match' to concentrate on a problem with his struggling Warrington outfit.

'There is no question of me quitting as England coach,' said Murphy. 'I want the selectors to retain me. I'm stepping down for this one match.'

The RFL's David Howes eased Murphy's worries.

'We accept that he has a good reason for doing so.'

Whether Murphy's absence made a difference or not, England, much changed from their previously successful meeting, were embarrassed 25-0 in front of just 7,680 at Headingley. Captain Millward was sent off to cap a dismal evening. It would be another sad end for one of the great characters in the game. Murphy would not get his chance to lead a Great Britain side into an Ashes series. Meanwhile, the England baton was about to be passed to Peter Fox.

With no senior international matches in 1976 the legendary Bradford Northern supremo would have to wait until the two European Championship matches in the early part of 1977 to make his mark. These matches effectively acted as an audition for the job of leading Great Britain at the World Cup later that year. (The shortened version of that competition would include just France, New Zealand and Australia this time around.)

The European Championship games did not go well for Fox. England lost 6-2 at Headingley to David Watkins-coached Wales. There followed even more ignominy as France ran out 28-15 winners in Carcassonne.

However, the new England coach was in no mood to take the criticism lying down.

Writing in a rugby league magazine Fox claimed that for both England games the players were selected for him and those picked did not respond to his his. He also said that his request that Nash be picked was turned down, while two others he wanted – George Nicholls and Jimmy Thompson – were added to the squad too late. Former Barrow player Reg Parker was still the Great Britain manager and it was no secret that he had wanted Wales's Watkins as coach, so Fox was always up against it. The other coaches on the GB shortlist had been Murphy and Dewsbury's Dave Cox.

Watkins was chosen and on 13 April Parker and the other eight GB selectors met to pick the new 20-man squad. Phil Lowe, back at Hull KR after his three-year stay in Australia, was not available because of a contract dispute with Manly, while Bill Ashurst was unavailable for similar reasons. Steve Norton, Jeff Grayshon and Paul Rose were all still playing down under. The absence of Norton and Lowe paved the way for the selection of Barrow's Phil Hogan. The Cumbrian side were struggling to avoid relegation and many of the selectors had their doubts but Parker had seen enough of him to champion his cause. He also got a helping hand when Saints second-rower Eric Chisnall withdrew to focus on a new business venture.

There was also much debate about the selection of Widnes powerhouse Mills. The prop was banned from playing in New Zealand for life after his disgraceful stamp on the head of Kiwi front-rower John Greengrass two years earlier and this time around

Great Britain would be taking on the Kiwis in Christchurch. Millward was once again captain.

Watkins, a man renowned for his intelligence, struck a positive note as he and the players – minus Warrington's Tommy Martyn who withdrew after the Premiership final because of a hamstring injury – flew out a week ahead of their first game against France.

'We are going out with the ambition of winning every game, not just the World Championship ones but the tour matches which follow. Australia feel the competition is as good as won by them but we hope to make them eat their words.'

The simplified format meant France, New Zealand, Great Britain and Australia all played each other once with the top two doing battle in the final in Sydney on 25 June. That meant the Lions' opener against Les Bleus was critical. Victory against the reigning European champions at Carlaw Park would give them a foot in the final.

The British game needed some good news after the awful death of 23-year-old Leeds half-back Chris Sanderson during the Headingley club's final league game of the season against Salford. His wife of 12 months, Sally, was watching from the stands and, after he was taken off on a stretcher, accompanied him to the dressing room where medics failed to revive him. He was hurt in a tackle and suffered head injuries. The game was abandoned after seven minutes.

Leeds chairman Jack Myerscough said: 'All we could see was a ruck of players at a tackle. When they moved away Chris was lying on the ground. He could not have had better medical attention.'

Once in New Zealand Watkins had the luxury of being able to pick from a fully fit squad, with Wigan winger Bill Francis having recovered from a stomach upset.

On a muddy pitch Wigan full-back George Fairbairn put in a superb effort to kick seven goals from eight attempts during a forward-dominated affair. Debutant Hogan led an inexperienced pack in fine style. Captain Millward, centre Dyl and winger Stuart Wright were the try-scorers.

With France also losing to Australia six days later, a victory over New Zealand on 12 June in Christchurch would secure Great Britain a place in the final with a game to spare.

Francis, who had spent the summer of 1973 playing in New Zealand, was called in to replace Holmes and was the only change. Millward was once again to the fore and his partnership with Nash in the halves proved highly effective, with Britain taking the spoils 30-12. Wright (2), Francis, George Nicholls, Eddie Bowman and Millward all crossed.

Brisbane would host Britain's final group game, with the match acting as a dress rehearsal for the final a week later.

Australia coach Terry Fearnley had been impressed by the efforts of Britain's dynamic half-back duo.

'Millward and Nash are accomplished halves, and it's obvious they haven't lost any of their flair – in fact I think they have picked up a few new tricks.'

The Australian top brass expected Watkins to make a number of changes ahead of the final but the Welshman only made one with fit-again flier Fielding coming in on the wing for Francis.

The home side ran away with it in the second half, securing a 19-5 win, with full-back Eadie once again proving a thorn in the British side. The Manly full-back claimed two tries to help his side reverse a 5-4 half-time deficit. Millward bagged his 16th try in 25 Tests but could not inspire another heroic effort thereafter.

Fearnley was quick to heap praise on his squad.

'We were too fast for them, and after we tightened our defence in the second half there was no way Britain could win.'

Watkins was not too downhearted, although his plans for the final were hit when hooker David Ward suffered an ankle injury and Fielding withdrew because of a shoulder injury. Both would miss the final, as would Nicholls, who picked up a late knock, although Dyl played with a heavily strapped ankle due to an Achilles tendon problem. Francis, Keith Elwell and Len Casey were their replacements.

'Our players are very determined to reverse the results and I think Britain will come out on top,' said the GB coach. 'Our boys ran out of puff in the second half. We are not used to playing in such a warm climate but the run under those trying conditions will do us a great amount of good for the final.'

Fearnley also had a few injury issues and the selectors brought in Parramatta's untested 5ft 3in scrum-half Johnny Kolc to replaced Tom Raudonikis, who had a rib injury.

This time around Watkins's side certainly did not run out of puff. They were incensed when English referee Billy Thompson failed to play an advantage for a first-half penalty, blowing up with winger Wright flying towards the try line. Australia won 13-12.

Thompson gamely admitted the mistake straight after, although the considerable recriminations that followed were unfair. There is no way of knowing what would have happened had Wright been allowed to score. There was still a long way to go.

Thompson said: 'I blew the whistle for shepherding by Australia and before I realised what had happened Wright was away. I knew straight away I had made a mistake and should have allowed play to continue but it's just one of those things that happen in the heat of the moment.'

It was an afternoon to forget for full-back Fairbairn, who had lost the ball twice in key moments. Firstly, Manly centre Russel Gartner had intercepted his pass in the first half, and then 17 minutes from time, Kolc was the beneficiary.

Watkins said: 'I'm proud of the way my lads played. They did well and it was just two silly mistakes by one of the most dependable players that cost us the game.'

Two days before the final the leading British players had learned they would not be able to play club rugby down under after the international committee agreed to a four-year ban on players moving between Great Britain and Australia. A number of English star names were said to be furious with the decision. The only way they could now play down under was to live there for 12 months beforehand, which would have meant a year without rugby. At the same meeting it was also decided to end the World Cup, and international rugby league reverted to a four-year tour cycle. It would be another ten years before the World Cup would return.

International board secretary Bill Fallowfield said: 'This ban will benefit rugby league the world over – for far too long England has been bled of its best players. However, by imposing the ban English clubs will lose the money previously gained from large transfer fees and Australia will not be able to buy the players.'

There was talk of legal action on the grounds of a denial of livelihood but the ban was largely enforced, although former Wigan hooker John Gray carried on playing with Manly (1978–80) and North Sydney (1981–83).

By early 1978 the RFL, aware that the chopping and changing of international coaches was not particularly conducive to long-term success, announced their determination to mirror what was happening with their team managers. Reg Parker had just finished his three-year stint.

The decision makers were clearly more sensitive to the forthcoming challenges ahead, with Australia visiting in the autumn and then another Ashes battle taking place on the other side of the world just eight months later.

However, no major changes could be agreed ahead of Bradford chairman Harry Womersley seeing off the challenge of four others to become Parker's replacement in June 1978. This was good news for Fox, who had just led Northern to second place in the first division Championship and then a 17-8 win over league champions Widnes in the Premiership final. Just a few days later he was made Great Britain coach.

Fox was a coach like no other. His way was to try and pre-plan each game in as much detail as possible. At one of his first international player meet-ups he turned to Millward and asked him what he would do on the third tackle at a particular point in proceedings. Non-plussed, the Hull KR legend explained that until he looked up he did not know what he was going to do. Doing things off the cuff was not encouraged.

New chairman of selectors Bill Oxley (Barrow) and his seven colleagues were going to have to get used to working in a new fashion. One of those colleagues was Womersley who could smooth over any possible grumbles of discontent, which meant the new way was quite simple: the coach would pick the team and the selection committee was there to rubber stamp his choices. The days of debating the merits of various players and then voting on each position were over, although nothing had been written into RFL law.

Buoyed by his new influence over the committee, Fox explained how the Aussies could be beaten.

'I know how the Aussies play. They don't take dummies and they use two or three in the tackle. That's why I believe we must have set pieces. I employ moves to make openings. I have four set moves from the tap but it takes time to teach them. In a one-off match the players are not playing for the coach they're playing for themselves. They're playing as best they can. I'm not going to train Great Britain ... I'm expecting them to be fit and ready to play for their lives when I get them. It's the responsibility of every club coach to make sure that any of his men selected are fit when they come to me.

'This year the selectors will have to make up their minds whether it's winning the Ashes or trying players for next year's tour that matters. The prime object as far as I'm concerned is winning the Ashes. This means that Test players have got to be both established internationals and in form.'

It was pretty obvious from what followed that those selected were very much chosen with the here and now in mind.

Frank Stanton, who had led Manly to Premiership glory in 1976 and 1978, was in charge of the Kangaroos and they arrived under something of a cloud. Queensland officials were livid that just three Maroons made the party – half-back Greg Oliphant, teenage winger Kerry Boustead and prop Rod Morris. Also in the squad was prop Graham Olling, just a few weeks after he admitted to taking anabolic steroids. It would be the first time British crowds would see second-rower Les Boyd, wing Chris Anderson, hooker Max Krilich and loose forward Ray Price.

Stanton, who had been part of the brilliant Australia squad of 1963, had a reputation for not suffering fools, and earlier in the year had easily won the New South Wales nomination ahead of Don Furner for the interstate series and then led them to a 3-0 drubbing of Queensland. Manly chairman Ken Arthurson lobbied hard for Stanton to get the top job. Writing in his autobiography *Arko*, he said: 'In 1978 I reckoned Stanton, such a firm disciplinarian and hard-edged professional coach, was just the man to take Australia's representative teams into a new era.'

Early Australian grumbles in relation to the standard of the refereeing were somewhat overshadowed by the manner in which they won their opening two tour matches against Blackpool (39-1) and Cumbria (47-4). They certainly impressed Clive Sullivan.

'They have all the physical power and drive of previous teams but seem to make better use of the ball,' said the former Great Britain winger.

Next up were John Whiteley's GB U-24 side at Craven Park in Hull, in a game full of blood and thunder – there were eight cautions.

The former Britain coach denied anything out of order was going on. 'Tough, vigorous play is what Great Britain–Australia games are all about.' Australia won 30-8.

But things were about to get a lot harder for the tourists. At Odsal, Bradford led 11-5 at half-time with 39-year-old Neil Fox crossing twice. The second-half comeback by the tourists was marred by a vicious brawl, sparked by a stray elbow from Northern hooker Tony Fisher that connected with Boyd. Blows were exchanged as the players spilled onto the track. After the melee the Kangaroos ran out 21-11 winners.

Three days later it was Warrington and the Aussies were up in arms after they lost 15-12. It was claimed that the hooter blew two minutes early. The match-winning try from Alan Gwilliam was deemed a farce with both Bobby Fulton and Steve Rogers appearing to have won the race to touch down. There was also controversy about Boustead having a try disallowed and the treatment of Balmain flier Allan McMahon, who was alleged to have been hit high on three occasions.

As well as the timekeeping there was clear discontent at the official attendance (10,056). With the Australian management receiving their cut of the gate in cash from the clubs themselves after each fixture, the suggestion that their English opponents were 'on the make' caused a great deal of animosity. But undeterred thereafter, the Aussies used non-playing squad members to monitor the turnstiles and also did their own timekeeping. It was a practice that continued on future tours.

The schedule was unrelenting. With less than a week to go before the first Test at Wigan, the Kangaroos would have to fit in tough-looking encounters with Wales and then Leeds.

Keeping players fit would be a huge issue for Stanton and the news was not good after he watched his side edge out an experienced Welsh team, which included Jim Mills, Tony Fisher, Trevor Skerrett and David Watkins, 8-3 at St Helens. Cronulla back-rower Greg Pierce was ruled out of the tour with knee problems. Canterbury hooker George Peponis had a less serious knee injury but was unavailable for the first Test.

The Australians were similarly unimpressive at Headingley. Leeds winger John Atkinson called his opponents 'the poorest side in my experience'.

Bill Oxley and the other selectors met on 8 October with the words of Fox ringing in their ears.

Stanton's biggest selection decision centred on his captain Bobby Fulton, who was nursing a torn stomach muscle. The Easts centre even went to warm-up on the Central Park pitch in his tracksuit bottoms and the decision to play him was only made at the last available moment.

Australia won 15-9, with 18-year-old winger Boustead and captain Fulton their try scorers. A report from the official files of the Australian Rugby League (ARL) shone a light on what the visitors made of it all: 'This disappointing first Test was marred by poor handling and shocking refereeing. The game was not a tough, gruelling international rugby league Test match but a brutal, rough, unfair spectacle in which anything went.'

Womersley accused the Australians of biting: 'A couple of Australians are fast getting reputations as biters.'

Australian manager Peter Moore retaliated, accusing the British of 'king-hitting, kneeing and kicking'. Fox was more concerned with the sending off of Nash and believed that was the turning point. The Salford scrum-half was dismissed along with his fellow number 7 Tom Raudonikis.

Commentating for Australian television that day was Rex Mossop, who, after a string of violent incidents, could not hold it in any longer when he saw George Nicholls using the knee on Olling after a tackle.'

Somebody's going to walk up and smack him [Nicholls] right in the mouth before the end of this game and I hope when they do they make it a good one because the referee doesn't appear as though he is going to do anything in the world about the knees he uses from time to time.'

Australian outrage continued into what would turn out to be the history-making Widnes encounter. A late Mick Burke penalty secured a famous victory for the home side but Kangaroos manager Peter Moore called the penalty 'one of the coldest things I've ever seen on a football field'. It would be the last time Australia would lose to an English club side.

The tourists righted the ship with more comprehensive successes over Hull (34-2) and Salford (14-2) ahead of the second Test at Odsal. For so many reasons it would be the stage for a hugely-significant 80 minutes of rugby league, not least because it would be the scene of a Lions win; we would have to wait another ten years for the next one.

Fox's selection of Brian Lockwood, Fisher and Mills is now enshrined in rugby league folklore. With a combined age of 101 they were coined 'The Dad's Army'. But it was another veteran, the evergreen Millward, who made the telling contributions, especially for the first of two tries scored by Widnes flier Stuart Wright.

Two late tries for Australia could not take the gloss off what was ultimately vindication for Fox and his methods. Age was just a number and an 18-14 success set up a winner-takes-all showdown at Headingley on 18 November.

Things then took a surreal twist after an impressive 26-4 win for the Kangaroos over St Helens in dreadful conditions at Knowsley Road. Once back at their base at the Dragonara Hotel in Leeds, Australian co-manager Jim Caldwell got into an altercation with Paul Weller, the frontman of the band The Jam.

Caldwell was moving a table which bumped into one of the other band members so Weller allegedly retaliated by smashing a glass over his head.

Balmain winger Larry Corowa was first on the scene and came to Caldwell's aid but later in the evening incensed Australian players went looking for revenge. Jam bassist Bruce Foxton ended up in hospital with broken ribs.

'I was in bed when Allan McMahon and a few of the others knocked on my door and said, "quick get up, we are going to chase a couple of blokes from The Jam",' said hooker Krilich. 'I was playing in the midweek game so I stayed in bed but I think they went and gave them a hiding. There wasn't much discussion about it afterwards because the deed had been done.

'They hushed it up but I am pretty sure that is what they would have done. The police came to the hotel a few days later to see Jimmy Caldwell, who has since passed away. He got glassed and that is why some of the players went out and chased these guys. They were scumbags.'

Police cleared the Australians of any wrong-doing, while Weller was eventually cleared of a wounding charge at Leeds Crown Court.

With Rod Reddy twisting his ankle in the final warm-up game against York, Stanton turned to the young Wests tearaway Boyd to partner Parramatta's Geoff Gerard in the second row, and his brilliant run and try in the first half was a standout moment in an eye-catching 40 minutes of intense, running rugby league. It was a poignant period of football because, while those watching would not have realised it at the time, it provided just a taste of what was to come during the next decade.

Australia's comfortable 23-6 success turned out to be a sad way for captain Millward to end his international career. He was picked for the 1979 tour but injuries kept him out of the Tests. Probably more than any British player since the war he deserved to go out in style.

'Millward was the best player pound for pound I ever saw,' said John Whiteley. 'He could kick goals from the touchline with a leather ball, he could kick to touch, his cover defence was brilliant. Despite his size (5ft 4in) I never saw him back off anyone in my life. His speed off the mark and speed of thought … he could find Phil Lowe past three men or in front of them. That try he scored in the third Test in Sydney (1970) … he must have jumped his height when he scored. And he was a superstar as a kid. When they started doing Sunday morning rugby league everyone wanted to watch Roger Millward. He created Sunday morning viewing. I was privileged to say I coached him. Alex Murphy was the best since the war in his position but Roger was the complete all-round player.'

Millward himself could only say: 'I'm sick. We lost our composure.'

Ray Price later wrote in praise of the 'hard-to-catch, clever' Millward and he also picked out John Joyner as someone he rated.

With just one win from six international games, Fox's future was in the balance and, despite still having the unwavering support of team manager Womersley, he was kicked out of the role in January 1979 in favour of St Helens coach Eric Ashton, who would also continue overseeing the England side.

Ashton had impeccable credentials as a player. He was a member of the 1957 World Cup-winning side and captained the Lions to Ashes glory five years later.

Womersley said: 'It is common knowledge my choice was Peter Fox, a man I know is capable of doing the job. But having said that I wish Eric all the best and I am sure we will have a good man for the post and that he will do a first-class job.'

The 30-man Ashes squad, surprisingly minus Leeds duo John Holmes and Les Dyl, was unveiled at the end of March and each player would have to pass a new fitness test. Those selected had to satisfy an RFL panel that they were able to tour, when put through their paces at Carnegie College in Leeds on 11 April.

'Jeff Grayshon has the biggest chest in the game,' said Womersley. 'His lung power exceeded that of some Olympic athletes. We've got some big forwards who can handle a big workload, such as Doug Laughton, Trevor Skerrett and Charlie Stone.'

While conditioning had been identified as a key factor, Womersley also believed there was only one skill needed for the quest ahead. 'We are a young side,' he said. 'But now have plenty of tacklers. When we chose the squad we asked, essentially, "can he tackle?" and anything else he had was a bonus. Playing the Australians you have to get up and knock them down. Otherwise you have no chance. We have been cleverer than the Australians but they have the fitness and power.'

Ahead of departure on 21 May the RFL set themselves the lofty target of making a £200,000 profit. They made the bold prediction based on having made "£148,000" on the 1974 Ashes trip. However, their actual profit from 1974 was £93,282 – £50,229 had been paid to the players. With seven more people in the party compared to five years ago it was an ambitious aim but with extra revenue coming from TV and sponsorship the theory appeared relatively sound.

Ashton said: 'This is a trip of a lifetime but with one purpose. Our aims are simple – win the Tests, make money and enjoy ourselves.' At least they would go on to achieve one of their aims.

Ashton's task of winning back the Ashes appeared to have been made easier with the stunning news that came out of Australia in late April. Captain Fulton announced he was making himself unavailable. ARL boss Kevin Humphreys was not impressed and claimed the star player was contractually obliged to play, however, the executive listened favourably to the 33-year-old and agreed to his wishes.

The awful winter of 1978/79 meant the Leeds v Bradford Premiership final was delayed until 27 May, two days after the opening tour match against North Queensland. Northern, who lost the final 24-2, were forced to squeeze in four matches in eight days while beaten semi-finalists Warrington had to play three fixtures in a week.

'I certainly don't think the players will be jaded,' said Ashton. 'Certainly not the younger players. They'll be full-time professional out here. The Australians are strong physical lads. We need three or four weeks to prepare ourselves for them.'

A car crash involving Ashton's daughter meant he would miss the first three tour matches. He stayed in the UK until it was obvious she would be OK. That left captain Laughton to oversee preparations during those early days until his coach, along with the delayed Bradford and Leeds players, finally made it to Cairns on 31 May.

It wasn't long before things started going wrong on and off the field. It became clear from early on that, despite all the promises of a fitness test, at least four of the squad rocked up carrying serious physical problems.

A knee injury for Oldham's Mick Adams in the second game against Central Queensland in Rockhampton – the Lions won 20-11 – would be a taste of things to come. At least for the second-rower it would give him time to finalise plans for his impending wedding, which would take place in Tamworth in four weeks' time. Centre Eric Hughes was his best man and fellow tourists George Nicholls and Jim Mills were groomsmen.

A third successive victory came against Wide Bay in Maryborough, but not before the visiting party had been embarrassed by the non-appearance of centres John Joyner and Mike Smith. The game kicked off ten minutes late after they both slept in and missed the bus.

'They are two of our best lads,' said Womersley. 'They have apologised. It was just one of those things. I'd put it down to a little lack of experience on their part.'

Both were punished but the GB manager refused to disclose what form their penalty took. It might also have helped matters if he'd explained what actually happened. The two young players had got up early to do some extra sprint training before breakfast and after eating decided to have a quick nap while dressed and ready to go. The management used a number system to check that everyone was on the bus so when two players' numbers were called out some joker decided to shout for them and the team departed for Maryborough two short.

'John and myself ran into town and got a taxi,' recalled Smith. 'Nobody would own up to saying our numbers. In retrospect it is quite funny but when your girlfriend hears about it on the *News at Ten* then at the time it wasn't. Obviously people thought we had been out on the town.'

However, the visitors were getting a reputation for enjoying the tour life a little too much and certainly Ray Price thought so.

'A lot of the guys we had met in 78 toured Australia the next season.' said Price. 'It was probably the worst British team I ever played against. They got stuck into Aussie beer like their lives depended on it, apparently they slept in till ten o'clock most mornings and generally they were as undisciplined as any Pom team that toured here.'

In the build up to the first Test the headaches piled up for Ashton, who appeared to have problems getting his message across.

Against North Coast, where 20-year-old Steve Evans impressed in a 33-6 win, Steve Nash was forced off with a serious eye injury. Three days later came Northern Division at Tamworth where a team of mainly young Aussies should have won. Ashton's half-time dressing down failed to have much effect and Britain limped to a 20-11 success.

The Lions coach did not mince his words either after Queensland were seen off 25-19.

'We are making it difficult for ourselves the way we are playing,' said Ashton. 'Nothing is coming easily to us. Our tackling in the first half was diabolical.'

His watching Australian counterpart felt the tourists were holding back somewhat, believing they were 'foxing'. Stanton told the Australian press: 'They looked good in attack but the men you expect to be doing things with the ball were particularly quiet.'

Respected Australian pundit Allan Clarkson feared for the Lions. He wrote: 'Great Britain's first serious encounter on the tour showed terrible deficiencies in the team in the way they played last night. Their defence in the first half was disgraceful. They failed to move up in defence, committing the cardinal sin of waiting for the attack to come to them. Unless they sharpen up the slick, professional Australian team will rip them to shreds in next Saturday's first Test.'

Former Aussie loose forward Ron Coote was even more damning in his assessment of the visitors' chances.

'GB are too slow, too fat and too unfit,' said Coote. 'They are too big in the belly to worry Australia. I can't remember ever seeing or hearing of a British touring team having such soft preparation for a Test match. I wouldn't be surprised if Australia won by 20 points.'

Ashton was not taking it lying down: 'The Australians always were all talk. We have been written off and perhaps rightly so on our recent performances. Yet the right spirit is there and we are fit. We haven't much to worry about.'

The final warm-up encounter came at now infamous Toowoomba, who won 19-16 thanks to Wayne Green's eight penalty goals from 11 attempts. Nash came back but damaged his hamstring, which ruled him out of the first Test.

Forty years later Bradford scrum-half Alan Redfearn recalled Toowoomba with something of a shudder.

'It was the worst game I ever played in for penalties. The referee and linesmen were terrible. They were blowing up all the time and stopping us scoring, giving forward passes when they weren't. A lot of tour teams lost there. They were a poor team.'

Hooker David Ward also remembered the game well: 'I think at one point we were penalised for a forward pass and we didn't even have the ball.'

Toowoomba was their first defeat and later that week the players were informed that there would be a curfew.

Womersley said: 'It took us a long time to come up with the decision but we do not contemplate any difficulties. There won't be any defaulters. We want to win that first Test. We want the lads together all the time – it's going to be early to bed and early to rise.'

Enforcing the curfew would be another thing, as Redfearn recalls.

'I think too much of a good time was being had to be honest. Fitness was good and we trained every day just about. I liked Eric. He was a good coach and taught well but once training finished at 12 or 1pm, you only had to turn up the next morning. There was no curfew. I could see why all the lads wanted to go out on tour. Folk kept coming and taking us out ... on boats and to golf clubs and the like. Taking us out for meals and nights out. It was really good from that perspective.'

Coote and Clarkson's prediction proved eerily accurate. With captain Laughton nursing neck and knee problems and leading playmakers Nash and Millward out injured, Australia ran riot in winning 35-0. A terrible night for Ashton's men was capped when Skerrett was ordered off for using an elbow.

Stanton did not hold back in praising his outfit. 'This side will be an extremely difficult one for anybody to get out of. They are a beautiful unit and complement one another in everything they do.'

To make matters worse for the tourists only 23,000 saw them demolished in Brisbane. With attendances at tour matches also down compared to 1974 there was a real danger the RFL would make a loss from the venture unless the management were able to rein in spending.

Two lacklustre efforts against Queensland (won 10-7) and Southern Division (10-10) in front of dismal crowds did not suggest good times ahead on any front and the lack of interest in the tourists was borne out by poor ticket sales for the second and third Tests in Sydney.

With the injury list continuing to mount, Hull KR full-back George Fairbairn and Wakefield's veteran prop John Burke were flown in as replacements. The arrival of the latter was something of a surprise bearing in mind his disciplinary record. At Castleford, following the 18th sending-off of his career in September 1977, he failed to turn up for training and subsequently spent six months out of the game before signing for Trinity.

The new arrivals did little to stem the tide of GB misery. In the final warm-up for the second Test, against Riverina, the hapless Nash became the 13th tour casualty. Coach Ashton was again happy to criticise despite a 37-10 victory, their biggest of the tour.

'We were lethargic, too slow to move up in defence and showed little imagination in our game. We have a heck of a lot of work to do before next Saturday.'

Just 26,837 saw the most competitive Test of the series. When Eric Hughes crossed to make it 17-14, the Lions' hopes of a brilliant comeback victory were raised, but a Rod Reddy try killed the game and the hosts eventually retained the Ashes 24-16.

The problems unfolding on and off the pitch was proving something of an embarrassment back home and, at the RFL's annual meeting in Scarborough just after the second Test, Womersley lost his place on the international selection committee, although there was no question of him not continuing as manager.

At a luncheon soon after, former Lion and then North Sydney coach Tommy Bishop did not hold back, with the squad in attendance. Suggesting that the British game had spectacularly failed to keep pace with its Australian counterpart, Bishop criticised the selection policy but did feel regret at the suggestion he was targeting the GB coach.

'I think a few people thought I was "having a go" at Eric Ashton, but I wasn't,' Bishop said. 'Ashton is an old friend whom I greatly respect.'

Two weeks later the lowest crowd ever to watch an Ashes Test (16,844) saw the Lions succumb 28-2. Warrington legend and former Australia coach Harry Bath said: 'I never thought I would see the day when a Great Britain team would play as badly as that.'

The squad could at least take solace in the fact that they beat New Zealand 2-1 but their efforts in late July and early August were overshadowed by what had unfolded before. However, hooker Ward felt the tour was subject to undue criticism.

'We lost three Test matches in Australia but I'm not having it when people say it was a bad tour. Yes in the outset you go to win Test matches but we didn't lose any other games in Australia.

There was Toowoomba but we 'won' that game and we beat New South Wales, Queensland and their second team. We won the series in New Zealand and beat their Maoris side when we were down to the bare bones. But sometimes that can help. It can pull a team together when you know you aren't getting any help and it's just down to you.'

Contradicting his pre-tour assessment, Ashton was much more specific in terms of pinpointing where the blame lie ... the clubs who played their leading operators in the week running up to the start of the tour.

'This contributed to us losing three key players just before the team left England,' Ashton said. 'We lost half-back Ken Kellett with a broken jaw and both our top wingers Stuart Wright and John Bevan with shoulder injuries only days before leaving for Australia. In addition, we had other players like Paul Rose, Phil Lowe and Bill Ashurst unable to tour. The loss of these players, compounded with our bad run of injuries, contributed much to our poor effort in the Test series.'

Financially the tour was even more of a disaster. In 1974 attendances for the Australia leg had totalled 277,631. Five years later it slumped to 153,803, which meant that the RFL's share of the gate receipts was just £109,927.

In New Zealand the story was little better. To make matters worse, spending had exploded from £44,545 in 1974 to £118,613. The players were guaranteed to receive 35 per cent of tour income, which meant that overall the whole adventure cost the RFL £31,590. In nine short years the British game, so lauded around the world at the start of decade, had just had its face rubbed in the dirt. On and off the pitch they just couldn't get it right and while there were those desperate to make serious changes at all levels of rugby league, the cartel running the game at the RFL just failed to grasp the nettle quickly enough. Ashton's replacement would be successful U-24s coach John Whiteley, brought in by his old friend and former team-mate Colin Hutton, Womersley's replacement as Great Britain manager. It meant the wheel had turned full circle for the Hull legend. The pull of trying to make a difference at the top of the game he loved so much just proved too strong despite the promise he had made to himself nine years earlier.

'I came back for Colin Hutton because he was my best friend in rugby,' recalled John. 'I virtually did it for love [of the game]. I never signed a contract. I got expenses and that was about it.'

Thankfully for the new GB management team the 1979 tour gave them leverage to implement changes to how players prepared for Test matches, although they still had to deal with an eight-man committee picking the team and a domestic game that was painfully slow in getting to grips with what was required to prepare their top performers for the rigours of modern-day international rugby.

Chapter Three

My Name is John

WHILE rugby league was getting itself in a tizz about the launch of Fulham Rugby League Club in the summer of 1980, the new coach of Great Britain, the GB U-24s and England was unveiled in a much more understated manner.

'I was in love with RL but not the management,' recalls John. 'I had helped run amateur rugby in this city and was still county coach. Colin Hutton rang me and said, "I would love you to come and be the coach." I don't need money. I was running two clubs in the city and was secure financially – I had bought my house.'

That beautiful, imposing, detached property in North Ferriby was the location for our interviews in January 2019. While chatting our way through 50 years of rugby you could not help but get drawn to the immaculate lawn stretching almost 40 yards from the French windows in John's lounge towards the fence at the back. It was the middle of winter yet looked good enough for a game of croquet.

'My six-year-old great-grandson lives close by and that's his training ground,' smiled a contented great-grandfather. 'We do laps together and throw the ball around.'

Another great Hull back-rower in the making? Who can tell at that young age but if anyone knows about the importance of early-years development it is John Whiteley. His extraordinary childhood ensured it was virtually a given he would carve out a successful career in sport.

While world-class athletes get to the top in a number of different ways they are united by one thing – early-life circumstances create an environment which allows them to be that little bit special. That mix of genetic predisposition to the physical side of life and any number of determining factors in the first few years set the groundwork for what follows.

It is difficult to imagine anyone having a better mix of early-life ingredients than John, even though he came within just a matter of yards of losing his life during the Second World War, when a bomb fell close to his school. Maybe that extraordinary and traumatic early brush with death would always give him a proper sense of perspective. It certainly did 40 years later when heads were being lost as the Australians rampaged to victory in the first Test at Boothferry Park in Hull, a venue that, ironically, was less than half a mile from his place of birth.

John Whiteley was born on 20 November 1930 in Scarborough Street, one of the many thriving side streets off Hessle Road, a main thoroughfare in the city famous for its fish docks. He was the eldest of four and lived opposite his grandparents. A gym owned by his Uncle Herbert was located at the end of the street.

'I learned to crawl on a wrestling mat,' said John.

Herbert Whiteley was a leading amateur wrestler in the city and a bodybuilder. In the years before the war he taught his nephew everything he knew about conditioning.

'He taught me all the rudiments of how to glove up, train and use things like the speedball and I was just hooked and have being doing it ever since. Never ever stopped.'

John would also spend a lot of time with his mum's brother Jack Howells, who was a professional sprinter and who also played for Hull Kingston Rovers, Castleford and York.

Jack was a fitness fanatic and before the war would regularly take John to his other grandmother on the other side of the city. While catching trams was an option, the duo would instead make the journey on foot and engage in a bit of sprint training on the way.

'We used to do this thing where we would run between lamp-posts and then walk to the next and then run to the next one and so on. I was just a little tot but I loved doing it. And when you combine it with my what my other uncle taught me I couldn't have had a better grounding for playing sport.'

Following the outbreak of war in 1939 his father joined the navy and Uncle Herbert became a physical training instructor in the RAF. John continued to use the gym and started showing the other boys in the street how everything worked. He would continue to teach the benefits of exercise for the next 80 years. He and his friends played a form of street rugby after John started at secondary school; the lack of organised sport could have been a block to his development but the gym was a great place to escape to, especially when the conflict intensified in 1941 and 1942.

'There was no rugby league during the war. We played in the streets and you would often play the next street. During the week there was no way you could get to the park, which was about a mile away, especially during 41 and 42 when we were getting bombed.'

In May 1942 the biggest bomb to explode on the city of Hull fell on Scarborough Street, killing ten and injuring dozens.

'I was in the air-raid shelter at my schools where, for two or three years virtually slept in there every night. The bomb went off about 200 yards from us and it blew the shelter door to smithereens. When we came out the roofs were off the houses and the chimney pots were everywhere and there were no windows. I tell you what: we didn't need a chimney sweep for years. I think every bit of soot came out. We had to go to the church hall because of the damage to our house but half the street had disappeared. When all the crap and dust subsided it was like fireworks because all the electric cables were flashing around.

'But when you are that age you don't really understand fear. One thing that I always smile about was a lorry that came down the street with a canopy over the top. It was mobile shower unit. Lads went in first and then the girls would go in. It was brilliant. We would go into the next street for another shower.'

His Uncle Herbert was eventually stationed in Canada and that twist of fate would open up a whole new world of opportunity. He sent John magazines and books on health and strength and the youngster became fascinated with American training methods. It became a huge part of his life and if anyone he knew was going to North America he would always ask them to bring back new material.

'At that time in America the boxers – Joe Louis was my hero – beat our boys easy. I looked at the physical side of what they were doing. For example, they were running up hills so that got me running hills.'

Tragically his Uncle Herbert did not make it through the conflict. When the 1,000-bomber raids started so many planes were being lost that the RAF was running out of rear gunners and Herbert volunteered. His plane was shot down over Germany where his body was laid to rest.

'It was really sad because he was my best friend,' said John.

As the war ended the centre of Hull was alive with children now free to start playing sport, and the day Hull Boys' Club re-opened, John and his friends joined.

'Five nights a week we went to Hull Boys. You would play rugby on a Saturday and Sunday against other youth clubs. We had a league of about 12. Because we were a big city with big companies like BOCM and Reckitts they also formed a works league in all sports. And then working men's clubs started again after the war.'

Aged 15 John already cut an imposing figure. Hull FC quickly became very interested in him and at 16 he was picked for a Hull rugby league boys' side against Featherstone and Hunslet. Scouts from all over the North were coming to watch him and his club-mates but as the boys turned 17 and with national service looming large, they agreed between them that none of them would turn professional until they got out of the armed services.

'What we did at Hull Boys' Club was make a pact. We knew Rovers wanted one or two of us and also Bradford Northern had got involved with us. Because we knew that conscription was coming, not one of us signed pro but the Army broke us up.'

Just 18, he had initially hoped to emulate Herbert and become a physical training instructor. Unfortunately his lack of education and the fact he had not been in the regular Army effectively dashed those hopes ... but only for a few weeks.

'I was swimming for Hull and the Army asked who could swim. They asked who could box ... I could box. They asked who could play rugby. I wasn't bad at soccer either. I had even been asked to go for a trial at Hull City. Major Buckley was interested. I was playing soccer for my works team, Fish Trades, at 15 or 16 – I was a filleter on the fish docks – and played a trial and must have had a good game. He wanted to see me, but I told him I wanted to play rugby league.

'Anyway, I am in the Army for the first two or three weeks. I am not doing Army work. I am boxing and swimming, a bit of everything, but soon, for the first time in my life, it was a case of being in the right place at the right time. The Army had had such an influx of national servicemen they had virtually run out of PTIs so they whipped me down to the PTI school at Aldershot for two days. They taught me how to project myself and how to run a class. I was only 18 at the time so had never done anything like that before.

'Anyway, they said pack your bag and I was on a train to Harwich from London and then a boat to Holland and then on night-sleeper to Austria. I was to be in charge of all the Army training equipment and when I got there had a room of my own with a four-poster bed. Absolutely brilliant. I was right in the middle of Vienna.'

Once he was in Austria one of the officers heard that the new arrival played rugby and wanted to see just how good this giant teenager from Hull was.

'I had never seen a game of rugby union in my life. I have only played rugby league. I know there are 15 players and I knew about the All Blacks. He got two or three of the lads together on this little grass area near the barracks. Anyway, we threw the ball out a bit and then he asked me what position I played and I said, "I played prop forward" because I was the biggest lad on the team. I was six foot two and fifteen stone. He said, "Well from what I have seen of you passing this ball on Saturday you will play stand-off half."'

John's half-back partner was a universities' international but even though John was a rugby union novice he quickly imposed his ideas on how he wanted the game to be played.

'I played two or three games with him and then I invited him to come to the park with me. I told him to stand where I would stand and then hit the ball against a tree – as if it was a scrum. I picked up the ball and passed him the ball. Then I did it again and asked him to stand a bit further away and then did it again before he told me, "You are trying to tell me something aren't ya." "Yes," I said. "Why the effing hell do you dive off from the scrum and finish up on your belly?"

71

'He said to me, "Well, Haydn Tanner is the best scrum-half in the world and he dives off." I told him that when he plays with me you don't dive off. When you pass to me you follow me because I want some support inside of me. Nobody had ever seen that. He said that by diving he gets another half a yard start on the opposition wing forwards but I just said not to worry. A ball will beat a runner any day if it is projected right. Everywhere we ran and nobody had seen it before.'

His Army side never lost and after six games John got picked for the British Army in Europe side to play the French Army. Playing at centre he scored five tries.

'A major came up to me and said, "Young man I'd like a word with you." He asked where I came from and then told me, "If I have ever seen an international in a young man I have seen one in you today." He asked me where I worked and what I did. I had no money ... I was working on a fish dock! He then said, "I want you to come to Scotland and we will give you a highly-paid job – you won't have to work – and all you will do is play rugby." But I said no because I wanted to play rugby league for Hull.

'Anyway, I didn't play for them again but did play water polo. I played against the British Army in Italy and remember getting taken in a private Army car from Vienna to Trieste. On the way I caught part of a stage of the Tour of Italy. I remember it so vividly because I had never seen a Lambretta before and there were thousands of them.

'What a view ... I couldn't believe it. Here I was watching this, travelling in a luxurious Army car and six months earlier I had been filleting fish in Hull.'

He left the Army in December 1950 and would not have to wait long to get his chance with Hull. He played two A-team games – against Huddersfield and Keighley – and, on the bus on the way home from Keighley, one of the directors asked him a few questions before he was asked to accompany the chairman back to Hessle, just to the west of the city.

'Mr Hardaker had a big posh house (he owned a removal firm). We were sat in his lounge, his big lounge, and he said, "We are very impressed and would like to sign you." I didn't have anyone around me to advise me – my dad was away at sea – and in those days you signed for life. No money was mentioned. He told me if I sign here he will put me in the first team on Saturday at York, so I did. I didn't get a penny for signing on and he said if you become an international we will give you £100.

'Anyhow I went to York and must have played well [Hull won 19-11] because they told me straight after I was playing the following week. I then never got dropped for all the 15 years I played. I got paid £8 for a win and £5 a game … everyone got the same. I played six games and got picked for England U-21s at Wigan so Mr Hardaker gave me a cheque for £100. I bought my mother a four-ringed gas oven, bought myself a radiogram and went to Butlins in the summer with what was left.'

In his first full season (1951/52) Hull became title challengers and made the top four, losing to Wigan in the semi-final of the Premiership. In the following season he gained full international honours, playing for England at the Parc des Princes. In the game, St Helens centre Doug Greenall claimed two tries as the visitors took the spoils 10-7.

He would have to wait a further four years to make a major international breakthrough, such was the competition for places in the back row at that time. When it came, however, his first experience in a Lions shirt was not a particularly memorable one.

A British side that included the likes of Tommy Harris, Billy Boston, Eric Ashton, Mick Sullivan and Lewis Jones was highly fancied to win the 1957 World Cup down under. Having beaten France in their opener in Sydney, defeats to Australia (31-6) and

New Zealand (29-21) meant the unbeaten Kangaroos took the trophy.

More than 60 years later John remembered it with great disappointment.

'On paper we had a hell of a side but we were a disaster. In my opinion we were as good a side that has ever gone to Australia. But we were mismanaged terribly. There was no unison or team spirit. We liked each other's company but had the team on the pitch been unified properly it would have been a different story. That was one of the big lessons I learned. It was an education. If I couldn't have done better than that ... there's no leadership or management. The RFL secretary Bill Fallowfield had to take over.'

However, the journey home turned into a remarkable adventure for him and the rest of the squad ... bar one player. After the World Cup the squad were informed that an unofficial three-match series with France had been organised in South Africa. It meant that Wigan's black winger Billy Boston could not go.

'We all said we're not going. We all vetoed it. So there was a lot of debate. Anyway, the RFL got hold of Billy on the side and said to him, "If we give you a holiday on the way home. ..." Anyway, he accepted and he flew back to Wigan via Honolulu and San Francisco. So we thought we had to go to South Africa.

'We enjoyed the trip and it was a hell of an eye opener in those days. We flew across the Indian Ocean and we were given a three-day holiday in Mauritius on the way ... Wow ... when you have been in back streets all your life. Anyway, firstly we landed in the Cocos Islands to refuel and then went on to Mauritius and had three lovely days. We had to stop to refuel because in them days it was the longest flight over sea you could make.

'And then flew to Johannesburg, and East London and Durban, and got vile reports from the South African press. They didn't want rugby league rearing its head in South Africa but we got good support from the black people. And we got on really well with them. In those days there were more black people watching us than white. We got on with them because we would ask them their first names plus we gave them all of our rugby gear, football boots and socks. They thought we were wonderful.'

The following summer John, fresh from helping Hull to the Championship after beating Workington Town 20-3 in the play-off final, was back down under as part of arguably the finest set of players ever to leave these shores. The 1958 Great Britain squad read like a Who's Who of league legends and at scrum-half was a teenage sensation called Alex Murphy.

John vividly remembers his first meeting with the precocious half-back.

'We were in the changing room at an international meet-up and I have never seen this kid before. Alex was stood on one of the benches and shouts across to the coach to ask who are the other 25 who will be coming on tour with him later that season.'

Along with Sullivan, Ashton and Challinor was the giant Barrow stand-off Phil Jackson, who captained the side in two of the three Tests. Hull's Tommy Harris was the standout hooker of his generation and packing alongside him was the formidable Wigan prop Brian McTigue, who grabbed his chance after captain Alan Prescott was injured in the first Test. John moved into the second row for the second and third Tests to accommodate loose forward Vince Karalius, while Whitehaven legend Dick Huddart was the other back-rower. As a three-man unit they had everything.

After losing the first Test, the tourists never looked back and sealed the series 2-1 with a quite brilliant 40-17 mauling of Australia in Sydney. Mick Sullivan ran in three of the eight British tries in front of 68,720 at the SCG. Overall, John played 18 of the 34 tour matches.

'Oh dear me playing with them two,' smiles John. 'Big Dick was in his prime, six foot two and could run like a gazelle, and Vince was as strong as a bull. I had the brain to weld the three of us together. It worked and we were good friends.'

However, before the good times rolled there were problems to sort out with tour coach Jim Brough. He had been sacked as Workington coach by tour manager Tom Mitchell just before the players left for Australia, but obviously both were RFL appointments so would have to get on. John remembered the early problems well and the drastic action that resulted in the coach being sidelined.

'Tom was a very clever man. He palled up with people like Vince and Brian McTigue. He infiltrated himself into the team to get their backing and pushed Jim onto the sidelines. Plus we had a fallout with him [Jim Brough]. We were in a hotel in Cronulla and unanimously passed a vote of no confidence in him before the Test matches. We told him we were unhappy with the direction he was taking us and we told him we will run the show but he can be part of it and stay friends. Senior players ran the team but what it ultimately did was unite the players. Between us we did it ourselves.'

During the tour John also had a meeting which had a profound effect on him. Australian petroleum company AMPOL were supporting the trip, which meant the Lions squad could fill up at their petrol stations free of charge. At one function John met the company's boss, who had a different attitude to those in authority back home.

'We got chatting and I said, "Oh, thank you very much, Sir, for inviting me." He said, "I am not a sir." He told me his first name and said, "Your name is John." And I said, casually, "Oh, I never knew my name is John." And I thought about it afterwards and realised he was the first person of any authority who called me by my first name. All through school, in the Army and then on to rugby league I was "Whiteley".'

Two Challenge Cup final defeats in 1959 and 1960 to Wigan (30-13) and Wakefield (38-7) respectively would be a bitter pill to swallow although the defeat to Trinity became synonymous with a remarkable effort from a clearly concussed Tommy Harris. Despite his sore head and Wakefield's dominance he was handed the Lance Todd Trophy.

By 1962 Hull's famous pack were beginning to show their age and when legendary coach Roy Francis was enticed to Leeds the following year, it was a natural progression for John to become player-coach. That was also the year he missed out on touring Australia for a third time, as an Achilles tendon injury meant he had to withdraw from the squad. He would have gone as vice-captain alongside Eric Ashton.

'I had always been interested in coaching. When Roy Francis took over at Hull he was superb. He was my coach for all my career. He was a million light years in front of everybody at that time. He had been a physical training instructor in the Army and was a sprinter. He was a fitness fanatic. And because of that I was his blue-eyed boy because I would have run through a brick wall for him. I worked in conjunction with him right from when he came. I even lived with him for a while.

'We built a running track at the end of the Boulevard and every player at Hull had to have a pair of spikes. It amazes me today that players don't own a pair of spikes. Every player at Hull had to have some spikes. In England at that time there were only six AAA [Amateur Athletic Association] affiliated coaches and one of them lived in Hull. Roy Francis employed him to teach us how to run and we would regularly go down to the nearby Costello Athletics Stadium.

'Even if you weren't a runner you were taught how to get from A to B by expending the least amount of energy. We were taught how to breathe, how to be balanced, how to stride. We used to do

400 metres and try and beat our times. In the winter we would cover the ground with straw bales and sprint through straw and it would be like running on a beach. Then we would have to jump on and off bales ... today it's called plyometrics.'

While John was in charge Hull would not be found wanting in the fitness department, although his stint as a player would come to an end in 1965. His last senior playing appearance came in the first round of the Challenge Cup at Warrington on 6 February, the Lancashire side claiming a 7-4 win. He turned out for Hull 415 times, scoring 156 tries. He also made 10 appearances for Yorkshire and 11 for Great Britain.

'I was having a problem with my shoulder and because I was the captain/coach felt I couldn't rollock anyone. I would also blame myself for everything. I would come home on a night and think about the game and I was getting upset. I was going on 35 and had had a tremendous career from day one. It wasn't really hard for me to stop playing because I was so interested in the coaching side. A lot of lads stop and don't know what to do. I was also teaching in the city and with some of the schools nearby. I had loads to do and 24 hours a day was clicking over with rugby.'

His retirement coincided with the launch of the Tuesday Night Floodlit Trophy, which helped create excitement for the sport as games were shown weekly by the BBC. The competition was used to trial the four-tackle rule.

The late 60s were dominated by Francis's exceptional Leeds outfit and although Hull were regulars in the play-offs they failed to challenge for league honours.

But there would be trophy joy for John the coach and it would be a very special one for all Hull fans. The Airlie Birds had not won the Yorkshire Cup since 1923 and after seeing off Leeds in the semi-final at Headingley, they beat Featherstone 12-9 in the 1969/70 final.

Missing star full-back Arthur Keegan and with centre Dick Gemmell playing with a broken bone in his ankle, Hull were able to edge it despite Clive Sullivan missing out on a try when he went over the dead-ball line in attempting to touch down by the posts.

That season John was a man in demand. He continued his work as Yorkshire county coach and agreed to help form a rugby league side at Hull University. He also received a circular from the RFL stating that nominees were being sought for the position of Great Britain assistant manager for the 1970 tour of Australia and New Zealand. Twelve men applied, with the RFL announcing it would decide between John and his good friend Joe Warham, who was chief scout at Leeds. Tour manager Harding made the decision to go with John.

But before heading out on what would be an incredibly successful adventure, in which the Great Britain Lions won series glory, John told Hull FC he would not be rejoining them when he returned.

'I fell out with the Hull chairman. I said when I go to Australia that's me finished. At that time no coach in England got involved with picking the team. Committees picked them. Directors picked them and I didn't know any different. I would go and sit in the boardroom with eight or ten directors and I am "Whiteley". Some would say Mr Whiteley and would ask, "What do you think about Saturday" and I would say, "so and so is fit" and offer an opinion. But they had the complete say.

'I would go home and think, "I am debating with a guy who has never played rugby or even watched it. He is a City [Hull City FC] supporter. Because they had been invited onto the board that gave them a complete say over me, who played the game, loved the game and had done everything in every aspect. And they were selecting players and I would cringe and would think "No way in the world is that young man ready to play, or is fit to play or should be playing against this team." So you start thinking, hang on, do I rebel? 'I remember one saying to me – maybe we had argued over an issue – "Mr Whiteley, remember you are a paid servant of this club." And then I would go back into my shell and think, "Yeah, you are getting your £8 … be thankful for that."'

'However, in 1969 I was doing really well. I was Yorkshire county coach and I had a really good young Hull side and this time I was beginning to become a bit volatile in relation to answering people back. Not being polite and not professional. I was thinking, "Hang on a minute … them people who don't know what they're talking about – what are they doing – they are jeopardising my professional ability." That's how I finished with Hull. The board was in such disarray but lo and behold I got into the last two for the Great Britain job and then won it.'

After John informed the club he was leaving, the board passed a vote of no confidence motion in chairman Joe Latus. His deputy Charles Watson moved up to the top job until the end of the season.

However, John's departure would not be formally announced until early August 1970. Boulevard board members had crossed their fingers all summer in the hope that he would change his mind, although Watson shamelessly described the news as a 'bombshell'.

'The board had no idea that he was going or why,' Watson told local reporters. 'He told us he was getting out because he would have to leave sooner or later, and this seemed as good a time as any. He [John] had nothing against the club in any shape or form – either financially or otherwise. The decision was his own. He was offered another contract here before his old one expired.'

In a move that shocked the city, John joined Hull Kingston Rovers for the start of the 1970/71 campaign and linked up with old friend Colin Hutton, who moved aside as Robins coach to become manager.

On being confirmed in his new position John said, 'I look on this post as a challenge and I am always open to a challenge. It may be difficult after so many years with Hull but I am sure players will accept me and I hope the supporters do too. My commitments are in Hull and I didn't want to move very far away. Rovers came along with this opportunity which fell in line with what I was looking for. It was all a bit sudden, though, and I will need time to assess the situation at the club.'

His stay at Rovers would be an unhappy one and he was sacked on 18 February 1972, just 15 days after losing 7-5 to Hull in the first round of the Challenge Cup. Speaking just hours after being told the news, John said, 'It came right out of the blue. It has shaken me very much. I have never had the sack before. I suppose there's always a first time but I haven't really had chance to think about it.'

The official Rovers statement from chairman Wilf Spavin read as follows: 'Both sides felt things were not working out as anticipated and that a change of policy seemed necessary. Whiteley was relieved of his post as coach and the team will continue to train under the remaining coaching staff until any further arrangements are made.'

Things had started promisingly for John at Craven Park. Victory in the Yorkshire Cup in the autumn of 1971 was just the tonic tonic, especially after their replay defeat to Keighley in the early stages of the Challenge Cup the previous January.

Meanwhile the sales of Cliff Wallis and Terry Clawson caused unrest in the squad. High-profile stars Roger Millward and Phil Lowe were said to be unhappy with the policy of selling top players. John remembers well how he found out he was about to lose one of his best players.

'We used to train in East Park on a Sunday morning and three of the directors pulled up in their car and told me they wanted to speak to Cliff. Anyway, he had a quick chat and came over to me and says, "I think I have just been transfer-listed." But they [the directors] had no obligation to speak to me.'

John's departure coincided with his appointment as full-time manager of the Eureka Working Men's Club in Hull, and with his commitments to his new amateur rugby league club, West Hull, plus his continuing efforts with the county team, he would still have plenty to keep him busy.

There would also be a short spell at York, where the players were threatening to down tools, but he left after six weeks with the ship righted.

A return into the rugby league spotlight would have to wait for four years. In November 1976 Great Britain U-24s were resurrected following a seven-year absence and John was given the task of guiding their development. With the World Championship taking place down under the following year and Test series against Australia in 1978 (home) and 1979 (abroad) to follow, giving the next generation of stars a platform on which to show how they could cope in elite company was considered crucially important.

Ahead of their first match against their French counterparts in Albi, John said: 'We want players who will eventually be able to stand up to the Australians and win. If a player has these qualities you do something with him.'

Captained by Castleford stand-off Bruce Burton, John's reign started with a 19-2 win, with the front row of Roy Dickinson (Leeds), John Wood (Widnes) and Eddie Szymala (Barrow) particularly impressive.

'This game proves more than anything that we have power and potential here.'

By the spring of 1977 John's good work with the U-24s meant that by the time the International Committee came to select the coach for the World Cup of that year, he was talked about as a strong candidate to return to the top job. Watkins would get it after John ruled himself out.

'I am not involved in the game full-time and I don't think it would be fair on other coaches who are. I know I took on the Under-24s but that was a different kettle of fish altogether.'

By November 1979 Whiteley's new-look and much-stronger-looking U-24s were set for their sixth meeting with France in three years, having come out on top in the previous five occasions. The team, and his philosophies, were proving a much-needed antidote to what was going on with the senior team, who had just suffered widespread derision for their efforts against Australia in the summer.

His 'play it naturally' battle cry was going down well in the press and his determination that the ball should always be made available for the full 80 minutes was much more in tune with the style of the Australian Test side had been encouraging for the last 18 months. He especially decried the sight of one forward driving forwards blindly without any options.

'There are 13 players on a field 75 yards wide,' said John, ahead of the U-24s' clash with France at Leigh on 24 November, 1979. 'No one should be isolated.'

Captained by Leigh's John Woods, they ran out easy victors and with the likes of Keith Mumby (Bradford) and Steve Evans (Featherstone) regularly impressing in the U-24s, the system seemed to be working in terms of grooming young talent for senior international rugby league.

Woods and Evans played for England against Narbonne in March 1980, a game marred by some of the worst crowd violence seen at a rugby match. Eric Ashton's side won 4-2 having beaten Wales 26-9 two weeks earlier in the comparative calm of the Boulevard.

In scenes not seen before or since, Huddersfield referee Billy Thompson was lucky to make it back from south-west France alive. He was pelted with missiles after blowing the final whistle and was locked in his dressing room for more than an hour as police battled with a 500-strong mob that was trying to force its way into the main stand. It took a diversion created by the English team to allow him to slip out unharmed.

The French were incensed when he disallowed what would have been the winning try because of a forward pass. The French touch-judge had run onto the pitch to tell him a mistake had been made. Thompson was adamant the pass 'was a yard forward'.

It was just the kind of story rugby league did not want at a time when hooliganism in soccer was rearing its head on an almost weekly basis.

Rugby league had so few examples of bad behaviour from those watching that one of its great selling points was its family-friendly nature for spectators. Cultivating that image would be one of the main themes going forward and, at a time of low attendances and poor performances for the national side, it was important the image of friendliness was maintained, not least for the plethora of sponsors who had backed the game. Under Oxley and Howes, the RFL's commercial activity had been ramped up dramatically, with sponsorship rising from £25,000 per year in 1975 to £153,500 annually five years later. By 1982/83 that figure would stand at £323,000.

In the 1970s Australia had shown how money could be generated by selling the game just the right way and in late 1979 the RFL agreed a £300,000 deal with Workington-based brewery Matthew Brown, makers of Slalom Lager, to sponsor the league. With deals already in place for the Challenge Cup (State Express), the John Player Trophy, the Floodlit Trophy (BBC) and Yorkshire Cup (Esso), there was some good news to cheer.

But every single successful sport needs successful teams and the job of selling British rugby league would have been made a lot easier if the Ashes could be won back.

The man tasked with overseeing that aim was Colin Hutton, the new Great Britain and England manager. In August 1980 his first decision was to turn to his long-term friend and former teammate with the promise that player conditioning would be taken to another level; together they were determined to try and give the players and clubs every chance to get their house in order ahead of the 1982 Australia series.

'At that time we were going through a not real good phase,' said John. 'Every club had good players but they were dominating the scene and were getting picked automatically and I don't think they were training to their true potential. I love this game that much and don't want to be detrimental and knock it but at that time we were in a terrible state.'

The duo had just over two years to execute their plans. The gap between Great Britain and Australia was clearly large and something fairly monumental would be required to close it in that time.

Chapter Four

The Countdown to 82

JOHN Whiteley and Colin Hutton hit the ground running in the summer of 1980 and straight away it was clear that the new team overseeing the three main international sides (Great Britain, the Under-24s and England) were going to spend a lot more time performing the role than previous incumbents. However, this was largely still a goodwill gesture from a now financially-secure John. His terms with the RFL meant he still only got paid £100 per game.

Hutton had a number of reasons for wanting his old pal back in the fold but critical was his availability to execute whatever plans they could. There was a lot to do. The new Great Britain manager had privately told others in the RFL that there was no chance of wresting back the Ashes because the top players did not possess the required skills and attitude.

'There was several reasons why I thought John was the right man for the job and one of them was his success with the Under-24 team,' said Hutton, whose stock was high having overseen the revival of Hull KR. 'We shall be dealing with a lot of players who have come through the Under-24 sides and [who] have worked with John. He has a rapport with these players and I know that they all have a high regard for him, but then John is tremendously well-respected in the rugby league world as a whole.

'Another big advantage is that he is completely unattached and for the amount of work we are going to have to do, it would be a burden for anyone with club commitments. Also, we both share the same kind of feelings for the game. I have had a long walk with John and our aims and ideals are on the same level.'

Hutton had already done his homework on the Australian game, and the pair's strategy became clear from the off.

'I have studied video recordings of a number of games and it is obvious from watching them and from my experience of Australian football that one of the main areas that we shall need to work on is fitness,' said Hutton.

'It has proved quite a difficult area in the past because, being a part-time sport, international calls inevitably cut across club training. My intention is to liaise with the experts at Carnegie College in Leeds and particularly Nick Whitbread, who was the fitness adviser to the Olympic team, using their facilities to ascertain everyone's level of fitness and to set players' individual targets.'

For the previous decade British rugby fans had been hearing coaches of all descriptions explain that English players were just not fit enough. Changing a long-standing culture of training on Tuesday (followed by a few beers), training on Thursday (followed by a few beers) and playing on Sunday (followed by a few beers) was going to take some doing. Their Australian counterparts were not full-time but elite-level performers did extra gym sessions before their day jobs. They were effectively training five days a week but it is worth remembering that they were being paid a lot more. Certainly, the top Aussie earners were raking in at least double that of the best British player

John's first task was to see for himself just how things worked in the Sydney Premiership, and, paying his own way, he joined a Former Lions Association trip to enable him to watch some of the Premiership play-off games in early September. He saw Canterbury beat Wests (22-17) and Minor Premiers Easts (13-7) on their way to the final. He also witnessed St George eliminating South Sydney 16-5 and then Wests do the same to St George (13-7). Canterbury, who included three Mortimer brothers in their starting line-up, would eventually take the title, beating Eastern Suburbs 18-4 in the final.

The Great Britain coach was impressed with the speed of play but felt there was a 'sameness' to the play.

'You'd still be too fast for us at the moment,' John told Australian reporter Ian Heads. 'The game is played at such a fast pace. But frankly I have been disappointed with what I have seen so far. There is a sameness about your football, a lack of variety. All the games have been played to the same pattern, all geared to speed and sheer endeavour. You seem to have a lack of ball-playing forwards and I would call what I have seen "flat" football.

'But at the moment we have no answer to you on the score of speed and fitness. My job is to close the gap that still exists between the two countries. I think we have turned the corner. So far, the fitness of our players and the approach to football at the top level does not compare with yours but that's changing.

'Canterbury showed that you don't have to knock heads to play winning football. They are a very professional club. They have some flair with their football and some individual skills. They are very aware of entertaining the public.'

John returned to ramp up preparations ahead of the three-match series with New Zealand, starting on 18 October. The Kiwis arrived in the UK on the back of losing 2-0 to Australia in fairly comprehensive fashion, but their squad was full of young, talented players, many of whom would go on to be household names at English clubs in the next five years.

Their oldest squad member was 29 and British fans would get their first chance to see the considerable skills of Gary Kemble, Dane O'Hara, James Leuluai, Fred Ah Kuoi, Mark Broadhurst, Graeme West, Kevin Tamati and Gary Prohm. They were part of a 26-man party under the stewardship of Ces Mountford, the ex-Warrington and Wigan playmaker.

'We have a lot of young players,' said Mountford. 'And they are going to pick up a lot of experience on this tour.'

Captained by the brilliant loose forward Mark Graham, the tourists were certain to provide a stern first test for Whiteley and Hutton, who, along with fellow selectors Bill Oxley (Barrow), Reg Parker (Blackpool), Tom Mitchell (Workington), Doug Alton (Bramley), Les Bettinson (Salford), Joe Seddon (St Helens) and Phil Brunt (Castleford), supported their new coach by spending the early part of the 1980/81 season watching as many international probables as they could, as often as possible.

So committed was Hutton, a fastidious man by nature, that he turned down an all-expenses-paid trip to Australia, to appear on *This Is Your Life,* which was featuring his great friend Artie Beetson. He would also have been well aware that a good start was needed to get his fellow selectors more in tune with the plan for more continuity and youth. A good start was also essential to make that plan a reality as he was just one of eight selectors.

'I am very much aware that both myself and the new system are on trial this season,' said Hutton. 'But I am hopeful that this method will prove to be successful and useful as a long-term pattern. Obviously our immediate aim is to win the forthcoming Test series against New Zealand but the long-term aim is regaining the Ashes. We haven't won a Test series against Australia since 1970 and we are keen to change that.

'New Zealand will be bringing a very strong team, particularly in the forwards. I have watched video recordings of the recent Test against Australia and I can promise you some of the forwards are pretty fiery.'

The selection committee met in Leeds on 25 September to select a 20-man squad for the first Tests, with ten of John's successful U-24 side making it in. There would be five training sessions to prepare in just 11 days – including two days focusing on fitness at Carnegie College – and the Great Britain management duo had a measure of discretion when it came to naming the starting XIII. Selectors' chairman Bill Oxley was prepared to offer this leeway provided that the committee's 'preferences' were taken into careful consideration. However, by 1982 there would be no such room for manoeuvre, although John was present when the teams for the Ashes were picked.

A foot injury suffered by St Helens forward Peter Gorley meant he missed out on joining his brother Les, while there were first-time call-ups for St Helens loose forward Harry Pinner, Leeds scrum-half Kevin Dick, Whitehaven half-back Arnie Walker and Hull KR prop Roy Holdstock.

'Dick is a very good young player,' said John, during an interview in Australia just after the Grand Final. 'He is rugged and quick and cheeky, but at times he can be a bit naughty. Pinner is not as big as the usual run of Great Britain locks but he is a very gifted player and very brave. Trevor Skerrett, who toured here last year, is in line for one of the prop spots. He was a little like General Custer out here last year but on that occasion, it was Australians and not Indians coming at him.'

Skerrett and Dick both played at Central Park while Pinner was a substitute. In total there were eight new caps. The Kiwis were hardly in top form having won just two of their first five tour matches.

Loose forward Len Casey stood out as the teams fought hard for a 14-14 draw. A late missed penalty from GB captain George

Fairbairn denied his coach a winning start but his Kiwi counterpart felt that the result was just rewards for both sides.

'If George Fairbairn had kicked Britain to victory with his late penalty attempt it would have been an injustice,' said Mountford. 'A draw was a fair indication of the game. I thought we played more attacking football than Britain.'

Excellent approach work from John Joyner paved the way for first-half tries for winger Chris Camilleri and his centre partner Mike Smith. In a hectic first half Ah Kuoi replied in kind after 25 minutes and five minutes later Graham's burst through some flimsy tackling and created the opportunity for second-rower Tony Coll to cross.

It was not the start anyone in the British camp wanted and for the second Test at Odsal on 2 November they would have to do without Skerrett, because of an injury he picked up in the Wigan opener. There were other injury problems which meant a Test debut for Widnes prop Glyn Shaw.

Also added to the squad were Leigh winger Des Drummond, Warrington half-back Ken Kelly, Widnes hooker Keith Elwell and Featherstone second-rower Peter Smith.

Hutton said: 'We have known from the beginning that this New Zealand side is competent. They have picked up some good ideas from Australia and while they are not as physical as the Aussies they can play a similar type of football.

'It was an eye opener for many of our players in the first Test. They came up against opposition which were thinking and moving quicker than what they are used to. They should go better now they know the size of task but it must also be considered that we had eight new caps in the first Test team and nerves are bound to affect performances to some degree.'

Pinner made his first start at Odsal with Casey moving into the second row, while Kelly replaced Rovers ace Steve Hartley at stand-off and Drummond came in for his Test debut in place of Keith Bentley. There was also a chance at hooker for Elwell, with David Ward and David Watkinson out injured.

Colin Hutton added: 'The men who have come in are similar in style to the ones who have dropped out. Shaw, for instance, is the same rugged, mobile type of prop as Skerrett and I have no doubt he will do a good job.

'The squad training also ensures every player is familiar with our pattern of play and we have not had to make any big changes in our plans. Like New Zealand we prefer firm conditions but that does not mean we are going to take them on at their own game. We will play it our own way because I believe we still have the players with enough skills to beat them.'

There had been worries about the Odsal playing surface but it can't be used as an excuse for a dismal effort. O'Hara's try 11 minutes from time sealed a 12-8 victory for the visitors, while the home side made just one clear break all match via Kelly and the crowd grew exasperated at seeing British forwards repeatedly barging forward on their own. It did not help that one of the pack was in no fit state to play having turned up inebriated.

'I think it would be wrong to pick on individuals,' said the Britain coach. 'Generally I have been happy with the team selected and I cannot see the point in bringing back the old names.

'It would defeat the object of our exercise which is to build for the future. The others have had their chance and not taken it. I'll take responsibility for today's performance which I thought was an improvement on the first Test. We put them under a lot of pressure but could not find the space to break through. At times we had them all over the place.'

Unfortunately for John, continuity was not a top priority for the selectors, whose patience with the new Hutton/Whiteley youth-based agenda had already worn perilously thin. With the threat of an embarrassing home Test series loss now a serious possibility, six players were dropped; in addition, Camilleri and Pinner were out injured.

Back came 'form horses' in the shape of Leeds winger John Atkinson (aged 34), who had made his Great Britain debut in the 1968 World Cup, plus seasoned back rowers Steve Norton (29) and Mick Adams (29). There would also be a debut for Whitehaven scrum-half Walker and, at full-back, Mick Burke was a late replacement for Fairbairn.

There was a new position for captain Casey, who moved into the front row alongside Elwell and the now injury-free Skerrett. The Hull KR firebrand also set the scene for the do-or-die third Test at Headingley by launching an astonishing defence of his coach in a newspaper column the day before the game.

'I am fed up with sneering, sniping and griping about our Great Britain set-up by those armchair critics,' wrote Casey. 'I'm directing my own counterblast at two or three well-known coaches in particular and only hope we can wipe those smirks off their faces in the final Test at Headingley tomorrow.

'They've been busy firing their bullets at Great Britain coach Johnny Whiteley, and, to a lesser degree international supremo Colin Hutton. Well, take it from me, our squad are sick of their snide remarks on the radio, TV and in the local press. Big Johnny, as usual, has shrugged it all off with a wry grin and a "we'll show 'em at the end of the day" attitude.

'But those know-alls have really got my back up. Coaches who should know better have been giving Whiteley and his methods some stick.

'Are their own track records and qualifications at highest-grade coaching superior to those of Whiteley? My answer is a firm NO. One of these knockers has been having a go at me as well. I can usually handle anything that is thrown at me but I can't stomach anybody who gives you a verbal clouting when you are halfway down and in need of a morale-booster.

'It's Whiteley's strength of character in all this "I would have done it my way" business that I've admired the most. There isn't one lad in our squad who doesn't rate him the perfect professional. Even the youngsters have quickly voted him tops. We accept all his driving in strenuous training sessions. On the other hand we thoroughly appreciate the way he gives us free rein.

'You see, Johnny is a firm believer in players being able to express themselves like they do for their own club sides. He expects 100 per cent fitness and honest endeavour and wouldn't tolerate any kidology or shamming.

'Some clubs haven't been much help to Johnny and team manager Hutton and I feel really sad about that. Yet my own Hull KR outfit have sacrificed a lot. Rovers' coach Roger Millward hasn't been quite so tough with his British members at club training – as though he's willing to give everything for Britain.

'It's high-time our national team was put before club football. Whiteley and Hutton, besides bending over backwards to give youth its chance, have also done their utmost to please Britain and the clubs.

'I know for a fact they could have had the players under their wing a lot longer but they knew they'd be depriving the clubs of their services. Completely unselfish and thoughtful to the last. That's Whiteley and Hutton, who temper their steel with care.

'Take it from me we will be pulling out ALL the stops for them at Headingley tomorrow ... and hopefully silencing those critics.'

Casey was a man on a mission and his 12 team-mates followed his lead in the opening exchanges as they opened up with some free-flowing rugby, but either side of half-time the British reverted to more conservative means of taking the ball forward. It took a brilliant effort from winger Drummond to reignite the game and his two tries in the final quarter settled the matter 10-2.

'It was an encouraging display because the players showed a lot of spirit but there is still a lot of hard work to be done,' said John.

The post-series statement from Howes spoke volumes.

He said: 'We have settled for a certain standard of play in our domestic football, while falling behind on an international level. It is now generally believed that we are just not fit enough to compete with the Australians and the New Zealanders. We have got to look to new, modern fitness techniques or we could fall further behind.'

Fitness apart the efforts of the players confirmed everything the British management team feared. The Aussies were going to be fitter and stronger but also were more dynamic. Hutton and Whiteley identified a lack of support play as a huge issue. One-up rugby still dominated the domestic game and getting the forwards in particular to change their ways was easier said than done.

Behind the scenes the Great Britain management had a plan. They knew the limited time they had with the players was not going to be enough and the internal politics of the selection committee ensured that gaining continuity of selection would be virtually impossible. It didn't help that at times selectors did not pick players from their own clubs because they didn't want to pay out international selection bonuses, or that they made deals with other selectors so that one of their players could be picked to help increase their value in the transfer market.

There was nothing John and his old friend could do about the tangled web of RFL politics but they were prepared to try and open the clubs' eyes to what they should be doing to get their players to the peak of their physical potential. In conjunction with Rod McKenzie, senior lecturer in physical education at Carnegie College in Leeds, four days' worth of clinics for club coaches were devised to be held across two sessions in March and May the following year.

McKenzie broke down the sessions into speed, strength, stamina and 'planning a training session', and on the first night guests would be shown a video, made by McKenzie, on the role of the coach. Attendees were also encouraged to give their thoughts.

Before that he was invited to put those players, who had turned out against New Zealand, through their paces. Whiteley and Hutton had determined that, long term, concentrating on getting 20 of the most likely players physically ready for the challenge of facing Australia was their best hope. That 'all-stars' squad would be given their own individual training schedules to run alongside what they did with their clubs. Obviously, there was no contractual obligation to follow the training plans. The Great Britain management hoped that players' ambitions to play for GB would be sufficient motivation. Certainties for this new elite training squad were Drummond and Mike Smith, who impressed McKenzie at their first meeting. University student Steve Evans also scored well, although it was less good news among the forwards. Reportedly, one player was told he needed to shed a third of his body weight. David Howes said: 'It's a myth that a forward needs to carry extra weight. A fully-fit man just needs powerful muscles.'

Looking back 40 years later the passion still burned bright in John Whiteley. Everything he had been telling rugby league bosses for years had hindered his ability to do his job.

'Because I had still been involved with U-24s and seeing a lot of the top players, it was clear the skill factor was getting them into the Great Britain side. They were entitled to be in that side. The same players were dominating the scene to such an extent they were becoming automatic selections because there weren't enough people coming through underneath. Too many of them weren't being pushed and were just doing enough because there just wasn't the same amount of quality coming through as in previous years. In Hull the Works League had to amalgamate with the local amateur league because there just weren't enough teams.

'We didn't have the volume of players like they did in Australia. Our top players were getting picked even if they were going on the piss too much or going through the motions at training. I'm not saying they were all doing that. Dessie Drummond was superbly fit, for example, and a lot of the lads were super. But they were in the minority. A third would run through a brick wall for you, a third would do just enough and another third would skive to the best of their ability.'

By the end of 1980 John still had time to play with before the Kangaroos arrived. He also had Great Britain games against France home and away at the end of 1981 plus England would play the annual European Championship with Wales and France earlier that same year. Nearer the time there would be four trial matches against France, in Venice on 31 July 1982, and then in early August there would be meetings with Hull KR, Leeds and Widnes. In the summer of 1982 there would also be a summer training squad of 31 for those deemed likely to make the side. It would be split geographically into three areas: Humberside, Rest of Yorkshire and Lancashire. They would be monitored and given final training instructions for the early part of the 1982/83 season.

In contrast the Kangaroos would welcome France in 1981 and New Zealand 12 months later, both for two Tests. However, the changes being made to interstate matches between New South Wales and Queensland were really starting to capture the public's imagination and by 1982 the State of Origin series – those selected played for the state in which they learned their rugby – as we know it was born.

The buildup for Britain's top players could not have started any more low-key if it tried. Just 3,229 paid to see England lose 5-1 to

France at Headingley on 21 February 1981. It would be the last European Championship as flagging interest in the concept and problems over officiating subsequently proved insurmountable.

In Leeds, French referee Guy Cattaneo so incensed everyone watching by his constant awarding of penalties to his countrymen that RFL secretary David Oxley paid him a visit at half-time.

'It is the first time I have done that and my main concern was for the public who were not seeing a game,' said Oxley. 'I wanted to clarify one or two points with him. It helped a little but he had murdered the game with his offside ruling.'

In the second half Cattaneo only dished out four penalties (two apiece) but refused to penalise the French scrum-half for feeding the scrum. The repeated sight of Guirard shoving the ball into his second row left the home fans incensed. Hutton called it the worst refereeing performance he had seen, while his coach added: 'How can I blame any of the players for that? In the circumstances they conducted themselves admirably. They were burning up at half-time but I urged them to keep control. It was embarrassing but we didn't play well. At home we should have overcome all adversities.'

Fairbairn's drop goal came in the 54th minute before Guirard scooted over for the game's only try three minutes later. He and his team-mates were given muted applause as Cattaneo was given a police escort off the pitch. It was France's first win on English soil since 1949 and meant they would be the last European champions.

Norton, who had threatened to pull out of the squad in the run-up to the Wales clash on 18 March, was again recalled, as was scrum-half Steve Nash. Neither had played for England since the 60-13 mauling of Wales in 1978. The Salford scrum-half was a late replacement for Featherstone's talented young No 7 Paul Harkin. Nash had not been seen on the international scene since knee trouble curtailed his efforts in the 1979 tour of Australia.

Nash's half-back partner Kelly stole the show at Craven Park. Playing his third match in five days, the Warrington stand-off scored one try and made another as England won 17-4.

Just a few days earlier one of the critical elements of the Whiteley/Hutton plan to exert change was finally enacted, with the inaugural Rugby League Coaching Conference in Leeds.

Beginning on 6 March, each of the 30 league clubs were asked to send their coach for an intensive two-day programme of instruction and discussion. There would be no representation from Huyton, Keighley or Swinton, who all sent their apologies. Alongside Whiteley and McKenzie were Dr Stuart Lunt, the secretary of the Rugby League Medical Association and Laurie Gant, joint national coach. Gant and Albert Fearnley had been two of the original advocates for the importance of coaching. Both had successful playing and coaching careers and in the early 70s their work evolved into what became known as the National Coaching Scheme although it received little backing from the RFL and the clubs.

Day one of the conference opened with a film and lecture called 'The Principles and Components of Fitness'. Then, with the help of players from Castleford U-17s, hour-long lectures and practical demonstrations were given on the specifics of speed, strength and stamina. Before a late dinner the coaches watched a video called 'The Role of the Coach'.

Day two started with a lecture called 'Planning a Training Programme'. There was then 90 minutes of practical training aimed at turning the theory into practice, before the conference was wrapped up with an open forum discussion that ushered in three very interesting ideas.

The coaches accepted the fitness deficiencies in the British game but offered the three following caveats (the following is taken word for word an official RFL report):

1) 'It was unanimously agreed that the four up and four down promotion and relegation system currently in operation since 1973 should be revised to two up and two down. They felt that 25 per cent of the clubs in the first division being relegated put too many clubs under pressure and forced teams to play safety-first tactics, thus inhibiting the adventurous style of players. It was also felt that the present system encouraged the yo-yo effect with too many clubs being promoted and relegated in successive years.

2) It was agreed that the management team in charge of an international side should be solely responsible for team selection, albeit with the aid of the selection panel. It was felt that the international coach to establish selection policies and team tactics during his appointment.

3) It was generally felt that British players were facing a much more demanding fixture programme than their international counterparts. Players with top sides were being asked to play between 40 and 50 matches a season plus possible representative matches for both county and country. This left little time for international preparation on the desired squad system.'

There had been efforts to make changes before to the number of games played and the way the season was structured.

As far back as the 1960s St Helens secretary-manager Basil Lowe came close to bringing about summer rugby. His proposal was expected to win the three-fifths majority vote, only for a number of clubs to change their mind at the last moment.

In June 1978, Castleford and Leeds pushed to reduce the first division to 14 and make relegation two up, two down rather than the long-standing four up, four down system. That failed to get the necessary support at the RFL's annual meeting in Blackpool.

With Division Two expanding through the early 80s only a modest change was made for the 1985/86 campaign when it became three-up, three-down.

Then, at the height of the awful winter of 1978/79, Bradford chairman Harry Womersley, once again led the call for summer rugby. John Stringer at Leigh was another prominent supporter of the idea.

'Games could be played mainly in the evening,' he said. 'We could even copy the Australian practice of playing colts, reserves and first-team games on the same programme in succession. Spectators would really get value for money and it is obviously more comfortable to watch in warmer weather.'

The idea did have support but had the obvious drawback of making summer tours an impossibility.

Bradford garnered enough support to call a special meeting of clubs. However, it was reported that TV bosses were not impressed, while Wigan supremo Sumner Baxendale pointed out that many northern towns had a tradition of closing down for a couple of weeks, which would create 'wake weeks'. David Howes said: 'The game could quickly become too parochial if it couldn't depend on the national and worldwide coverage given on TV.'

If Womersley and Stringer were frustrated there was also a degree of annoyance surrounding events at the second Rugby League Coaching Conference at Carnegie College on 15 and 16 May 1981. This time eight clubs did not send a representative and the goodwill and platitudes after the first two-day clinic were not followed up with actions. It was so symptomatic of the attitudes of the time.

On the field, the team who would start the first Ashes Test at Boothferry Park was beginning to take shape when on 8 November England played their first match in Wales for 31 years. With 12 months to go their coach was starting to feel the pressure.

Ahead of the fixture at Ninian Park, home of the new Division Two side Cardiff City Blue Dragons, John said: 'In many ways the pressures are even greater than I have felt for Test matches. There is so much at stake ... for me, the teams and the game in general. Winning is the priority but we have also to put on a good show to impress the Welsh public.'

In five international matches he had only managed two wins and his policy of building a young side, based around the core of his successful U-24 squad, had been effectively given the thumbs down. The selectors decided to continue to choose players for the here and now, emphasised by the return of Leeds stalwart Les Dyl in the centres. With Fairbairn returning at full-back and Drummond one of the few no-brainer selections on the wing, three of the five backs who would tackle the Kangaroos in Hull were picked. Wigan's exciting teenage winger Henderson Gill, on his international debut, and Hull KR centre Mike Smith made up the backs. Gill's selection was also important in a wider context. At a time of headline-grabbing racism on the terraces of soccer grounds up and down the country, the selection of two black wingers for the same international rugby league team was a big moment for all Afro-Caribbean sportsmen.

The half-back partnership of Woods and Nash would also be the same in 12 months while soon-to-be Ashes players Jeff Grayshon, hooker Ward and Norton were part of a hugely experienced pack. Alongside them in Cardiff were 31-year-old Phil Lowe, 32-year-old Hull KR prop John Millington, whose previous England appearance was back in 1975, and 30-year-old Saints second-rower Peter Gorley.

'The younger players have to prove they are better. In sprinting you do not replace a veteran who does even times with a youngster who only does 10.2 seconds.' John was being a diplomat to the last.

Against a Wales side that lacked the stardust of recent incarnations, England's quality shone through although they had to withstand a late fightback from the home side as tries from Wigan scrum-half Ness Flowers and Hull winger Paul Prendiville left the final score at 20-15. The really good news for the RFL was that their major publicity campaign drew an impressive crowd of 8,102. That was 2,000 more than saw Cardiff City v Norwich and Cardiff RU v Munster 24 hours earlier.

While Millington and Lowe had played their last international games it was obvious that Norton was still central to the selectors' thinking. The Hull loose forward's ball-playing skills would be pivotal to future strategy and he would play in what were effectively the last two major GB games before the Ashes.

Norton, Drummond, Woods, Grayshon, Skerrett and Widnes second-rower Les Gorley would all play in the home-and-away double header against France in December. To offset the refereeing issues that had dogged recent fixtures between the two, Australian whistler Greg Hartley was flown over to take charge of both encounters.

Stage one would be at the Boulevard on 6 December before an interesting trip to the football-mad city of Marseille 14 days later.

Norton, still to really bring his excellent club form to the international stage, had been the cornerstone of a resurgent Hull side and across the city Rovers, buoyed by some big-money signings, were also on the march. That rise to prominence was reflected in the selection of the turbo-charged Hartley at stand-off. The Robins star, who had made one GB appearance against New Zealand a year earlier, was the country's leading try-scorer (15) when the French arrived in Hull and his international coach was excited at the prospect of the two linking up.

'There is no [other] forward with Norton's ability to put players through gaps and when Hartley puts his head back there is no stopping him,' said John. 'Unfortunately ground conditions could be against speed men and there may have to be a change of plans with more concentration on forward play.'

It would be the one and only time both Gorley brothers would start in an international; Woods was moved into the centre to accommodate Hartley. Widnes's 20-year-old highly-regarded scrum-half Andy Gregory also got his chance to stake a claim. One pundit described him as the new Alex Murphy although one has to hope he didn't do so within earshot of Murphy.

However, they would all be overshadowed by the efforts of wingers Gill and Drummond, who ran in five tries between them as a 12,743 crowd lapped up a 37-0 thrashing of the French.

'We aimed to get 30 points and should have had 50,' said a delighted coach minutes after the final whistle. 'There is little wrong in the backs with Drummond and Gill the two most exciting wingers we have had for a long time. But we have to get all six forwards working together for the full 80 minutes. Until we get that I won't be satisfied.'

The only bad news for the GB camp was an injury to Hartley after 30 minutes. He had combined brilliantly with Norton just as predicted and the two linked up to make the first try, the Rovers flier scorching past two French defenders on his way to the line.

With Woods scoring the other try it appeared things were clicking into place and pundits and supporters alike were hopeful of more of the same in Marseille. But as he and his players flew out from Heathrow John was playing down expectations.

'It would give me great satisfaction to nil them again. We won easily enough at Hull but I am looking for an improvement that cannot be measured in points. There has to be more combined play from our forwards with none of the them going alone, even the defence can be tightened.

'If the forwards do their jobs right the backs will pick up the points again. And looking ahead to Australia next season that is important when one point could be the difference between winning and losing.'

Both he and Hutton knew too many of the forwards were being picked for their strength rather than their speed and stamina but finding others to fit the bill was not easy. It didn't help that a few of them didn't seem able to resist the bright lights and 24-hour drinking available in the southern French port. Reports that four squad members – both Gorley brothers, Skerrett and Norton – were caught up in trouble in a French bar in the early hours of the morning did not bode well.

Hartley had recovered in time to resume his partnership with Gregory while Burke got his chance at full-back. Watkinson was finally fit to come in at hooker and there was an opportunity handed to Barrow's tenacious tearaway Eddie Szymala in the second row. He replaced his fellow Cumbrian Peter Gorley, who was the substitute.

The French made wholesale changes and had a field day as a remarkably ill-disciplined performance from Great Britain contributed to the hosts running out 19-2 winners. Les Gorley was sent off and referee Hartley even threatened to end the match early if both sides didn't stop the niggling.

'We made the mistake of being drawn into the trap of niggling by the French instead of concentrating on football,' said John.

In nine months the Australians would be arriving and John and Colin had some big decisions to make. At the end of the 1981/82 season a 31-man summer training squad was picked and they faced an intensive few weeks, starting with a three-day camp on 4 June. In the meantime, whoever was going to lead the Kangaroos would get three more opportunities to watch them against New Zealand (3 and 17 July) and Papua New Guinea (PNG, 2 October).

The leading candidate for the Ashes tour was long-standing incumbent Frank Stanton, who had led the side so well in 1978 and 1979. He was impressed with the 31 names announced by the RFL on 25 May 1982.

'There is certainly a lot of ability in the backline,' said the Balmain coach, who also admitted to not being familiar with a few of the names. 'The forwards are an unknown quantity. If they are young and keen, they could cause Australia some problems. The lessons from the last tour to Australia and the Kangaroo series in England in 1970s have been absorbed by England's selectors.'

The training squad read as follows:

- Full-backs: Mick Burke (Widnes), George Fairbairn (Hull KR).

- Wingers: John Basnett (Widnes), Des Drummond (Leigh), Henderson Gill (Wigan), Paul Prendiville (Hull).

- Centres: Steve Evans (Hull), Eric Hughes (Widnes), John Joyner (Castleford), Mike Smith (Hull KR), David Stephenson (Wigan).

- Half-backs: Kevin Dick (Leeds), Andy Gregory (Widnes), Steve Nash (Salford), John Woods (Leigh), David Topliss (Hull).

- Back rowers: Mick Adams (Widnes), Les Gorley (Widnes), Steve Norton (Hull), Ian Potter (Leigh), Alan Rathbone (Bradford), Peter Smith (Featherstone), Gary van Bellen (Bradford), Kevin Ward (Castleford).

- Props: Jeff Grayshon (Bradford), Mike O'Neill (Widnes), Trevor Skerrett (Hull), John Wood (Fulham).

- Hookers: David Ward (Leeds), Ray Tabern (Leigh), David Watkinson (Hull KR).

It might not have been the 'super squad' of 20 the GB management team had initially wanted but there was a clear indication of the direction in which they wanted to go with the inclusion of a number of young, mobile forwards.

O'Neill was just 21 and while many questioned his ability in the prop position because of his perceived lack of size, he had done well for his national coach as part of the Great Britain U-24s.

Potter, part of Leigh's title-winning side in his first season with the club, was only 23 and his selection was widely expected. Rathbone's inclusion was also due reward for his efforts with the U-24s and his all-action style was very much in keeping with what was required, although managing him proved hard work. But few foresaw a chance for van Bellen and particularly 26-year-old Wood, who was part of the Fulham team relegated and who had no previous international experience.

In the backs new Wigan arrival Stephenson had a big fan in his coach. Alex Murphy lauded the 23-year-old with typical hyperbole.

'This youngster reminds me of Reg Gasnier,' Murphy told Australian journalists. 'He's all power and class and should be the first selected in my book.'

Whether Murphy believed it himself is unclear but whatever ability Stephenson had – and he unquestionably had plenty – you can't reach the top without application.

'He always seemed to be injured when we wanted him for training,' reflects John. With Stephenson largely absent Rovers' Steve Hartley would also get called up. In the summer of 1982 the Yorkshire players came to my gym and were amazed at the standards my amateur players set them! Mike Smith for example, will tell you to this day that for the few weeks I had him that was the best he felt. He is proud to say it. In fact I never had one problem with any of the Yorkshire lads once they started training.

'But it was too late. We hadn't got enough if it. So you always knew you were going to be fighting an uphill battle. When people say they can get athletes fit in six weeks … I wouldn't show them through the door. Nobody in the world can get fit in six weeks to play professional rugby. It takes you a year and more.'

Injuries and unavailabilities would become something of a theme for John, who was overseeing the Humberside players at his training pod, while Mal Reilly agreed to help out with the rest of the Yorkshire players. Over in Lancashire, Graham Starkey, the former part-time RFL coaching co-ordinator, took charge of regular sessions near Warrington. However, attendance was still a voluntary thing. There were no extra payments from the RFL for these players to come to night-time sessions after work and fit them in around pre-season training with their clubs.

O'Neill remembered them well.

'Graham was very strict. He pushed us hard and would constantly talk about the Australian physiques and show us pictures of their players. He wanted us to look like them.'

David Ward recalled running up slag heaps and through woods in Kippax, and sessions in a gym in Castleford.

'We worked hard and I enjoyed the sessions but we didn't work on ball skills,' said Ward. 'Obviously you have a number of guys who were very switched on in terms of tactical awareness … the likes of John Holmes and 'Knocker' Norton. But collectively, as a group, we were behind the Australians. At the top level tiny details make a big difference when it comes to teamwork and cohesion.'

Peter Smith had to withdraw because of work problems, Woods had an injury concern while Adams, Burke and Gill were kicked out of the squads – Leeds centre Dyl coming the other way – after failing to report for at least one session. With numerous holiday commitments also adding to the coaching staff's headaches, it would be tough to keep enough of the players up to scratch. Mind you, not everyone liked the idea of regional training camps. Alex Murphy was one who didn't think they would produce results.

'A training squad is fine, provided all the players are together regularly,' said the Wigan coach. 'But at present half train in Lancashire and the rest in Yorkshire. Fitness is a major factor, but we'll need teamwork to topple the Aussies.'

With just weeks to go, and Reilly and Roger Millward added to the coaching team, the final countdown for the Great Britain squad started in the most unlikely of places. Venice would be the location for a warm-up match with a French XIII. It was hoped that it would be the start of a push to get the game noticed in Italy; the resort at which they played paid for the British party to fly over. Monsieur Cattaneo was put in the charge ... obviously someone at the French equivalent of the RFL had a sense of humour.

Prendiville, O'Neill, Wood, Potter and Rathbone all started and Topliss captained the side as they lost 8-7. Joyner was Britain's solitary try-scorer at the picturesque Stadio Pierluigi Penzo. Officially there were just 1,500 in attendance.

'We had a good spirit but were beaten fair and square on the night,' said John.

Once back in the UK finding available players for the final warm-up did not bode well. On 15 August against Widnes (in Mick Adams's benefit match), manager Colin Hutton was forced to call in extra players. Veteran Wakefield full-back Harry Box, Leeds stand-off John Holmes and Castleford second-rower Dave Finch all played, and the team lost 13-5. Burke, ironically, improving both tries – for Stuart Wright and Fred Whitfield. One-time GB hopeful Chris Camilleri also crossed for Widnes while Finch registered Britain's solitary try.

Burke's appearance in the white and black of Widnes was something of a surprise. Two days earlier it was reported that he had made his peace with the selectors and was due to play for the national side.

Hutton said: 'Burke has had a talk with me and his attitude has been just what we had been hoping. He has kept himself fit and has now rejoined the squad.'

The Great Britain line-up had had a much more familiar feel to it in the first game against Hull KR seven days earlier. Ray Tabern got his chance at hooker while Basnett was given a run on the wing and Dyl partnered Joyner in the centres. Hughes teamed up with his club-mate Gregory at half-back while Wood and Potter got another go in the pack and Casey also came into the second row. A late flurry of scoring eased GB to an encouraging 30-0 success. They scored four tries in the final 15 minutes against severely-weakened opposition. Rovers were without Hartley or Millington, who were having a joint benefit match, but were able to call upon big-money signing Andy Kelly, who had just arrived from Wakefield for £60,000.

'We shall be ready physically and mentally when the Aussies come,' said John after the game. Rovers stand-in coach Roger Millward played 31 minutes in the second half and confirmed that the match would be his final appearance.

Four days later Leeds were the opponents in a fixture that acted as a testimonial for David Ward. The hooker was set to be a substitute for the national side until Watkinson withdrew because of injury.

Van Bellen got a start and both Peter Smith, also now back in the fold, and Rathbone played in a pack that also included Fulham prop Wood.

The way in which Leeds fought back from 16-5 down to win 22-21 did not do much to enhance the chances of the younger British forwards on show. A drop-goal from John Holmes secured a dramatic win for the home side and the experienced stand-off combined superbly with his teenage half-back partner Mark Conway. Along with the outstanding David Heron, they outshone their opponents. Veteran winger Alan Smith and Conway both crossed twice while Neil Hague got the other Leeds try. Joyner, Hughes, Drummond, Fairbairn and Gregory were Britain's try-scorers.

RL secretary David Oxley said: 'Don't read too much into the results of the Great Britain squad in recent warm-up matches against club sides. We have learned some valuable lessons. The Aussies may be formidable but are not invincible supermen.'

However, privately the Great Britain coach was worried.

'I knew we were short of enough quality players and the attitude of the selection committee always seemed to be just make and mend,' recalled John. 'Then some players were picked because his club director was a selector.

'Having been to Australia I knew they had left players behind that if you made a third team out of would have given us a good game. Colin and I could have picked a better side, and I'm not making any excuses, but we didn't have control and we were the ones watching the players and could see how they could fit into a team.'

With six weeks to go before the Ashes started a further five players were added to the now 35-man training squad, who were now meeting weekly with John and Hutton.

Dave Heron's early-season exploits for Leeds had not gone unnoticed while Wigan hooker Nicky Kiss was also called up along with Saints' impressive half-back Neil Holding and the experienced Hull forward Paul Rose. In addition, Woods returned to the fold; his creative talents made it hard for the selectors to ignore him.

However, the intensity of the summer sessions was lost once the 1982/83 club season started, according to Hull KR centre Mike Smith.

'We did all our weights work and training and then once the season started all that evaporated. We'd have one night at Huddersfield or one night at Castleford. But people had jobs and would have injuries and a lot of times I think it was a cop out. Plus I think some of the clubs wanted the players for themselves. I don't think Great Britain was a priority.'

Hutton was also putting on a brave face: 'Although we lost two of the three pre-season games we have been delighted with the progress of the players on the fitness front. Suspensions and holidays disrupted our plans for those matches. Now we are to look at the tactical side of our play in preparation for the Test series.'

Six days after the British squad was increased in size, Parramatta and Eastern Suburbs met to decide who would play Manly in the NRL Grand Final. It would be a critical few days with Australia's selectors set to announce their own final 28 players.

On a mudbath of a pitch at the SCG, Parramatta defied the slippery conditions to put in an extraordinary display of running and handling to blow Easts away 31-0. Dazzling, length-of-the-field tries by Eric Grothe (twice) and Brett Kenny caused a sensation in Australia.

On 26 September Kenny, Grothe and Steve Ella were all on the scoresheet as the Eels claimed their second successive Premiership title 21-8. On the very same day back in the UK a proposed player strike over changes to the injury insurance scheme was narrowly averted.

The contrast could not have been starker. The disjointed and insular British game was still in a never-ending firefighting mode while a new breed of Australian superstars, ten years in the making and part of a cohesive and targeted training programme, were about to send shockwaves around the world.

Chapter Five

The Kangaroos

'INVINCIBLES humbled' screamed a headline in the *Sydney Morning Herald*. The story had nothing to do with the 1982 Kangaroos. The team they were referring to were Jack Gibson's Parramatta after their 31-14 defeat to Manly on 5 July 1982.

It wasn't untypical of the time for Australian newspapers to go overboard with their headlines but it was indicative of the esteem Gibson's champion side were held in and, although it was their fourth league defeat of the season, there was a growing consensus that his exciting young outfit were going to dominate Australian rugby for years to come. Their backline, in particular, was making waves, not least because they were all so young. Peter Sterling, Brett Kenny, Steve Ella and Eric Grothe were all 22 or under and they were brilliant.

Two days before that epic league meeting, Parramatta's standout second-rower John Muggleton had saved Australia's blushes in the first Test against New Zealand at Lang Park. A great offload in the tackle from St George prop Craig Young sent substitute Muggleton through for a try three minutes from time to make it 11-8.

It was hardly the stuff of nightmares if you were a British rugby league fan, but the closeness of the game had more to do with the staggering total of 45 penalties handed out by English referee Fred Lindop.

'The Australian team is one which needs a good supply of ball so they can move the opposition around,' said Stanton. 'This did not happen, and our fellows chased the ball for a lot of the match.'

Lindop reluctantly agreed to meet the Kangaroos coach and his New Zealand counterpart Cecs Mountford. Sorting this out was especially critical for Stanton. This was more than just about the next Test match with the Kiwis.

The previous month, Queensland had come from one down to beat New South Wales in the State of Origin series. They had last won an interstate series in 1960 but the new rules, which meant players didn't have to play for the state in which their clubs were based, levelled the playing field considerably in their favour.

It meant the likes of John Ribot, Paul McCabe and Kerry Boustead, all stars of the Sydney Premiership, could represent the state where they learned to play rugby and from that moment the annual competition quickly grew into a stellar event renowned for high quality and high drama.

Many expected the Maroons' victory in 1982 to be hugely significant for their coach Artie Beetson and there was plenty of Queensland backlash when he did not replace his New South Wales counterpart for the New Zealand Test matches.

Most vociferous had been Queensland Rugby League President Ron McAuliffe, who believed Beetson should have automatically been given his chance against the Kiwis after winning the second State of Origin on 8 June.

But in 1981 Stanton had seen off Beetson for the New Zealand series with the casting vote of ARL President Kevin Humphreys, and 12 months later the exact same thing happened with the caveat being that Stanton's efforts in leading Australia for the Tests at Lang Park in Brisbane and Sydney (3 and 17 July) would be closely monitored. Back then performances in Tests were still more important than Origin games as a guide for future internationals.

It was widely considered that Queensland stand-off Wally Lewis had stolen the State of Origin show while his half-back partner Mark Murray was another to press his claims. Against the Kiwis, pundits were particularly looking forward to seeing Lewis combine with Canterbury's box-of-tricks scrum-half Steve Mortimer, who had played in all three Origin games for New South Wales. Unfortunately for both men and Stanton, the stop–start nature of the first Test played into the hands of New Zealand's more forward-dominated approach.

Mountford called Lindop 'the best referee in the world'. He added: 'We have every confidence in him and are satisfied with his interpretations.'

The Australian camp were less confident, especially after he offered to sit with both coaches and watch a videotape of English scrummaging.

'Every game is played by the rules,' said Australia team manager Frank Farrington, who admitted a free-flowing match suited his side. 'The question is how Lindop interprets those rules. Frank [Stanton] will approach Lindop privately and will ask him about his interpretations of the rules, especially scrummaging. But the fact remains that Lindop's interpretations are very different from Australian referees.'

In Sydney for the second Test, Queensland's exciting young centre Mal Meninga got a chance instead of Steve Rogers, while, in the pack, Parramatta duo Ray Price and Muggleton started with Paul Vautin and Rod Morris stepping aside.

Whatever Stanton said to Lindop did not really work as Australia, fighting a determined New Zealand – the game accruing a 17-8 penalty count – put in a defensive masterclass to run out 20-2 victors in front of a modest 16,775 crowd.

Second-rower Les Boyd and prop Rohan Hancock played half the game with injuries while Price marshalled the green and gold wall brilliantly and was named man of the match. The Parramatta loose forward also grabbed a try, as did Boustead, Lewis and fullback Greg Brentnall. Stanton could breathe a sigh of relief. It wasn't pretty but in the circumstances he had effectively managed his battered and bruised troops well. In many ways it was just like a tour match and ideal preparation for what the Kangaroos could expect when they made the long trip north.

On 20 July Stanton was confirmed as coach for the tour of Great Britain and France and two months later the Ashes squad, selected by Ernie Hammerton (chairman, NSW), Les Cowie (NSW), Mick Falla (NSW), Jack Reardon (QLD), Dud Beattie (QLD) and Bert Quinn (QLD), was unveiled once all medicals were passed. There were six players apiece from grand finalists Manly and Parramatta and seven from Queensland-based clubs.

The initial reaction in Australia focused on significant absentees, perhaps most noticeably the versatile Easts playmaker Kevin Hastings.

'I thought I was in but the selectors obviously enjoy kicking me in the teeth,' said Hastings later. 'I devoted the rest of my career to proving them wrong.'

That year the 25-year-old was named player of the year by the prestigious *Rugby League Week* magazine for the third successive time.

Another who came close was South Sydney hooker Ken Stewart. Australian captain Max Krilich had not even been a regular for Manly and in the Grand Final was on the bench while Ray Brown, who also made the tour, played.

Queensland full-back Colin Scott was another near miss and with only one specialised full-back in Brentnall, his claims appeared justified.

There was criticism for the selections of St George second-rower Rod Reddy, who had not been a regular with his club, while the inclusions of injury doubt Ian Schubert, who had last played for Australia in 1975, and 29-year-old Chris Anderson were said to have been done on past glories. Schubert almost missed the trip because of a chest-bone problem but was cleared just days before the Kangaroos left.

It led former international Ian Walsh to write: 'To me it is a mediocre Kangaroo team. The demands of youth have been ignored and the team looks like a squad from an old men's home.'

Many of the old guard had ruled themselves out, noticeably the imperious Parramatta centre Mick Cronin, such a star of the 1978 trip, and his vastly experienced clubmate Graham Eadie, who had made such an impression with British fans in 1973 and five years later. Others who might have got a place but didn't want to come included Wests' brilliant half-back Terry Lamb, who would have his day on British soil four years later but passed it over because he was getting married in 1982. Manly centre Alan Thompson and Easts try machine Terry Fahey also ruled themselves out for personal reasons.

Stanton applauded the boldness of the selectors for picking a lot of younger players with limited international experience. Balmain's inspirational back-rower Wayne Pearce, Parramatta's new half-back wizard Sterling and his club-mate, the bulldozing wing Grothe, had not featured in any of the State of Origin matches from just three months earlier.

'Every Australian player has been catalogued by the English team management in one of the most comprehensive preparations for a Test series in history,' Stanton told Australian reporters.

'They [the selectors] already know the strengths and weaknesses of every player selected for the tour. The schedule of matches is a lot tougher than previously and we will play four matches in the first week.

'This team is well balanced with a blending of youth and experience, and it has a lot of pace. Our forwards, particularly, will be required to work very hard because of the intensive buildup by our opposition. With strong play from our forwards, we will then be able to capitalise on the skill and the pace of the backs.

'The team does lack a little in the experience of the previous Kangaroo teams. There is no Bobby Fulton, Mick Cronin, Alan Thompson, Graham Eadie, Greg Pierce or Tom Raudonikis with us.

'And the players will have to be wary of a more relaxed way of refereeing in England. In Australia the players are not accustomed to being tackled around the head but it will happen in England. They must be disciplined, not react to this sort of treatment, and keep their minds on the job.'

Captain Krilich, who had also toured in 1978, was full of confidence that the squad had the dynamism and physical attributes to be a huge success.

'I don't think there is any way the English players will handle the power of our defence,' Krilich said. 'In the past three years our game has become harder than when we were last in England.

'The big forwards are hitting harder than ever and the punishment handed out and absorbed is incredible. I can't see any way they will be able to handle the size and power of the team.'

While being interviewed for TV after the series Krilich reflected: 'Before we went away we were panned as a very weak side because we had people like Peter Sterling, Wally Lewis, Brett Kenny, Eric Grothe and Steve Ella. There was also Wayne Pearce but nobody knew how good they were. These blokes were the next crop of superstars. I was just lucky to tag along with them.'

The full squad read as follows:

Coach: Frank Stanton

Co-managers; Frank Farrington (NSW), Tom Drysdale (Queensland)

Medical officer: Dr Bill Monaghan

Trainer: Alf Richards.

Players – full-back: Greg Brentnall (age 25, Canterbury-Bankstown).

Wingers: Chris Anderson (30, Canterbury-Bankstown), Kerry Boustead (23, Eastern Suburbs), Eric Grothe (22, Parramatta), John Ribot (27, Manly-Warringah).

Centres: Steve Ella (22, Parramatta), Gene Miles (23, Wynnum-Manly), Mal Menninga (22, Southern Suburbs), Steve Rogers (28, Cronulla-Sutherland)

Utility back: Ian Schubert (26, Eastern Suburbs).

Half-backs: Brett Kenny (21, Parramatta), Wally Lewis (22, vice-captain, Fortitude Valley), Steve Mortimer (26, Canterbury-Bankstown), Mark Murray (23, Valley Diehards), Peter Sterling (22, Parramatta).

Hookers: Ray Brown (25, Manly-Warringah), Greg Conescu (22, Northern Suburbs), Max Krilich (32, Manly-Warringah)

Props: Don McKinnon (26, North Sydney), Rod Morris (32, Wynnum-Manly), Craig Young (26, St George).

Back row: Les Boyd (25, Manly-Warringah), Rohan Hancock (27, Toowoomba Wattles), Paul McCabe (23, Manly-Warringah), John Muggleton (22, Parramatta), Wayne Pearce (22, Balmain), Ray Price (29, Parramatta), Rod Reddy (28, St George).

The Australia coach had gained a reputation as something of a disciplinarian but perhaps more importantly Stanton was smart, driven and a winner, having led Manly to Premiership victories in 1976 and 1978.

For just over 20 years he was associated with the Sea Eagles – except in 1974 when he took a year out to helped build his own house – having first played reserve grade for them in 1958 before making his first-team debut in 1961.

His efforts as part of the New South Wales interstate team two years later earned him a place on the 1963 Ashes tour, which is fondly remembered down under as the Kangaroos had not beaten their old rivals in a series since 1954.

The tourists secured the series in the most extraordinary fashion, demolishing a shell-shocked Britain side 50-12 at Swinton. The then 23-year-old Stanton would not play in any of the Tests but remembers the game well as he was commentating on it for one of the Sydney radio stations.

'It was amazing to see some of the tries that were scored. That was the start of the fitness era in Australian rugby where players were fitter and stronger than they had been in the past and they wanted to play free-flowing football and were quick enough to do it. Most of the British players were brought up under that old one-yard rule, I suppose where you kept the ball as long as you could and starved the opposition of the ball. Australian rugby league was a bit more free-flowing than that.'

In 1963 Australia played an incredible 36 matches in the UK and France – including on Christmas Day in Albi. Stanton played in half and was used as a utility back. He would fill every position behind the scrum and saw first-hand how the power pendulum had swung back towards the Australian game.

'A lot of the 63 squad were younger blokes and there were a fair few country blokes who were naturally fit because they worked on farms, and, as you will understand, every one of those players had to have another job. They weren't paid enough to be professional footballers. But those young blokes that came into that 63 Kangaroo team were all products of a decided improvement in Australia's approach towards rugby league. Normally you would go to training two nights a week after work and then you'd go down the pub and have six beers. It was good for bonding but not all that good for fitness. It was part of a change of attitude in sport generally towards alcohol, which wasn't the be-all and end-all anymore.

'Some of the blokes on that 63 tour were fitness fanatics for instance, like John Raper. Michael Cleary and Ken Irvine were Olympic class sprinters so they would be training for running all the time.'

Stanton's career would be dogged by injuries. After coming home from the UK he had two operations on his fibula bones and only played four games that season, and then two years later dislocated a collar bone in a strange way. The bone popped into his windpipe and he had to be placed in a figure of eight brace and remain as immobile as possible for between six and eight weeks. By the time he got back on the field the season was virtually over.

'By the time I was 30 I was stuffed,' recalls Stanton almost 50 years later. 'But I had a good job. I was working in a finance company and was appointed manager of the finance company on the basis I gave up rugby league. But rugby league was giving me up at the time anyway. I was at the age where I had had enough and went straight into coaching.'

He took over Manly's reserve team and stayed for three years before taking a year out. Manly legend Ron Willey stood down from the main job in 1974, leaving Stanton some big shoes to fill on taking the top job the following year. He inherited a team with some stellar names, including the inspirational Bob Fulton.

'A lot of players who have been good players for Australia have been players who did extras. Now every player talks about doing extras. One that springs to mind that I coached was Fulton. As a young player he came to my club at 18 but even then after training he would go and do sprint training and other stuff like that to improve himself.'

With Fulton pulling the strings Manly would win their third Sydney Premiership title with a team that also included Eadie, star centre Alan Thompson and the bruising forward Terry 'Igor' Randall. Also in that side were Englishmen Steve Norton and Phil Lowe.

Two years later Manly were in contention for honours again and the closeness of the league season – just five points separated all five play-off contenders – was reflected in a remarkable series of knockout games. The biggest margin of victory, apart from the Grand Final replay, came when Parramatta beat Canterbury in the second qualifying final by just seven points.

Manly were involved in two replays, the second of which was the Grand Final with Cronulla. It was their sixth fixture in 24 days. Randall defied injury to play in every one of those games with the help of painkilling injections, and against Cronulla helped his side to a 16-0 win. Eadie was named man of the match.

Stanton and seven of his champion Sea Eagles were in England less than two weeks later and he could see how attitudes towards touring had developed something of a generational split.

'In 1978 we needed to maintain our fitness levels and make the English teams move around because they weren't at the same levels of fitness, but we had a saying, which transferred through to my whole era as Australia coach ... "Make them play at our pace." If we stopped playing at our pace and allowed them to play at their pace and dictate then we were in trouble. So we didn't allow that to happen.

'There was still a number of older players in the squad in 78. Touring wasn't just a holiday, it was a job. A lot of older players looked at it a little bit differently than it being a job. They trained hard when they had to for a game, and especially a Test, but generally they were on tour.'

The series is remembered for the Britain's successful 'Dad Army' selection at Odsal, and that and the bizarre 2-0 series defeat in France would represent the only Kangaroo defeats while he was coach.

'I wouldn't say we were outfoxed in Bradford. You can fall into the trap of playing at their pace and some of those players, if you allowed them to play at their pace, had a fair bit of skill. We had to emphasise our better fitness all the time. I think you can see from the results of the games our points were scored in the second half when they had run out of steam.

'In France the refereeing was diabolical. We played one match there, not a Test, where the penalties were 32-4 against us but that was symptomatic of their attitude. The main reason why they were like it, I was told, was the French RFL was trying to get rugby league included in the curriculum of French universities, and in their endeavours to get that included on the curriculum the people who were responsible were saying, "Well, who have you ever beaten?" So they said "Australia". Against us one of their blokes ran behind the back of the dead-ball line and came back in and scored a try. I was told French rugby league was trying to broaden its outlets and broaden its attitudes.'

Following his overseeing of Australia's emphatic home Test series drubbing of the 1979 Lions, he headed north to Queensland for a season, leading Redcliffe to fifth, before heading back to the Sydney Premiership and Balmain. The Tigers finished bottom in his first year but two years later he had turned the club around and during his six-year spell would help them reach the play-offs three times.

But before he could focus all his attention on Balmain there was Australia, and in 1982 the serious planning began the day after he learned just what type of hand he had been dealt.

'There were a couple of players who I was a little bit surprised didn't make the squad but at that time there were so many options to pick from. You could have picked six different teams and got the same result. They were all benefitting from this attitude towards fitness and conditioning and training and doing it four or five days a week.'

What happened now for Australia was in the hands of Stanton and his co-managers – Frank Farrington from New South Wales and Queensland's Tom Drysdale.

Farrington was a stalwart of the Newtown club. He played for them between 1946 and 1955, combining his time as a prop with a career as a professional boxer. He also had three stints as secretary (1968–70, 1972–74 and 1977–91) and was a member of the New South Wales Rugby Football League's executive committee between 1975 and 1977. He brought Jack Gibson to Newtown in 1973 and also helped Warren Ryan build a brilliant team in the late 70s with the highlight being their 1981 Grand Final appearance.

Meanwhile Tom Drysdale was an integral part of the Eastern Suburbs side that made six successive Grand Finals in the Brisbane Premiership between 1946 and 1951. A back-row forward, he led his team to Premiership glory in 1950. Post-retirement he became a director on the Brisbane division of the Queensland Rugby League and a director for the state in 1980.

The first job of Stanton, Farrington and Drysdale was to pick two separate teams for the final warm-up games. One group of 15 would visit PNG with Stanton while the other 13 would take on a representative side from Western Australia.

'At that point we hadn't played any games so we decided to send some experienced Test players to both areas. For instance Krilich was captain and Wally Lewis was vice-captain so Krilich went to one area and Wally Lewis went to Perth as captain.

'We wanted to make sure everyone had a game under their belt before they arrived in England. There wasn't any selection criteria as such at that stage. It certainly wasn't done on form because we hadn't played a game.'

Ten of the players who would wear the green and gold in the first Test at Hull would head north for the full Test match, while Grothe, Pearce and Boyd travelled west to Perth.

Grothe carried his brilliant late-season form to Western Australia and claimed four of the 13 tries shared between nine players in a 57-5 mauling.

It was much tougher in PNG where a packed crowd in Port Moresby made for a special atmosphere. Officially the attendance was 15,000 but, with locals perched in every conceivable vantage point, the actual number of people watching was a good deal more.

The playing surface proved the biggest cause for concern.

'That ground was like concrete – even harder than the SCG,' said captain Krilich.

Grothe's main rival for the other wing spot – Boustead was considered a certainty – was Ribot, who scored four tries as the Kangaroos eased to a 38-2 success. Brentnall (2), Boustead, Kenny, Meninga and Rogers also touched down.

Muggleton sprained his ankle and became the first doubt for the opening match against Hull KR in just eight days' time. 'Satisfactory under the circumstances,' was the typically economical and to-the-point assessment of coach Stanton.

While the coach was always trying to rein in expectations, not everyone could contain their excitement as Australian journalist Ian Heads had discovered on the night before the PNG clash.

'I always got on well with Ray [Price], a forthright and unusual character, but a terrific player,' said Heads. 'We were sitting together at the big function to welcome the Australian party, chatting informally about the tour ahead. His declaration was this: "We won't lose a game … I'm telling you." He reminded me of that prediction back in Sydney long after the tour.'

It is doubtful, though, that even the supremely confident Price could have anticipated just how good a show he and the other 27 Australians were about to put on.

Chapter Six

Six Out of Six

AUSTRALIA clearly could not wait to get started. The fact that they arrived two days earlier than the RFL expected caused a few early problems for their hosts.

'Communication is one of the things the Aussies are not very good at,' said Howes. Meanwhile, RFL chairman Jack Grindrod, had set the bar high for Colin Hutton and the rest of the British party as he and other leading officials welcomed the Kangaroos.

'I think we've got to win because if we don't the Australians will think we're a lot of no-hopers and we're not.'

Chief selector Bill Oxley, who had been party to all the warnings from the British management team, was less demanding: 'You can only give your best and I think our boys will give 80 minutes of sheer endeavour.'

Stanton had clearly done his homework on his opposite number's preparations and there were early Australian concerns that the British side would be able to match the Kangaroos.

'We have brought an exciting squad which has a lot of youth and talent,' said Stanton on the coach from Heathrow to Leeds. 'We lack experience, but this should be overcome if we adapt quickly to the conditions. The Australian public would like to see us win and we haven't come here to lose. We realise it is going to be an extreme challenge and probably one of the hardest Australian rugby league has had for a long, long time but we are prepared to meet and work hard to get there.'

His manager Drysdale was extremely positive as he was interviewed by a reporter who was part of a team making a documentary about the tour.

'We think the selectors have given us the nucleus of a side that can match it with anyone around the place. It is a good blend of youth and experience which should go very well.'

Also interviewed on the bus were captain Krilich and a softly spoken Sterling. The experienced man was as stoically positive as he had been in the run-up to the tour.

'The competition is going to be very hard and all the young players are very skilled in their game and they will come through. They all play in the top leagues in Sydney and Brisbane so will come through OK.'

For Sterling it was his first taste of life on tour and the realisation of all the hard work and endeavour was obvious.

'Obviously I'm looking forward to it as much as everyone else. It's a bit of a dream come true for me so I'm looking forward to a good tour out here. It was the greatest thrill of my life to be selected. Since a young kid I've always wanted to play for Australia and it is something I have worked very hard for.'

The Australian party had stayed overnight in a hotel before travelling north the next day to their base at the Dragonara Hotel. Waiting to greet them as they stepped off their coach was Howes and he was asked for his opinion on how the series would unfold.

'The Tests will be tremendous football and the Australians are undoubted favourites – they've won their last nine games on the trot – but we think we can pinch it 2-1.'

It was going to be a big few weeks for Howes, who had overseen much of the logistical work and the itinerary. Many keen eyes noted that the Hull match had been placed on the Tuesday before the second Test, traditionally a date where a touring side might take the opportunity to rest a few big hitters. It was not an accident.

Howes also wanted to make sure that there was a good geographical spread and that matches at host clubs who were close in proximity would not be close in date. He came up with the following programme:

- 10 October: Hull KR
- 13 October: Wigan
- 15 October: Barrow
- 17 October: St Helens
- 20 October: Leeds
- 24 October: Wales
- 30 October: Great Britain (Hull)
- 3 November: Leigh
- 7 November: Bradford Northern
- 9 November: Cumbria
- 14 November: Fulham
- 16 November: Hull
- 20 November: Great Britain (Wigan)
- 23 November: Widnes
- 28 November: Great Britain (Leeds).

With Hull KR the first of four matches in eight days, Stanton took advantage of the extra time to watch Rovers play on the Wednesday before they met the following Sunday. It would also represent something of a reunion for the former Manly coach and Phil Lowe, who had been such an integral part of the side that won the Sydney Premiership in 1976.

The first major official obligation for the Kangaroos came at Headingley with a press day. There was even time for a light-hearted moment. Photographers stunted up a publicity shot with a model wearing a T-shirt emblazoned with the logo of series sponsors Dominion Insurance. She was held aloft by Krilich, Craig Young, Rod Morris and practical joker extraordinaire Rod Reddy, who was holding the young lady's midriff.

'Look no hands,' laughed Reddy as he lifted his arms in the air to the amusement of all those watching.

The first major drama centred on the Kangaroos' training based at McClaren Field, home of Bramley Rugby League Club. The club were worried that regular training would destroy the pitch. They had a regular season fixture list to honour.

'They've given us notice,' said Stanton. 'And now it's up to the English Rugby League to find us another ground.'

Their new base would be the old playing fields owned by the Burton clothing factory in the centre of the city, a facility which proved 'more than adequate'.

The short studs that the Aussies used on their harder grounds were not sufficient to do the job on the softer English pitches so they had to find a supplier of longer studs. With eight players fined for being late to board the bus for training those early days were not all smooth sailing. There were also some ground rules to be sorted for new room-mates Sterling and Wayne Pearce, who certainly wasn't one of those fined because he set the tone by deciding to make the daily four-and-a-half mile journey to training in Bramley on foot ... or fleet of foot in his case.

'I am a Rip Van Winkle,' Sterling later told an Australian TV reporter. 'I like my sleep and to be awakened at 6am in the morning to the sound of skipping was a little bit off-putting but when he [Pearce] found his skipping rope in 200 pieces the next morning he took the hint and never skipped again, and we got along fine.'

Hull KR went into the clash having only won one of their last four fixtures but the Kangaroos' coach was taking nothing for granted.

'They have some good players who will see this game as a chance to impress the Test selectors so they will be going all out to do well. Coming to Hull is always a pleasure, the people enjoy their rugby and the atmosphere is special.'

Australia's first XIII included Sterling and his Parramatta team-mate Brett Kenny alongside him in the half-backs but Stanton remained adamant that their selection was no indication of how his team would line up for the first Test.

'In the first game against Hull KR, Kenny and Sterling played as the halves and then the next game was Wigan and in our minds it was a stronger club and would be a harder game so we picked Mortimer and Lewis, who were incumbents, and we had to give the other half of the squad a run ... the players who didn't play in the Hull KR match.'

Rovers coach Roger Millward was able to call on Britain hopefuls George Fairbairn and Mike Smith, who got a bit of a shock when he set his eyes on Meninga.

'I remembered Meninga from 1979,' recalls Smith. 'Him and Gene Miles. They were both tall and skinny and then they came over in 82 and were both massive. I don't know what they had been feeding them but I guess they were pretty much training as full-time professionals.'

The home side received a blow on the eve of the showdown. Len Casey, who had been sent off in the previous match and had been given special dispensation to play against the tourists, failed to respond well enough to intensive treatment on a groin injury.

That opened the door for a 21-year-old recent arrival from Wakefield to slot into the second row.

Andy Kelly's promotion into the first team for what turned out to be an explosive and remarkable first clash of the tour capped a fairly incredible start to his Rovers career having just arrived from Wakefield for what then was a record fee for a forward (£60,000). Two months earlier he had made his first appearance in the famous red and white against Great Britain. It was a rare international-themed start to a club career for a man who would get his own international chance a few years later.

'Roger Millward was probably ahead of the game in terms of the other British coaches at that time,' recalls Kelly. 'He had been over to see the Chicago Bulls. He had been in their training environment, which was unheard of at that time. We trained really solidly on our fitness and our defensive work and that was a massive cultural change for me. Training was much more intense and the approach to games was more professional. I even think we had an extra training session. One week we would do four nights and the next three and alternate like that.

In terms of preparation, of the Aussies was hard to come by but obviously we had heard of many of their players and we knew who to look out for. It was the younger end that were the problem and there were a good few that came over, as there normally would be with any tour. When the teams came into the dressing room an hour before, that was your first look at them and everybody crowded round the team-sheet. There was none of that announcing your squad two days before or declaring your team on the morning of the game like there is now.

'When the team came in that's when the buzz started and you could see who you were up against. Their pack was full of people who already had a reputation and you could not help but pay attention to a couple of them. Boyd and Reddy came with good reputations. Ray Price was a tough, old hombre ... Mr Perpetual Motion. Everyone knew about him. He wasn't a dirty player but was a tough player. In terms of the skulduggery side of it … that was very prevalent in those days. People would be in hysterics now at the stuff that went on.'

Officiating was Stanton's old friend Fred Lindop, who was clearly determined to stamp his authority on affairs. However, with the atmosphere febrile and both sides determined not to take a step back, it was not going to be long before tempers frayed.

Kelly remembered the first scrum well.

'At that time scrums were an aggressive area of the game and you well knew that as you were binding, if somebody took their arm from around your waist that arm is there for a purpose … somebody's catching a whack. A number of punches were thrown and the referee could not see a thing and we had a very aggressive hooker in David Watkinson. He demanded that you were aggressive. I can't remember exactly how many punches were thrown but it was enough to bring the scrum up and a fight started.'

The first major flashpoint came on 16 minutes and unsurprisingly Watkinson was in the thick of it. He and Price exchanged blows. Temperatures were rising. Lindop took no action that time but certainly did two minutes later when Rovers' prop Steve Crooks made a dart from dummy-half before being tackled by his counterpart Morris. Following up was Reddy who swung a stiff left arm into the collision point with the referee just three yards away. The burly second-rower was given his marching orders.

Just five minutes later it was 12 against 12. While Roy Holdstock and Boyd tussled, off the ball Watkinson's punch in the direction of Price was spotted by Lindop as he ran back from the other flashpoint. He had no hesitation in dismissing the Test hopeful. It could well have been the decisive factor in the Rovers' hooker's absence from the Ashes opener. From the subsequent penalty Young crashed over for the first of Australia's 97 tries in 15 games on British soil. It was also probably their least flamboyant.

Rovers' powerful second-rower Chris Burton was one certainly making a good impression, breaking a number of tackles and making good yardage. From one of his surging runs, the home side were awarded a penalty after Steve Rogers was adjudged to have held him down too long in the tackle. Boyd was following in and as he retreated said something to the referee, who immediately sent him off. The 'baby-faced assassin' refused to admit he had called Lindop a cheat and his fury was evident as his captain had to escort him off the field. Fairbairn kicked the penalty and it was 2-5 with ten minutes to go before half-time.

The incident sparked a remarkable ten minutes of brilliance from Millward's men and even more incredible is that Australia conceded two tries in that time. While in the UK, they would play a further 1,160 minutes of rugby and concede only five more tries.

Clever play by substitute Lowe opened up the Australians on 33 minutes. Burton's great run and offload was followed by a clever kick-ahead from the veteran. John Ribot should have collected but slipped as he went to smother the ball and only managed to knock it into the path of Steve Hartley flying up on the outside. The Robins stand-off pounced to level the scores.

Hartley was a player who could carve open teams with his blistering pace and nimble feet and the next Rovers try was all of his making. Picking up the ball inside his own half he left Sterling and Krilich for dead before finding Gary Prohm superbly just as Hartley was clattered by Grothe, enabling the Kiwi full-back to slide over the line despite a gallant last-ditch tackle by Kenny. Fairbairn missed again. Had the full-back had his kicking boots on it might have been a different story, especially with the man advantage.

However, the first indication of the Australians' fabulous physical condition came with their impressive second half effort, with Sterling central to their comeback.

A penalty for offside afforded Meninga the chance to cut the gap five minutes after the restart and just a minute later the Hull KR crowd were treated to their first bit of Sterlo magic. Collecting the ball from a scrum there appeared to be no danger to the Rovers' line but the Australian No 7 had other ideas. He stepped inside his opposite number James Walsh to the gasps of those close by and managed to hand off 17-year-old winger Garry Clark and Fairbairn for just long enough to make it over.

Rugby league fans in the city would be treated to a lot more of the same in the not-to-distant future. Meninga's conversion left the visitors 12-8 ahead but Rovers hung on in and a penalty from their full-back halfway through the period kept alive their hopes of a famous victory.

But in the final 15 minutes those dreams were shattered in emphatic fashion. Firstly, Krilich broke a couple of tired tackles before laying it on a plate for Sterling, and three minutes later the game ended as a contest as Sterling, Kenny and substitute Muggleton combined beautifully to send Rogers over. The knowledgeable crowd offered warm applause.

Wally Lewis, on for Ribot, was next over after a beautiful bit of interplay between Price and Sterling and the scoring was rounded off in breathtaking fashion by a glorious piece of individual brilliance from Meninga, just seconds before the final hooter. Kelly certainly recalled that final try as one that showed early signs of just how special they were.

'Mal Meninga's last try I remember very vividly. I think he beat everybody twice and went around George Fairbairn. He was a phenomenal athlete and I think he got the ball on his own "20" on the left-hand side, travelled left to right, palmed a few off and all of a sudden displayed this turn of speed people didn't expect from such a big man. And I think that's what caught out George [Fairbairn].'

The big centre hit the line perfectly and sliced through the Rovers' defence but it was the way he rounded Fairbairn 20 metres out which made it something of an iconic moment. Here was a man, bigger than virtually any forward in the British game, out-sprinting some of Britain's quickest backs.

Stanton described the try as having 'the stamp of international class' while the man himself had clearly responded to the urgings of his coach.

Meninga said: 'In the first half we kept it in close and didn't swing it out wide too much. At half-time he [Stanton] said to move it and we got results.'

In the immediate after-match Stanton was unhappy at Boyd's dismissal.

'Obviously it is a case of mistaken identity and that was fairly obvious to everyone in the ground. However, he's [Lindop] got to wear that. We shouldn't waste too much time on that though but we should concentrate on talking about the way we carried the day. Some of those blokes did tremendously well.'

Boyd, Reddy and Watkinson would have to wait until a disciplinary hearing on 28 October to find out if they would be free to play in the first Test just two days later.

One man who already looked well placed to appear at Boothferry Park in just under three weeks was Sterling, who delighted Stanton.

'It was a great international debut and I look forward to seeing many better things from him, but we've got a couple of other fellas yet to come out and it's going to be a great battle for Test berths.'

The players he was referring to were Steve Mortimer and Mark Murray.

Mortimer, the favourite to play scrum-half before the trip, would get his first chance to impress at Wigan three days later but the Canterbury star knew he was in trouble from that game on.

Having seen at firsthand Sterling's development into a top player he knew what type of pedigree he possessed.

'Peter Sterling is one of those guys who was born to be a footballer,' wrote Mortimer in his autobiography. 'As far back as 1971 when I was playing with Turvey Park U-15s, I can remember a day at the Tumbarumba knockout carnival when the class of Peter Sterling became obvious to me. He was a little blond-haired kid playing for Wagga Panthers U-11s and you couldn't help but notice him. Maybe it was the hair. He was certainly spectacular. But to me it was the things he could do with a football that set him apart and at that stage they had to be natural things that were simply part of him.

'For a kid so young he was absolutely magic, and I remember wondering even then how such a scruff of a kid was at a carnival like that. You had to be special to be noticed and he certainly was special. When he bobbed up seven or eight years later in a Parramatta jumper I was hardly surprised.'

In later years Mortimer also wrote about his conviction that Price's 'support' for Sterling and Kenny was a factor in their selection for the Test side. Even before the Hull KR match he was convinced that his chances of playing in the Tests were slim.

'As I busily unpacked in the room at the Dragonara Hotel that I was to share with Wally Lewis for the next couple of months, I had a terrible sinking feeling that my tour, from a Test match point of view, might have been over before it had started.

'The first side played extremely well and Sterlo and Brett Kenny had a dream run. From Stanton's point of view, I suppose, there was no real reason to change the side that had started so well on tour. Sterling certainly played very well and I have no beef whatever with him. My beef, and my only beef, is that I was not given, and neither was Wally Lewis, the opportunity that should have been our right to protect our Test positions in that first game.'

But Mortimer and Lewis had not really sparked as a pair playing for Australia and the scrum-half partially attributed that to a lack of chemistry.

'Similar ions don't attract each other,' he said after the Wigan clash. 'Wally had his own thinking and for us to synchronise I had to let Wally call the shots, which was fine. I'd come back to my conservative half-back style, provide good service, loop around, restrain my game but then it was said, "Oh, Mortimer was quiet."'

Australia edged it 13-9 and the press pack were already reporting this side as the 'second string', much to the frustration of their coach. To be fair to the British media it was traditional for the midweek game to be the domain of the reserves and the side selected to tackle Alex Murphy's outfit lacked most of the established Test stars.

Manager Farrington gave Wigan the compliment of saying: 'We won't get a harder club match on this tour.'

The game itself was dominated by York-based referee Gerry Kershaw, who handed out 28 penalties, ensuring it became a stop–start affair and thereby blunting the flow of the tourists.

One of the few Australians to impress was Paul McCabe, who gave his side the lead midway through the half after Ella and centre Colin Whitfield had managed two penalties apiece. The big second-rower finished off the best move of the half after Pearce, who collected a wayward kick, combined brilliantly with Boustead to set up the score. In his autobiography Mortimer also recalled that his first meeting with Stanton in 1981 had begun with a very specific instruction not to chip over the top.

If that exchange did happen then the exciting No 7 did not heed the advice as, just before half-time at Wigan, he collected a quick play of the ball, darted forward and kicked the ball directly into the face of home full-back Barry Williams. The action led to a try for Muggleton but only thanks to a fortunate series of ricochets plus a mistake by hooker Nicky Kiss, who tried to fall on the ball only for it to squirm out of his control.

Another Whitfield penalty left the score 10-6 at half-time but Australia took control early in the second half with McCabe avoiding a couple of tackles and finding Boustead. The winger had to dive full length to collect the pass but there was no Wigan defender in the immediate vicinity and he simply got back to his feet and dived again for the three points.

Price and Rogers were introduced into the fray midway through the second half after Wigan had reduced the deficit to four points. A brilliant burst from Kiwi substitute Danny Campbell set up the score but Henderson Gill still had plenty to do when he collected the ball 20 metres out. With Ella covering, the winger looked second favourite to make it but somehow managed to squeeze past the Australian centre and in at the corner.

That would end the scoring for the night. Never again during that tour would the Kangaroos fail to score at least two tries in the second half.

Coach Murphy was beaming with pride as he was interviewed on the pitch straight after the final hooter.

'I was quite pleased with our lads tonight. Thought they put in a tremendous performance and competed to the end, which must be very heart-warming for the England selectors to see we can beat the Australians if we take the ball to them. If the man in the middle had been a little bit more kind to us who knows but they [Australia] played well and they are not a bad side.

'There were 28 penalties in the game and when you have 13,000 spectators in the ground I think the man in the middle should be seen a lot less than he was seen.'

McCabe was named man of the match and was impressed by his opponents.

'It is truly a great honour for the boys to elect me as their man of the match. There were a couple of other very good performances in Wayne Pearce and I think Donny McKinnon took the ball up well all night. It was a good all-round effort and a great all-round defensive effort. Wigan have the best defensive record in the league over here and I can see how they have earned that and it was really a great effort from the Wigan side.'

For the people of Barrow, getting the Australians back to Craven Park was special. Those who could remember the last time they played there (in 1967) were able to recall some heroics as their illustrious visitors were held 10-10.

Barrow's insular location and its pride in its rugby side were always going to ensure a special atmosphere on the evening of 15 October, particularly as the match coincided with the official switching on of their new floodlights. Shining especially bright that night was their loose forward Derek Hadley, who marshalled an exciting young team brimming with excellent Cumbrian youngsters. He, as much as any other British player during the tour, gave the Kangaroos most to think about.

'I was right at the top of my form when they came,' recalls Hadley. 'I was a bit of a ball handler and I don't really think they had seen a player like me before. Also my fitness was as good as it could have been for a part-time player and the team had such a good blend.'

Rogers, who was sitting on the bench, welcomed Hadley off at the final whistle with the following compliment: 'Tidy player.'

Hadley, a local hero brought up in nearby Walney, was one of those offered the opportunity to stand aside with a league game just 48 hours away.

'Frank Foster offered some of us the option not to play. He wanted to keep his playmakers for a match against Castleford couple of days later [a game they would win]. However, none of us would take the offer up. You couldn't miss this. This was a once-in-a-career opportunity, especially where we had come from in the Second Division. And obviously it was great for the town. There was a fantastic atmosphere on the day and the fact the attendance was double what we were normally getting speaks volumes, really.'

Foster, a tough taskmaster by tradition, said: 'I would have liked to have stood two or three of them down but nobody wanted to miss the chance of playing the Aussies. In the end I suppose I could have put my foot down but it would not have been fair to disappoint the players. I just hope we don't get any injuries for the Castleford match on Sunday.'

Stanton brought in third-choice hooker Greg Conescu and scrum-half Murray for their first starts, which meant all 28 had seen some action in the first week. Ribot, Morris, Boyd and Reddy all came back in and for 40 minutes the visitors were embarrassed by their supposed journeymen opponents.

A brilliant early break by Barrow winger Mick James was met with a roar of delight from the packed crowd and Murray did well to ground him in full flight. In the first quarter there was also a glimmer of a chance for Hadley, who jinked to within ten yards of the line. Just before half-time scrum-half David Cairns' up and under gave Schubert all manner of problems and he was lucky to recover and touch down having dropped the ball oon his own goal-line.

Barrow were 2-0 ahead through a Cairns penalty by the time the tourists got going and just before the quarter point Schubert crashed onto a Wally Lewis pass and showed great determination to touch down, despite Hadley and full-back Steve Tickle being in close attendance.

Stanton might have hoped that the score would spark his side into life but they rarely threatened. Only Boyd's excellent run, just before the interval, hinted at the quality running through the Australian ranks.

Nearly 40 years on Stanton remembers that half as one to forget and cannot recall his half-time team-talk, which has passed into Cumbrian folklore. Legend has it – this came from Rod Reddy – that he told his team to forget about everything he had said prematch and to just stop the Barrow No 13.

'Up until half-time we were doing it really tough,' said the Australia coach straight after the match. 'I don't think they realised that if they wanted to be considered for Test selection they couldn't just go through the motions and the second half changed a bit.'

Manager Farrington was even more damning. 'I thought it was a terrible first half from our players. One of the worst performances I have seen our players turn in for a long while. The coach Frank Stanton gave them a little bit of a dressing down at half-time and they rose to the occasion and played a hell of a lot better football in the second half. Seeing it as though it is early in the tour it is going to take the team time to settle down. Changes do make an effect. The players don't get to know each other properly until they get on the field but as we go on I think we will mould into one real good team and possibly two really good teams.'

In the other dressing room the mood was very different, as Hadley recalls: 'Frank [Foster] more or less gave us a free licence to have a go and it worked for a while. I remember him saying: "You have got the best team in the world on the rack" and he was right because we were pressing and so that built us up for the second half and we did well for the first 20 minutes after half-time but the floodgates opened at the end. We never expected to win but after where we were on 60 minutes, we all came off and were really disappointed.

'You could sense their frustration building and I think, because it was so early in the tour, they hadn't really gelled yet as an attacking force but, defensively, they were so good and that's how Australian teams were built in those days. They always seemed to be back in line so fast. You could never get a quick play-the-ball against them. They would also get three into the tackle so to get all of those players off … that extra two seconds would be all they needed to get the line set again. That was probably something we learned from them.

'We made a couple of decent breaks but they were snuffed out so fast. Two days later we made those same breaks against Castleford but we finished them.'

The Green and Golds were a different proposition after their rollocking and would blaze over six second-half tries. Conescu got the ball rolling as he forced his way past three defenders and there was a great deal more finesse to the next, scored when man-of-the-match Pearce skipped past two tackles after a quick release from the scrum.

The visitors were surging through the gears and Murray tore through a gap to put the game to bed at 18-2. Barrow were also starting to slip off the tackles and that allowed Schubert his try ten minutes from time, with substitute Brown the provider. Immediately after the restart Pearce threatened to run through the whole team on his way to the line but instead his bulldozing effort set the platform for Ella to score after some quick hands along the line. Substitute Rogers finished things off but his job was made easy by a clever sniping run and perfect pass from Murray.

Barrow secretary Bill Caine was not particularly impressed with what he saw.

'We competed well until half-time but once they started getting more possession they put us under pressure and they were just a bit too strong.'

Stanton added: 'We allowed ourselves to be rattled in the first half, and I thought the players panicked at various stages.'

Queensland prop Rohan Hancock became the first major injury worry with a torn hamstring – he would be out for four weeks – and the front-row department was certainly an issue with Young and Don McKinnon both struggling with neck problems.

With St Helens up next, Boyd was moved to prop alongside Krilich and Young, the three men who would make up the front row for the opening Test. In fact, the team that took the field at Knowlsey Road that bright Sunday afternoon would be the ones who faced Great Britain in just under two weeks, with the exception of Muggleton, who would have to make way for Reddy.

Saints did not provide the test anyone expected, especially the RFL who had deliberately left the period around the St Helens game free of competition matches to maximise the crowd, which in the end was half the size it had been in 1974. With a Lancashire Cup final against Warrington six days later, coach Billy Benyon was left with a side that only included six first-team regulars, a move which did not even help as they were beaten 16-0 in the final by their local rivals. With a more generous win bonus for a cup final it was suggested that a few of the first teamers did not want to risk getting injured with such a large financial incentive looming.

'We expected a harder game than the one we received,' coach Frank Stanton said. 'We came here to entertain yet the paying public was robbed. They saw a reserve grade side play.'

In the grand scheme of things the home side, without the likes of Peter Gorley, Harry Pinner and Roy Haggerty, did reasonably well just to lose 37-0, considering the opposition they faced. Their undoubted highlight was the performance of scrum-half Neil Holding, who on more than one occasion used his vision and pace to punch holes in the visitors' fearsome defence.

That apart it was something of a procession and by half-time the contest was over with the scoreline at 16-0. Certainly full-back Clive Griffiths remembered the contest with plenty of affection even though he came off the field with a head full of stitches, a broken thumb and a dead leg.

'Having played in Wales against touring rugby union teams from Tonga and Australia, I always felt it was an honour to play against any international team and it meant I played against Australia twice even though you knew you were going to get your arse spanked.

'I wanted to play whatever was going to be thrown at me and, playing full-back, there was a lot thrown at me that day. I was exposed, they were coming through like it was Custer's last stand sometimes. I remember thinking I had got hold of Meninga's legs and it was one leg I had got hold of. The bigger they are the harder they fall … Christ, whoever said that needs to be taken off in a straitjacket.

'I was so glad I played against them. They were the best team I played against in either code … there is no doubt about that.'

An excellent piece of imagination from Muggleton created the first try for Boustead. The second-rower received the ball from Sterling, who had switched the play, and, with the Saints winger drawn to the ball, he grubber-kicked ahead leaving Griffiths hopelessly exposed. The winger was able to collect the ball over the line and dive on it.

Boyd's quick thinking, determination and strength got him over the line for the next. Five yards out he was brought to ground by three defenders where he quickly took a tap and surged for the line; those same three Saints defenders were unable to stop him grounding the ball.

One of the training drills that the Australians were becoming renowned for was one that encouraged them to twist their body in the tackle and get the ball away. This was evident three times in the build-up to Boustead's second try. Firstly, Sterling contorted himself into trouble but somehow managed to get the ball away to Muggleton, with a pair of home players wrapping him up. The exact same thing happened again before Steve Rogers was next in possession and as he was in the process of being upended he somehow managed to flick the ball to his winger, who had the freedom of St Helens to scoot over on 34 minutes.

Moments later Boyd charged onto a Sterling short pass, smashed through tackles and bounced off two other Saints players who were clearly surprised to see him. The inspired Aussie then pirouetted brilliantly before crashing over. He looked a natural in the prop position. Two minutes after the restart Grothe collected a kick from Holding but still had 70 metres to go. Once he had broken the first tackle he was in the clear and no Saints player could get near him.

The St Helens faithful were then treated to one of the greatest tries ever seen at Knowsley Road. It was started and finished by Grothe, who was looking more like a Test winger by the second. Firstly, the Parramatta powerhouse collected a superb long pass from Kenny deep inside his own half and broke one tackle before finding Rogers just a split second before being hauled into touch.

The experienced centre evaded one attempt to stop him but, just as he was collared, displayed great awareness to twist and loop the ball to the onrushing Muggleton, who seemed to have let things slip with his subsequent pass going to ground. However, Sterling was just in the right place to tidy things up and he slipped the ball to Boyd, who handed on to Kenny, who in turn flipped the ball out to Grothe on the charge. The bearded wonder handed off two desperate attempts to stop him crossing at the corner. He was brought to ground by David Fairclough but was not stopped and he got to his feet and touched down.

The tourists were really turning it on now and Rogers finished off a wonderful flowing move down Saints' left. Pearce's final pass was just sublime – he hooked it round one defender while another brought him down.

Sterling had the easiest job of the day in scoring the final try. All the hard work was done by Boyd, who appeared to have been stopped and restrained. However, he somehow freed his ball-carrying arm and flicked out a perfect pass for the Australia scrum-half to gratefully collect.

Once again the Kangaroos had turned on the style and, despite concerns that Meninga might have done something serious to his wrist, their leading Test hopefuls had all come through the game unscathed. Now all eyes were on the Great Britain selectors who were meeting the next day to pick the 13-man team, two substitutes and a travelling reserve. John Whiteley had watched every Australian game and his worst fears had been confirmed. While he was saying nothing about who should or would be picked, he was clearly unhappy at suggestions that the Kangaroos were not that good.

'I think the forwards can be mastered but we can't afford to let the back have the ball because there's a lot of potential there,' said the GB coach just before his squad was announced. 'If anybody says they're not a fair outfit they're in cloud cuckoo land. It won't be a Test for the squeamish.'

Other leading rugby league personalities were a lot freer to speculate on who might get in and Alex Murphy, writing in the *Manchester Evening News*, summed up the diversity of opinion that was swirling around at the time. Apart from Des Drummond and Trevor Skerrett, nobody could agree on what constituted a winning formula.

'I want to plead with the selectors not to go for the old brigade,' said the Wigan coach, who would be commentating on the match for the BBC alongside Ray French.

'Of course we need some experience but if it's a choice between a youngster and a veteran they must go for youth. While winning the series is paramount, we must also be looking ahead to the 1984 down under tour and we need new faces.'

On 18 October the selectors took just two hours to decide on the line-up, leaving those aligned with Murphy's view disappointed.

Most of the media led with the call-up of Lee Crooks, the teenage sensation from Hull. At just 19 he was thrown into the heat of an Ashes battle but the second-rower was no ordinary young player. He had led the Great Britain Colts on their summer tour of Australia and PNG – that was why he didn't take part in the summer training squad – having played 42 matches for his club the season before.

And those who saw his stunning effort for Hull against previously unbeaten Leeds just a few days earlier would not have been surprised in the slightest. He claimed a hat-trick of tries as part of a personal 23-point haul and that almost certainly secured his place.

'He has proved he can do it at the top level and has the perfect temperament for the big occasion,' said John. Now was the time to really build up his players.

Crooks apart, the selectors played it safe with six of the side aged 30 or over. Salford's 33-year-old scrum-half Steve Nash led his country for the first time but the fact that the seasoned campaigner had just spent a year playing in Division Two was not lost on the critics, especially those in Australia.

Manager Hutton said: 'From what we have seen so far the Australians are a very powerful team and are superbly fit but we can beat them. All the players are good footballers and they're physically equipped for the job. We have gone for players of proven character and all are in good form at the moment.

'The attitude of Nash during our squad sessions has been superb and his overall influence has been exemplary. He is a natural leader and a good organiser in tight play. As captain he will take much of the weight off David Ward, who will be in charge of the British forwards.'

The full team read as follows: George Fairbairn (Hull KR), Des Drummond (Leigh), Eric Hughes (Widnes), Les Dyl (Leeds), Steve Evans (Hull), John Woods (Leigh), Steve Nash (Salford), Jeff Grayshon (Bradford), David Ward (Leeds), Trevor Skerrett (Hull), Les Gorley (Widnes), Lee Crooks (Hull), Steve Norton (Hull). Substitutes: Ken Kelly (Warrington), David Heron (Leeds). Travelling reserve: Mike Smith (Hull KR).

The attitude of many seasoned watchers was best summed up by a line in a piece by the highly-respected *Yorkshire Post* reporter Raymond Fletcher, who said: 'Plans to rebuild after the last disastrous Test series in Australia in 1979 have been thwarted by the lack of genuine new talent. Nine of the 1979 tour squad are retained and it is difficult to imagine they have improved.'

Brian Lockwood, one of the heroes of the last British victory over the Kangaroos in 1978, was already quoted as calling the new crop the best Australian team ever to come to Great Britain.

The growing sense of foreboding in the British game was intensified by concerns over injuries to key Hull forwards Skerrett, who was struggling to overcome knee ligament damage, and Norton, who had banged his hip. Australia would name their Test team in seven days' time. Before that there were games with Wales and firstly Leeds at Headingley.

Robin Dewhirst's experienced outfit were top of the table and he named his strongest possible side for the midweek clash. The decision was made easier by Leeds not having a game the following weekend and he took advantage of his close proximity to the Australia training base to watch his Wednesday-night opponents in the run-up to the clash.

'It will be a great experience for our younger players and they are bound to learn something. I did just watch them training. Their attitude is so different. While English players walk between exercises the Australians jog.'

The Leeds coach was unable to give Kevin Dick the chance to show the selectors they had made a big mistake in leaving him out of the Test team. The scrum-half, who was the leading try scorer domestically, had a back problem, which gave 18-year-old Mark Conway a dream opportunity against the best team in the world in only his second start.

At the other end of the scale 38-year-old Leeds stalwart Alan Smith got the nod ahead of Mark Massa, and he would have to utilise every ounce of his experience to deal with the in-form Grothe. Test players Dyl, Heron and Ward were also included alongside the similarly experienced John Holmes and Neil Hague.

The appearance of Smith, the last of Britain's stellar 1970 side who would face the Aussies this time around, generated mixed feelings having seen first-hand how the game had deteriorated in the decade before.

'By the mid-70s our game changed. For amateurs it was Sunday League football and in the Brookhouse, Leeds, Doncaster, Dewsbury areas ... the juniors weren't playing rugby anymore like they used to be. There weren't a lot of players coming through the system. I played until I was 39 and I should not have been allowed to play to that age. Not at Leeds. There wasn't enough coming through to take my place and I think it was the same in a lot of clubs. Our A team, the attendances ... everything was dropping off.'

He could also see the parallels between that great British side he had been part of and what John Whiteley's 82 outfit were going to be tackling.

'Us in 1970 and them in 1982 had the same mix of quality. There was pace, power and skill. We had all that. Whatever team we faced in Australia we could deal with it and that Australia side were the same. We always said they would beat us at fitness but we could beat them at football. They tackled us so hard and in 1970 we had the skill. But they came over in 1982 and Sterling and Lewis and the rest of them had the lot.'

The efforts of Sterling were certainly making a lot of people sit up and take notice and he would get another chance to show off his dazzling array of skills at Headingley. In fact, Australia's back line and front row was unchanged from four days earlier, while Pearce switched to his more accustomed loose forward position in place of Price, and Paul McCabe slotted in easily alongside Muggleton in the second row.

Many of the Australian squad had enjoyed an afternoon at the illustrious Moortown Golf Club the day before and that bit of R&R had clearly worked as they tore into Leeds from the off. For those who had seen all the matches this felt as if they had raised the bar that little bit higher, such was the intensity of their play. It was a good job that Ward managed to win the scrums 9-6 and the hosts enjoyed a favourable 17-7 penalty county.

A typical piece of Sterling's scurrying approach work after just four minutes laid the platform for the first of seven top-class tries. The manner in which Rogers brushed off the attentions of new international Heron on his way to the line might have set off a few more alarm bells for the Great Britain management. The Leeds back-rower's attempt to stop the Aussie centre by going high was dismissed in a contemptuous manner as he barely broke stride in fending off the raid.

Dewhirst's team were lucky that Rogers, Grothe and Boustead had missed out on gift opportunities beforehand but the latter did convert after being fed by Meninga, who had taken two men out of the game with a top-class take and pass. There was a huge gasp from the crowd as he stepped inside Hague, leaving the Leeds full-back sprawling on his back. A Conway penalty earlier meant the sides turned around at 12-2, although one piece of elusive running from Dyl had given the Headingley faithful some hope.

Unfortunately for the experienced centre he was hauled down five metres short.

Pearce had the freedom of Leeds to charge through a gap to create the first try-scoring opportunity of the second half and with the home defence funnelling back in desperation, Boustead's inside ball found Meninga at full pace and, despite a host of blue and yellow shirts in front of him, the powerhouse centre was not going to be stopped 15 yards out.

Australia's next try has lived long in the memory for Smith.

'Second half Johnny Holmes kicks the ball from inside our own half towards Grothe's wing. I chase it down and Eric Grothe catches the ball and I am going to push him straight to the wing. I can't let him go infield and behind me the cover is coming. Anyway, he gets the ball and sets off … boof! He brushed me aside like I was just a twig. When I got my head on someone I could tackle but he was so strong. I looked around and he had done the same to one or two others on the way up. Neil Hague was the last man and he was flat on his back near the stand.'

It was a score to further confirm Grothe's fearsome reputation, especially considering the manner in which Hague's diving tackle attempt was dealt with. The big winger did not break stride as he dived over.

In the final quarter once again the Kangaroos started to unload. When Meninga crossed for his second try there were four of his team-mates in support as Leeds were exposed on their left-hand side.

Leeds were well beaten and substitute Steve Ella feasted on their carcass with two late scores to make it 31-4. The post-match comments of Smith caught the essence of the task facing Great Britain perfectly, although he remained hopeful of a shock in ten days' time.

'Believe you me these lads, the Australians, are very professional. The last time I played them was nine years ago and they are improving all the time. The fitness … they play the basics so good and so fast.

'Our lads need to get among them because there were just one or two times tonight where we just put them under pressure, but we could not sustain any flow.

'I do hope the GB lads have lived together and trained together well and all being well can match them and beat them. It's going to take a good side to beat them and I hope our lads rise to the occasion.'

Grothe and Smith chatted afterwards and the young star did his opposite number the honour of giving him the benefit of the doubt in the lead-up to that iconic try.

'I got pretty lucky more than anything. He [Smith] lost his footing which let me get past him and then it was a pretty straightforward run to the line. I had to get him back because he beat me in a tackle earlier. Overall I think we are getting the referees a bit more on our side compared to the last tour [1978]. Apparently they gave Australia a hard time which made it hard for them to win games.'

With his team looking unstoppable coach Stanton might have had more concerns over the appointment of inexperienced French referee Julien Rascagneres for the Test match.

Having done a good job taking charge of Leigh's clash with Castleford earlier in the month, the 34-year-old postman was appointed to the match having been groomed for the Hull showdown by the RFL. However, concerns that his English was not strong were dispelled by David Howes.

'His control of the game at Leigh did not suffer even though he does not speak fluent English. He proved the language difficulty was no problem.'

Stanton appeared more exercised by a feature in a British rugby league magazine which suggested Craig Young was not among the top-five props in the world while two other Aussies – Geoff Gerard and Royce Ayliffe – were.

'The Poms don't respect us as ball players. I don't think they expect us to come up with moves to get us out of trouble, but I'm confident Young will become our key man.'

Young was a certainty to pack down against Great Britain and, while officially the Test XIII would not be announced until the Monday before the game (30 October), it's make-up was all but confirmed by the unveiling of the side to face Wales in the final warm-up match on Sunday 24 October.

Chris Anderson recovered from a hamstring problem to take his place on the wing and only Reddy of the future Test line-up was named to take on Welsh team lacking Skerrett. There was no way he could be risked; such was his importance to British hopes.

Wales' coach David Watkins and his captain, centre John Bevan, had a lot to bring to the table but with just a couple of practice sessions together, and steering a side containing nine Division Two players, it was always going to be tough for the men in red to give the Australian second string a game.

Those tourists not in the frame for a Test pick started to call themselves 'emus' (the other animal along with the kangaroo on the Australians' Commonwealth Coat of Arms) and this was definitely a team full of big birds.

Ella took his try-scoring form into the fixture at Ninian Park and bagged four of the nine tries that afternoon. Murray and Mortimer paired up well at half-back while Lewis captained the team from the centre.

In Cardiff the Green and Golds took a while to find their feet – they did not cross until the 23rd minute – and even conceded a try to recent league convert Brynmor Williams, their first for four matches.

For coach Watkins, who had overseen the Great Britain set-up five years earlier, the future prospects for the Ashes series were keenly anticipated.

'Obviously we are disappointed but one has to be a realist in sport and not let the situation run away with you. They were far better organised and a far better team on the day and they have already played exceptionally and already posed Great Britain many threats for the Test series starting next Saturday.

'We got together on Friday and it is very hard when you have a team together for just two training sessions to then go into an international match against a side armed with all the armoury they had. They looked good. I think they gave the Welsh public a good impression with good backing up, good running and good tries which people appreciated.

'I think at this moment in time rugby league, apart from the very top sides, is going back somewhat. We play the ball slowly, we don't back up as well as we should do, we don't lie deep enough to run onto the ball and we don't straighten the line-up often enough. I think this is a basic fault at the moment and today it was good to see a side [Australia] doing all these basic things properly and one can only realise how effective a side can be when they are done properly, no matter what the opposition is.'

Watkins was as astute as they come and his downbeat assessment of the state of the game should have been listened to. However, the fragility of British rugby league was about to be laid bare on live TV and in front of an audience of millions. The single most important match in the history of the British game was just six days away.

Chapter Seven

The First Test

ON Monday 25 October, in a function room at the Dragonara Hotel in the centre of Leeds, Australia's co-manager Frank Farrington rose to his feet to address all 28 players and the rest of the backroom staff. The mood was sombre. Those who knew they weren't going to play were downbeat and those who knew they were playing weren't much happier. As much as you are pleased to have grabbed the jersey you are equally unhappy your mate has missed out.

Farrington pulled his glasses case from his back pocket and put on his spectacles. There was little in the way of introduction as he listed the side from 1 to 17 (two subs and two on standby were also listed) and not a word was uttered from anyone else in the small room as he did so. He also read out the names of the men who would be 'duty boys' and others who would fulfil a number of non-playing tasks on the day of the match.

Australia operated a lockdown system in the week before Tests which meant that those 13 players not likely to be involved were given extracurricular duties or were encouraged to go exploring. This is where it got really serious and any kind of potential distractions were minimised. Meanwhile, the three duty boys –

Ian Schubert, Rod Morris and Rohan Hancock – were expected to help out around the dressing rooms, assist medical staff and take care of the bits and pieces that you would associate with training … sorting bibs, cones, other equipment and drinks.

At Boothferry Park for the first Test there were three extracurricular activities. Mortimer and Conescu would check that the official timekeepers were doing their job accurately, Murray, Anderson and McCabe would help log all the in-game statistics and Ribot, McKinnon, Lewis and Miles would be stationed at different points of the ground to count the fans as they clicked through the turnstiles. This was a hangover from a time when countries were regularly cheated out of their share of gate receipts because of the under-reporting of attendances.

Lewis looked surprised as his name was read out for this unwanted job and the tension in the room was palpable but as Farrington said, 'sand boy … Ray Brown', laughter rippled around the assembled ranks. He would be required to bring out a bucket of sand whenever Meninga needed some for a kick at goal. The reserve hooker would be a busy man.

The Australia team read as follows: 1, Greg Brentnall (Canterbury); 2, Eric Grothe (Parramatta); 3, Mal Meninga, (Souths Brisbane); 4, Steve Rogers (Cronulla); 5, Kerry Boustead (Eastern Suburbs); 6, Brett Kenny (Parramatta); 7, Peter Sterling (Parramatta); 8, Craig Young (St George); 9, Max Krilich (Manly); 10, Les Boyd (Manly); 11, Wayne Pearce (Balmain); 12, Rod Reddy (St George); 13, Ray Price (Parramatta); 14, Steve Ella (Parramatta); 15, John Muggleton (Parramatta). Standby: 16, Wally Lewis (Fortitude Valley); 17, Rod Morris (Wynnum-Manly).

'The current side has been chosen on current form,' Farrington told British reporters. 'It represents our best line-up from our squad of 28 players.'

The only real issue for most of the travelling press pack was that Reddy had beaten off the challenge of Muggleton and McCabe for a second-row spot. His reputation as an enforcer may have just given him the nod. Ashes Test matches were notorious for their brutal early exchanges. There was also the caveat that Reddy and Boyd would have to escape punishment at an RFL disciplinary hearing held two days before the match for the red cards collected in the tour opener at Hull KR to be able to play.

'Reddy was chosen because of his consistency and form and his greater experience compared with the lack of consistency and form of his rivals,' said Stanton.

The absence of Lewis caused a stink back in Queensland and discussions surrounding the decision reached the top echelons of the game and eventually the tour management.

'Wally Lewis was supposed to be the best player on the tour but his form didn't always allow him to be picked,' recalled Stanton. 'In terms of the players, to my knowledge, they all understood why Wally wasn't being picked but there was some kerfuffle back home. Ron McAuliffe (Queensland's rugby league chief) complained bitterly to Ken Arthurson who reached me and eventually flew over to England and one of his questions was "why wasn't Lewis playing?" Of course I gave him all the reasons and he said, "You must have a bloody good team" and of course I said "Yes I have".'

Lewis himself took the news better than many of the other squad members. On the flight over, the stand-off had acquired a hamstring problem that would ultimately dog him for two years, plus he had added more than a stone in weight in the first four weeks in the UK. His response to the Test snub was to change his diet which essentially met cutting out the extras.

The Dragonara Hotel had a casino which offered its guests free food, and many of the squad had taken to buying a few chips just to enjoy the sandwiches and drinks. However, before Lewis turned to salads to help him shed the pounds, he joined a few of the non-Test-playing boys on a night out to drown their sorrows at not being selected. He awoke at 3am to find his room-mate Mortimer doing sit-ups; the Canterbury stand-off, had his own way of dealing with the frustration. Schubert led the way in organising social stuff for the non-Test players, as Lewis recalled some years later. The Queensland legend wrote: 'Schubert founded the Emu Club, calling the inaugural meeting when Stanton took the Test team aside for tactical conferences. Schubert sent out invitations to all non-Test players. "You are invited to an emu party, all grog supplied, please tick the I accept/I decline box." There was no "I decline" box.'

With time on their hands many of 'the emus' decided to buy second hand cars in which to explore, including Lewis, Murray, Miles and Conescu who clubbed together to purchase a Hillman Imp. Reddy couldn't help himself in offering to help, and phoned the car's owner pretending to be John Ribot, an Australian film director who was in the country making a film about the Yorkshire Ripper. Before the day was out a befuddled Ribot was being questioned by West Yorkshire detectives in his hotel room. They bought the car after Reddy told the owner he was the last remaining Hillman Imp mechanic in Australia but blew his cover after trying to find the engine at the front of the car.

Meanwhile Mortimer, McKinnon and Brentnall paid £50 for a Morris Minor while Ribot and Boyd clubbed together for something a little more fancy, a black Ford Cortina. On the Tuesday, with many of his unselected players chugging around the narrow lanes of Yorkshire, Stanton and the Test squad began to work in earnest on their final preparations. The interest in his team was such that he was forced to interrupt their first workout to clear a number of overly-keen local schoolchildren from their training base.

Seventy miles to the east, the British players met up in the Lincolnshire seaside resort of Cleethorpes and those who watched them preparing noted a decided lack of timber around the midriff, of many of the well-known players in particular. Dyl, for example, was reportedly 10kg lighter than he had been during the 1974 tour.

The Britain coach was asked about his focus on fitness, the resistance he had experienced to forming the summer training squads and the absurd suggestion that they were being overworked.

'We know we are novices compared to Australia's approach to fitness,' said John. 'But our lads have so much ability that it's a crying shame they haven't been used to their full potential.

'Although the lads have been working at it for four months now we've only just reached the tip of the iceberg and the players are so keen that they are doing extra training on their own.

'They're discovering a new pride in their fitness. Previously, a top player in his position would not have to worry about his level of fitness. He would be selected for a Test and know that he didn't have to do any more, but that's all changed now.'

Those who thought John was tiring out his players should have seen what their Australian counterparts were doing back in Leeds. On the Wednesday, led by Price and Rogers, the Kangaroos were put through a punishing schedule culminating in a 'rocking-horse' workout in which players locked arms and legs and, in a motion similar to a sit-up, repeated the exercise almost 200 times.

The next day (Thursday) the Australians focused on ball work while manager Farrington accompanied Boyd and Reddy to their RFL hearing. Both were cleared to play although the latter was fined £10. Boyd was found not guilty of calling referee Lindop a cheat but was warned about swearing. It would have been a shock if either had missed the match. The last time a tourist received a ban was back in 1967.

The RUGBY LEAGUE NEWS

JOHN HARDING
Manager

JOHN WHITELEY
Asst. Manager
and Coach

FIRST TEST

AUSTRALIA
v
GREAT BRITAIN

Under the auspices of the
AUSTRALIAN RUGBY LEAGUE
SOUVENIR PROGRAMME

**LANG PARK
BRISBANE**

20c

**JUNE, 6
1970**

Registered in Australia for transmission by post as a newspaper.

This is the programme cover from the first Test in Brisbane in 1970

The front page of the Sunday Mirror *(Australia) following the second Test where crowd violence marred proceedings*

England's Roger Millward tries to duck through a gap during their titanic tussle with Australia in the 1975 World Championship Series in Sydney which ended 10-10

England scrum-half Steve Nash has his black eye examined by coach Alex Murphy after the tourists beat Western Australia 40-2 in 1975

Australia winger Allan McMahon touches down for a try despite the best effort of George Fairbairn in the final of the 1977 Rugby League World Cup

Two of the key figures in helping to modernise the RFL… long-time league secretary David Oxley and long-time PR officer David Howes pictured in 1977

The Great Britain squad ahead of the 1979 tour of Australia and New Zealand

Great Britain coach Eric Ashton in 1979

Teenage John Whiteley

Great Britain manager Colin Hutton

The Hull side of 1960 captained by John Whiteley (holding the ball)

Ray Tabern, Mike Smith, Paul Prendiville, George Fairbairn and John Joyner enjoy an ice cream in Venice during their trip to Italy in the summer of 1982

1982 Australia squad

Australia co-manager Tom Drysdale

Australia co-manager Frank Farrington

Australia's front row of Craig Young, Max Krilich and Rod Morris prepare to pack down against Hull Kingston Rovers in the opening match

*The maestro Wally
Lewis battles
through an injury
for Australia against
Wales*

*Steve Norton, Mike
Smith, Jeff Grayshon,
David Ward, Steve
Evans, Les Dyl and
Lee Crooks in a
publicity picture
ahead of the first Test
in Hull in 1982*

Great Britain hooker David Ward is caught during the first Test at Boothferry Park in Hull

First Test man of the match Wayne Pearce

Mal Meninga kicks the ball clear in the third Test at Headingley

Mick Harrison, pictured in action for Leeds, returned to Hull for a remarkable swansong effort at the Boulevard against Australia

*Australia captain
Max Krilich bursts
through a gap to score
a try under the posts
in the third Test*

*Victorious Australia coach
Frank Stanton (left) is
welcomed home at Sydney
Airport by Minister of Sport
Mike Cleary*

Great Britain coach Frank Myler leads a practice session with full-back Mick Burke in 1984

Wayne Pearce leaps high to collect a ball with Great Britain winger Des Drummond waiting to challenge the Australia forward in 1984

International scrum-half rivals Steve Mortimer (left) and Peter Sterling in 1984

Australia forward Noel Cleal tries to power his way past Great Britain winger Barry Ledger (right) and Garry Schofield in 1986

Andy Gregory throws out a pass for Great Britain in the 1988 Ashes series. The scrum-half would have a huge part to play in the history-making third Test

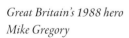

Great Britain's 1988 hero Mike Gregory

Joining Great Britain in training on the Boothferry Park pitch that day was Warrington forward Bob Eccles, freshly arrived from scoring a try in six successive matches. That meant that 17 players were now preparing to tackle the Aussies. The call-up was described as precautionary, with Norton and Skerrett 'flat out' in the session at the home of Hull City although goalkicker Crooks would not get the chance to practise kicks at goal with the erection of the goalposts being delayed.

The GB coach was interviewed for TV while watching his players being put through their paces. 'Preparations have gone very, very well,' said John. 'The attitude of the players has been tremendous and the weather has been very kind to us and we have got plenty of training in and we have worked very well and I hope on the day it all comes together and it comes good.'

He was also asked about the threat of Grothe but wouldn't be drawn on how his wingman would cope.

'Well I think you should reverse that and ask how is Grothe going to handle Des Drummond? I mean in sheer movements Grothe is a straight runner, a very big straight runner and he needs room to run. Dessie needs half an inch either side and it's night night.'

He was also questioned about the pressure on his teenage goalkicker, Crooks.

'At this particular stage he will be handed the kicking job. He was going to use today but there was no sticks up, so that's put the kibosh on that. But it will be a crucial factor because it will be a very tight game. People have been talking about the Australians playing with a lot of flair but they won't get that room to move so it could revolve around goalkicking and it should be a tight game.'

It was a time for final instructions on both sides. Both countries were reminded that, for the first time in an international in the

UK, the sin-bin would be in operation. RFL media man Howes confirmed how it would work.

'The referee will indicate a five- or ten-minute period for the offender who must leave the field and go to the dressing room. He will be recalled in time to resume when the cooling down period has been completed.'

With Huddersfield official Billy Thompson named as the official reserve referee – he would act as a touch judge – everything was now in place.The bookmakers were giving the hosts a ten-point start and if you wanted to back the underdogs you could get odds of 4-1.

Stanton would be asked one last time about his thoughts.

'We expect Britain to play a physical, defensive type of spoiling game, trying mainly to take advantage of any mistakes we may make. We are ready for that kind of approach. The side we have chosen has a lot of pace and flair but at the same time I think we are tough enough to handle whatever tactics Britain employ. We will probably find out in the first 20 minutes.'

Back in north Lincolnshire his British counterpart also had one last duty to perform for the press.

'There is a tremendous spirit among the players and a great sense of occasion. I've been through it all before as player and coach and know the feeling from both sides. I've been written off and won. Anything can happen.'

Rugby league historians were happy to point to the fact that we had seen previous Australian incarnations win all their fixtures ahead of the first Test (1921, 1933, 1973) and then lose. There was a genuine sense that Whiteley could work his magic, as he had in 1970. After all, it wasn't that long ago and back then he was also working against a backdrop of successive Australian series successes.

But this would be different. One man who encapsulated how things were changing was Australia's newest second-row forward, one of six youngsters playing against the Lions for the first time. The others were Brentnall, Meninga, Grothe, Kenny and Sterling. It was easy to forget that second-rower Pearce started the tour as a Test possible, such was his impact during those early tour games, but his selection was the culmination of an extraordinary dedication that was unparalleled in the sport at the time.

His national coach had also watched him blossom at Balmain over the last 12 months and had a special reason to be pleased for the likeable 22-year-old. Four years earlier he suffered a potentially career-ending bout of hepatitis. Overcoming the disease was typical of his extraordinary resolve.

'Fitness was his hobby,' recalls Stanton. 'He didn't drink or smoke like the others. He came from a semi-hard background. He used to have to work as a kid at Balmain, selling hot dogs at the games and stuff like that. He was always going to be an achiever. He obviously worked hard. Football became an outlet for him to achieve something for himself and through that he put himself through uni. He was a fitness freak. He watched what he ate and was one of the originals.'

At the end of the 1982 domestic season in Australia, Pearce, who would soon gain his teaching degree from the University of Sydney, had paid for his own ticket to visit Hawaii as part of Balmain's end-of-season tour. It meant making a frantic effort to sell the ticket to someone else after hearing he was in the Ashes tour party.

'Because Price was the established lock I hadn't even played for New South Wales,' said Pearce. 'I really didn't think I had much of a chance. I'd only been in the first grade for a year or so ... I had to find someone to buy the ticket to Hawaii off me at the last minute.''

'Junior', as he would become known to his team-mates, was a man ahead of his time. He did not eat red meat for health reasons at a time when there was just a dawning realisation that eating

163

the right things at the right times could give you an edge on the sports field. This was 13 years before Arsene Wenger arrived at Highbury and started a dietary revolution with Arsenal the English Premier League.

It is hard to imagine a sportsman, anywhere in the world at that time who was better prepared for an international introduction than Pearce.

In contrast his fellow second-rower in red, white and blue Lee Crooks who was also making his full international debut, was far from fully aware of what was about to hit him. In making it to the top, the Hull-born teenager also had it tough. He learned to play rugby at Ainthorpe Junior School but at secondary school received little help although that did not stop him becoming a teenage rugby sensation. Much of that was down to his own self-reliance, borne of having to do many of the jobs that parents would normally do. He was barely out of primary school and he would, among other things, have to come home and make dinner for his younger brother while his mum and dad were out working.

Critically his mates were generally two or three years older than him and playing those knockabout games with them on the nearest bit of grass they could find after school and at weekends meant he had to find ways of 'not getting beat up'.

One of his first proper coaches was Sam Burgess's granddad, who looked after Yorkshire U-16s, and while he was still only 15 Crooks played for England Schoolboys and a year later captained them.

A whole host of top English outfits wanted to sign him but Hull was his club and after some to-ing and fro-ing with Rovers, he joined the black and whites just a few days before the famous Hull derby Challenge Cup Final of 1980.

He made his full debut just six months later against Salford at the Boulevard and during the following campaign (1981/82) became a mainstay of the pack. That summer he captained the Great Britain Colts on their summer tour of Australia and PNG. Had that tour not happened he would almost certainly have been among the 31 players named in the summer training squad.

He only joined in Great Britain training following his first Test call-up, although his blossoming friendship with his boyhood idol Steve Norton would mean he had a seasoned international to help him through the last few days before the match. However, the enormity of the occasion hit him in the final few hours before the game kicked off at 3pm.

Crooks recalls: 'I was bricking it to be fair but Steve was just so calm … mind you, he had seen it all before. And we had watched the game against Hull KR and Rovers had given them a good game. We sort of had that feeling they were not that good. Everyone was saying how good they were but we thought we had a chance of beating them.'

The weather in the build-up to the match had been unseasonably warm and that lasted until matchday where the high temperatures created something of a carnival feel, although as kick-off time approached it started to grey over. With drums banging and the sell-out crowd settling into their positions the arrival of legendary Australia supporter Laurie Nicholls caused something of a stir. The Balmain fanatic, dressed in a bright yellow T-shirt, skipped down the steps of the main stand singing 'C'mon Aussie, c'mon, c'mon' while shadow boxing. A couple of his right uppercuts nearly took himself out. In the changing rooms, beneath the bouncing Nicholls, both sides were going through those final few motions and captain Krilich had one more surprise up his sleeve.

He later wrote: 'Probably the most incredible experience of my life happened at Boothferry Park in Hull where we played our first Test in 1982. We had put our heads together and decided to do something typically Australian before the games. Something that would lift everyone.

'And so we got into a boomerang formation as we stood waiting for the national anthem.

'It was a very moving moment – every time we did it it affected me. Nobody could realise what it's like. I find it hard to express my feelings ... but there would have to be something wrong with a bloke if it didn't touch him.'

The buzz was special and made all the more memorable by the state of Hull City's ground. The North Stand behind one of the posts had been demolished to make way for a new supermarket so hundreds of supporters watched the drama unfold from what was essentially a building site.

On the other side of the world 1978 tourist Geoff Gerard, who many thought should have been selected for the following series, would act as a pundit for Channel Seven. The Manly prop said: 'A lot of people thought I should have gone this time but I missed out and good luck to the fellas who are over there.'

When asked about the team, Gerard added: 'In my two seasons at Manly whenever Les [Boyd] has been asked to fill in at prop he's not really enjoyed it. Apparently he's had a couple of good games in that position and the only other one is Rocket [Reddy]. He must have had a good game last time to get in ahead of Muggleton and McCabe. They reckon against Wales he had a bit of a blinder to clinch his spot but we will see whether he is worthy of it today.'

Asked about the Britain side, Gerrard said: 'There are a hell of a lot of players over 30 but there are a lot of crafty buggers in there and maybe they realise this Australia side is a pretty hot side and the way to beat them is unsettle them and get them off their game. In most of the Australia games it has been pretty close at half-time so far but Australia's superior fitness has come good in the second half and I think that will probably be the case today.'

The final act was the playing of the national anthems. Channel Seven commentator Rex Mossop estimated that around 2,000 of his fellow countrymen were in the crowd. All that expense and time was about to be made very worthwhile.

The waiting was finally over.

Rogers swung his right boot to kick-off the 101st meeting of these two old rivals. The ball drifted long and bounced twice before popping up nicely for Drummond. He made 15 yards before slipping into the legs of the onrushing Young. From the next play of the ball the tourists were penalised for offside. Monsieur Rascagneres made an early and positive impression and he would maintain that impressive form throughout.

Fairbairn's kick reached the halfway line and hooker Ward took the opportunity to take a quick tap and go while the opposition were not quite set, barging into his opposite number Krilich. Nash orchestrated what was clearly one of Britain's set moves, flicking a reverse pass to Grayshon, but he was submerged under three tacklers. On the next tackle Gorley pounded into the opposition line. The crowd were eager to voice their support.

Woods switched play again, finding Norton who handed off to his club-mate Crooks. But they were both coming from a standing start and not committing tacklers before releasing. It was easy enough for the best defensive side in the world to cope with these safety-first early forays.

Boyd took an age to let Crooks get to his feet and even kicked out at the ball as it was played to Norton who found Dyl at pace, but Krilich was there like a flash and hauled him to the ground.

There was more pace about the way Grayshon hit the line from Nash's pass but the way he was picked up and unceremoniously dumped to the ground by Pearce was an ominous early sign and even in those early moments the Aussie second-row's physical stature stood out. So broad were his shoulders you could have built a small dwelling on them.

As Ward prepared to play tackle six the referee blew for another offside just 25 metres out. The sand was brought out for Crooks and he had the perfect opportunity to settle everyone's nerves. The 19-year-old did not disappoint and he put Great Britain ahead for the first and what proved to be the only time in the series.

The crowd chanted as Rogers restarted with another low, deep kick. This time Fairbairn collected but he was felled by the scampering Sterling, who went low while Boyd followed in to prevent a quick release.

Next, Skerrett had his first dart but he had barely got into his stride by the time Pearce led three into the tackle. Ward was then able to get away quickly and Pearce missed his tackle, but the Leeds hooker slipped and was jumped on.

Norton managed to get the ball away out of the tackle on the next play but his pass went to ground. Gorley tidied things up but there was no pace and even though the Widnes forward evaded a couple of despairing dives he only made five yards.

An early kick in the set from Woods headed towards the left wing where Grothe did well to catch it with Boustead in his way. The crowd cheered as the bearded powerhouse got to his feet and headed down the wing, Drummond coping well as the wingers fell into each other close to touch.

Meninga was threatening to cause mayhem when the referee awarded the visitors a penalty for something Grayshon had said and Brentnall's kick gave his side their first major opportunity to apply pressure. The ball took an age to be returned from the East Stand terrace. Young had first go and was held well by Ward and Hughes. Boyd then ploughed forward to little effect before Krilich got his side to within five yards of the line. It would soon be level pegging. With Sterling heading down the blindside, Australia were awarded a penalty for offside. The kick for Meninga would be a formality and it was 2-2 after six minutes.

As both teams retreated commentator Mossop noted that 'looking at the size of some of the British players I am sure they will be grateful for the odd break. I know Frank Stanton is very anxious that his side should move the ball a lot. He stressed the point to them that this is a large ground and there are many open spaces.'

Woods restarted with a high kick that dropped perfectly for Sterling, who had plenty of time to look up and find Boustead. The winger tried to release Kenny but Nash did superbly to cling on to the speedy stand-off's right leg and Dyl, charging in, ensured he did not get the ball away. It was the first real inkling of how things would ultimately pan out. Pearce beat one tackle but could not get past Crooks before Boyd had a run, bouncing off Gorley. The Hull youngster was again on hand to complete the tackle. It was hardly scintillating stuff but Sterling took everyone by surprise by chipping through on the next play of the ball, and with Evans having got a hand to the ball before Kenny fell on it, the Kangaroos had six more tackles.

Sterling was afforded a quick tap-and-go and already the British looked in trouble but Reddy let them off the hook by kicking on the first tackle and his poor attempt to find the corner was snaffled by Fairbairn, who was brought to ground by Sterling.

It got worse for the Aussies. Price was penalised for a kick on Grayshon after the Bradford prop had been felled on the first tackle. It was just the break the home side needed and the Scottish star pushed his team to just shy of the halfway line.

Once again Ward ambled forward to start the set and his perceived lack of pace made this tactic hard to fathom. On tackle two Nash used Norton on the runaround – we had already seen this move once – but this time his pass was dropped by Skerrett and the forwards packed down for the first time with Australia given the head and feed. It took a while for the scrum to right itself and the ball barely made it in before popping out. Sterling was as alert as ever and released Kenny who headed wide. He was halted by a trio of backs.

The Aussie No 7 seemed to be everywhere and he dummied to Price before having a go himself, but Norton stopped his dart after a ten-yard gain. Reddy made a similar distance with a gun-barrel-straight charge before Pearce bounced off a couple but was restricted well. Price was more effective on the next play, beating two flailing arms and taking his side into the danger zone. It was still one-up stuff and Brentnall's attempt to test Fairbairn with a bomb was a poor one as the ball barely made ten yards. Crooks tidied up possession well after some scrappy attempts to regain the ball.

Britain, for all intents purposes, were holding their own and the crowd were cheering every drive with plenty of gusto. On the third tackle of the next set they got another penalty when Boyd was penalised for a stiff arm in a collision with Grayshon, who took a while to get to his feet because of a sore left leg. The volume increased dramatically with Fairbairn's massive clearing kick, which took his side to within 15 metres of the line.

The crowd roared as Ward surged forward but he was driven back by Kenny and the sound was sucked out of the ground as Krilich came up with the ball. Boyd was pushed back in similar fashion on the next play but he managed to find Reddy and the big second-rower eased the pressure with a powerful drive to the ten-yard line.

The penalties were coming thick and fast. Norton was next to feel the wrath of the tangerine-shirted Frenchman for coming into the tackle knees first. Both sides were struggling to find any kind of rhythm. Australia had given the ball more air while Britain's wingers Drummond and Evans were anonymous. In fact Hull player Evans, who was more used to playing at centre, had not touched the ball. The home side were then afforded another good possession with their second penalty in quick succession but we got the first groan of the day when Ward once again used the first play to drive straight into two Australian defenders. On the next play Nash used the runaround move for the third time with Norton the shield and once again Skerrett dropped it. In those early stages it felt like it was going to be one of those tight, dour affairs with the winning team being the one who made fewest mistakes.

But the game exploded into life with the first piece of Australian brilliance. After Brentnall had injected some pace into proceedings with a good burst on the first tackle, Pearce took the ball forward and brushed aside Norton's attempt to go high. He found the perfect pass to Kenny just as Crooks snagged him around his ankles. The Kangaroos stand-off evaded his opposite number in emphatic style but Fairbairn did a splendid job of stopping his progress and his chances of finding a colleague in green.

Rogers evaded another tackle with the sound of applause fading away. The crowd desperately wanted a home win but were more than happy to show their appreciation of brilliant rugby. Boyd stomped all over Nash but thankfully Gorley did enough to stop the prop. It was noticeable that things were speeding up around the play of the ball and with 21 minutes on the clock, Australia struck. Reddy switched the ball to Young who looped the pass out of a double tackle to Pearce, who wasted no time in releasing Meninga. It appeared he was well covered but the manner in which he handed off a renowned tackler like Dyl was sensational. His pace got him past Fairbairn for the first try. An exasperated Mossop bellowed 'Dyl should be shot for not going low on a man the size of Meninga'. With the try-scorer failing with the touchline conversion the score was 2-5.

The try gave Stanton's side confidence and with each play that followed the gasps from the crowd increased with regularity. Krilich made good ground from the restart and on the next play Pearce broke another tackle. It took three to stop him and in the BBC commentary box Murphy and French were full of praise for the efforts of the dynamic second-rower. Young was next to join the party, beating off two tackles before Skerrett just about managed to halt his thrust with the help of Nash. Kenny could not step out of danger to the relief of the home bench, who could see that the momentum was flowing one way, although their anxiety must have lessened somewhat as Sterling's attempted kick to the corner went too far.

In response Skerrett took the ball up but as he was felled his isolation spoke volumes. On the next play his prop partner Grayshon was also grounded at the first attempt. Les Gorley was then upended as the British forwards gamely tried to get the ball out of their half but the difference in speed of pass was evident as Crooks was was brought to ground ten yards behind where the play had started. There seemed little in the way of structure, which was confirmed when Norton looked confusedly for help on the next play. There was none coming, Sterling easily stopping him and, as Ward funnelled the ball back to Fairbairn for the clearing kick, the sight of British players clumped in a disorganised manner almost made it impossible for the full-back to be found. Fairbairn responded by chipping ahead in a valiant attempt to beat the press but Kenny collected superbly under pressure and smartly brought it back to halfway.

Another well-timed charge from Brentnall set the tone once again for Australia, although Reddy's run on tackle two was snuffed out well. It was the calm before the storm. Sterling dummied left to Price which took out Ward and Nash. Crooks tried to cover but only ran into a colleague and the young scrum-half was just too quick for Gorley. There was panic in the British ranks. Sterling sucked in Dyl before releasing Rogers, who got the ball away just in time for Kenny to fling the ball out of the tackle. For a split second it appeared that his wild pass had killed the Kangaroos' chance of a second try but Boustead calmly collected and Pearce, of course, was in support. The second-rower looked inside straight away where Boyd had made up the ground, and drew in Fairbairn before putting in a perfect pass for the Aussie prop to scoot over unopposed on 26 minutes.

'Oh yeah,' crowed a clearly pumped-up Mossop. 'What a try!' He had a point. The score was enough to send a similarly excited Nicholls to the front of the Main Stand and again the nearby VIPs were treated to a bout of his best shadowboxing.

Pearce took a while to get to his feet. Replays confirmed that Fairbairn had gone in late and high and he was lucky to escape the ignominy of the sin-bin.

This time Meninga was able to convert a slightly easier chance. The chanting of the crowd had dissipated and as the players got set for the kick a thousand conversations were taking place. It didn't take a genius to realise what they were talking about. Those who said these Aussies were special were right all along.

As if to prove the point, Sterling cleverly flicked the restart behind him and zipped off a pass to Boustead who set off menacingly and drew in four white shirts before releasing Kenny, who sidestepped Nash and beat Grayshon's despairing dive. They were off again, Woods and Hughes eventually combining to fell him just shy of the halfway line. Boyd was less effective on the next drive but the Australians flung the ball wide and already they were threatening to play Harlem Globetrotters-style rugby. Gorley did well to keep hold of Meninga as the crowd feared another free-flowing score. It just took the edge off the Australia assault and Reddy was easily stopped on the next play, as was Krilich who was isolated for a change. The Kangaroos had slipped out of top gear but they demonstrated their intent by running on the sixth tackle from deep and it nearly worked, but Drummond did just enough to force Grothe into touch.

There was a welcome moment of respite as Australia were penalised at the subsequent scrum for failing to bind properly, and Fairbairn's kick made about 20 metres. There were audible boos as Ward restarted play by running straight at his opposite number – where had we seen that before? – and Gorley also ploughed forward on the next play. Thankfully for the British they were awarded their ninth penalty of the half, this time for offside. The French referee was certainly harsh on the Aussies as they tried to give themselves every advantage at the play-the-ball, but at least he was consistent. The visitors could have no reason to grumble.

After another excellent kick from the British full-back, Crooks had first go and he made good ground to set things up. If the home side were going to do anything they had to capitalise on every opportunity. But the sameness of their forays was becoming all too evident. Once again they used a runaround move involving Nash and Norton. This one at least had more pace about it, although once Gorley was picked out, Sterling was waiting for him with a textbook tackle.

The Widnes second-rower took an age to get to his feet. The physical effects of the opening half hour were beginning to take their toll and you wondered whether the insipid display of supposed star forward Skerrett was down to his lack of match fitness. On the next he tiptoed forward only to be flattened by Pearce and Boyd, and again struggled to get upright. Crooks dropped the ball to kill British hopes of a try but it was something of a hospital pass and as the players retreated Gorley received treatment to his leg.

The subsequent scrum collapsed into a heap. You had to wonder if some of the forwards just wanted a slightly longer break. The good news for the home fans was that Nash appeared with the ball. The scrum was always going to be one area where Britain held the upper hand. The sight of Woods dancing around a couple of golden and green shirts was enough to get the crowd exhorting for more and he managed to get to within ten yards of the line. On the next play Grayshon finally was able to pass the ball out of the tackle to Crooks but Meninga buried Crooks' hopes of keeping the play alive. The fans shouted their encouragement again, desperate for a try, but Woods took the wrong option on the next as he darted back into trouble. Luckily Pearce was penalised for a kick out at the tackle (he hadn't) and Crooks could not miss with the kick. It reduced the gap to six points with seven minutes to go before half-time.

From Rogers' restart Drummond got his second touch of the ball – Evans was still yet to see it – and the Leigh wingman made good yardage before being held by Krilich. There was a lot more purpose to Skerrett on the next play and he had a great chance to get the ball out of the tackle but when he looked around there was no one in support. Grayshon also managed to evade one tackle as he got his side close to the halfway line. The British boys were starting to take more chances with Norton and Crooks both finding a team-mate while being snagged, but again it was mainly from a standing start and Woods virtually fell over his own man to kill a lot of the momentum. Nash's skip and surge briefly threatened to open things up but he was caught and Ward received the ball with men all around him. More excellent work from the veteran scrum-half put him in a good position and a driving kick proved too hot for the retreating Boustead, who could only palm the ball dead.

Rogers restarted from the goal-line and hit it straight at Evans, whose bright white shirt stood out like a sore thumb. He beat one tackle on his first possession but not Young. At least the game was being played in the Australian half.

Ward's predictable take-the-ball-forward response was met with the usual double tackle. Skerrett had another go and was clearly growing into the game after a terribly shaky start. With 20 metres to go Nash went on the runaround for the fifth time and in this instance could not even get the ball away. Then, finally, the ball was flung wide and kept going wider. Fairbairn hit the line and was felled within eight yards of glory. On the final tackle the ball was dropped backwards. The full-back recovered it but could not make any serious headway. This was much more like it. This is what we had been promised by the coach.

Australia won a relieving penalty from the scrum and Sterling, ever the optimist, took a quick tap and piled into a sea of British bodies. Reddy made more good ground before Skerrett halted his progress and Krilich did likewise on the next before Price threatened to trample his way to the line. His bullish run was halted at the fourth attempt.

A rare piece of miscommunication killed the Kangaroos' hopes of a try just before half-time, with Boyd being called for offside as Sterling threatened to expose another crack in the crumbling red, white and blue wall. Fairbairn kicked for touch yet again as Norton received treatment to his right leg.

Gorley kicked things off as the home side tried one last time to close the gap before the interval but his run did not threaten. There was purpose to the next foray with Crooks linking well with Hughes and the Widnes centre evading one tackle. But with the Hull teenager losing the ball on the next tackle the momentum flipped 180 degrees as Grothe set off on a typical charge up the line that only ended with a superb double assault by Ward and Hughes.

Australia wasted no time in flinging the ball wide and Boyd took control for the next two plays, tapping and going to good effect. His captain followed in a similar vein and another try looked on but Woods was able to steal the ball. There was more home relief as Young was penalised for taking too long to roll out of the tackle.

For the ninth time Fairbairn successfully kicked for position and there was just time for Grayshon to take the ball in before the hooter blazed around Boothferry Park. There were just six points in it. As Dyl walked off Millward was waiting to give him the hard word.

'I thought I was having a half-decent game,' recalled Dyl. 'But Roger gave me a bollocking for missing Meninga. "You've got one chance," he said to me. I was like "I know...."'

Back in Australia Gerard and the his co-presenter were all smiles. The Manly prop's keen eye for things meant he was able to see what was coming down the road. However, couldn't have possibly imagined just what carnage was heading Britain's way.

'Yes, they are doing it reasonably easily and in the second half will only get better. Towards the end of that half the Englishmen were starting to walk.'

While the then British coach can't recall exactly what he said to his players at half-time his abiding memory nearly 40 years on chimed very much with that of Gerard.

'For the first 20 minutes we were doing OK but then the walls started crumbling. But even today I tell people that if you have got 13 batteries in a torch and you put a dud one in, those 12 other batteries have got to help that one.

'And it's the same in rugby. If you haven't got 13 players who are fit, then those fit players start hedging their bets to cover for the dud. And sometimes you are in positions you have had to go but then you are left floundering and then get blamed for a situation where you have already tried to appease someone else's position. But we've all done it. If you are intelligent enough you realise that sometimes that is what team games are all about ... being able to hold your position and have a fitness level where, whatever's thrown at you in that particular space and time, you can withstand that.

'I would have known in "those days", like I do now when I train my kids, I know I can blow my kids to a level that normal kids can't get to but then I know their limits. And back in 1982 the physical barrage we had taken and absorbed … we weren't used to it. It was the same back in the day when English boxers used to go to America. On their own patch they were world champions but go to America and the physicality of their opponents wore them down.'

John often used boxing parallels in rugby. Unlike many of the watching public, he knew deep down that his team were already on the ropes without the option of being able to save the situation with one knockout blow.

The second half began with a high kick from Woods which found Boustead who bamboozled Ward with his footwork, although Grayshon was on hand to tag him. Price then did brilliantly to take a wild pass one-handed above his head to keep things ticking over, before the ball went wide to Boustead who demonstrated how things were going to be for the visitors by flinging the ball in risky fashion back in-field. Sterling maintained possession as Nash closed in and the referee blew up for an Australian penalty with their opponents adjudged offside.

Brentnall, with the breeze behind him, took play up to the 20-metre mark. Price, Boyd and Krilich all took their turn to edge their side nearer a third try, which would not be long in coming. First there was a brief respite as Australia were penalised for crossing and Fairbairn cleared deep upfield.

Skerrett and Gorley trundled forward in response before Norton was handed possession in what appeared to be a promising position. Crooks' dummy run took out Reddy but Hughes could not take the pass. Thankfully Drummond was close and he appeared to retain possession but only he knows what he was thinking when he shuffled the ball backwards under pressure from Krilich and into the hands of Grothe. The winger had a lot to do but once he had got past Ward he was in the clear with Fairbairn charging across. The full-back did all he could but the winger's momentum carried him over the line. Meninga's touchline conversion made it 4-15 on 43 minutes.

With the crowd still buzzing about the power of Grothe, the game restarted with a rare mistake from Price, who dropped a quick pass. Sterling then had two goes at feeding another messy scrum and again it came back the right way for the home side. It was a great position from which to really have a go but once again Woods' decision to hold on to the ball with men outside him was met with groans. It did not get much better as Skerrett charged into the busiest part of the Australia line. Young was never going to let him get away.

There was much better play from Grayshon who did well to offload out of the tackle to Gorley but Kenny hit the Cumbrian second-rower hard and low and Price followed up high. Norton had space on the next tackle but came back inside where Price was waiting to gobble him up. On the next play Skerrett definitely should not have tried to pass out of the tackle as he was spun 180 degrees by the collision, allowing Kenny to dart through and fall on the ball.

The Kangaroos then spread the ball wide but as Rogers tried to switch play he was met with a posse of home players. As the tacklers rolled away Crooks was clearly in agony and held his knee while the visitors ploughed on. His afternoon was over.

Les Boyd got to the halfway line on the fourth tackle and Sterling twisted and turned himself into Norton to momentarily halt his flow. It was already evident that the Kangaroos were only going to get more and more expansive.

On the next tackle Rogers did brilliantly to keep the ball alive after making a half-break, and Meninga also defied attention to find Boustead, who in turn returned the favour. But the big centre was overwhelmed by British bodies.

Australia kept possession from the scrum as Dave Heron entered the fray in place of Crooks, with Roger Millward frantically trying to pass out some instructions from the sidelines. Ten seconds later the tourists appeared to have crossed again as Brentnall powered through a huge gap but his overhead pass to Price was deemed forward.

In response, on the second tackle, Grayshon again lifted British spirits with a powerful burst and offload to Nash but Reddy was perfectly placed to put the diminutive scrum-half on his back. Woods then spun round and round to no effect once more and again it was the Bradford prop, showing his younger team-mates what was required, who was next to have a go. He did brilliantly to find Heron after a collision. It was Heron's first taste of action and, in keeping with what had gone before, the Leeds youngster was prevented from keeping the ball alive by yet another textbook double assault.

Woods infuriated the crowd in response. With the ball flung along the line he inexplicably turned back into traffic with three of his team-mates positioned perfectly on his outside. For a man slightly built, relatively speaking, his strength was broken-field play running and his decision-making this day was truly abysmal.

With the home side retreating after losing crucial yardage Gorley ran into Meninga and bounced off him in a such a way you could not believe this was a forward running at a back.

Britain were able to win the scrum that followed and Heron's decisive move forward was met with appreciation by all hoping for a Great Britain comeback. There was more good news when Kenny was penalised for not letting Skerrett get on with it; here was Britain's window of opportunity. It was now or never.

With the Australia line less than 20 metres away Ward could not resist the temptation to have another dart. The result mirrored what had gone before but there were five more tackles ... well, in theory. Price ripped the ball from Grayshon as the Bradford veteran was hauled down. With two in the tackle it was tough on a player who was clearly playing at the level required and he followed up the disappointment by stopping Boyd in his tracks almost straight from the restart.

Grothe came in off the wing to give his forwards a breather and he made good ground, from which Sterling did not waste the opportunity to ease his side from danger with the opposition defence still retreating into position. With the Australians set for another assault Rogers was the fall guy as he dropped a good pass and the teams packed down.

There was just time for a little bit of history to be made as both hookers were sent to the sin-bin for continually disrupting the scrum ahead of the feed. Krilich realised straight away what had happened while his British counterpart was less sure.

With two fewer players on the field the situation played into Australian hands and 20 seconds later they were 80 metres up the field with Drummond desperately hanging on to Kenny for dear life. Price had created the space for Grothe to tear up the line with a brilliant shimmy and pass to his stand-off after drawing his man, only for the Leigh winger to haul Kenny back.

Grothe had another go as home players funnelled back and this time Dyl managed to intervene with Drummond there as backup. The danger was far from over, though. Rogers doubled back and was stopped a yard from the line but then Price linked with his clubmate Sterling on the loop to crash over by the posts on 54 minutes. It was game over at 4-20. Now it was just a question of how many and with Meninga's dead eye with his kicking, the answer was that Australia would double their tally before the final hooter.

Sterling, as ever, asked a lot of questions from the restart but it helped that Britain's chase of Woods' chipped kick lacked the impetus of previous restarts. Boyd piled over the halfway line and you could see the tourists were starting to enjoy it. Price dummied and maintained the relentless pace, flying away from dummy-half straight up the middle. On the next play Rogers escaped Dyl's tackle and freed Kenny, who was being dragged back close to the line but was not stopped. He correctly calculated that Boustead, free of any attention, was a better bet and the winger crossed on 57 minutes despite a valiant attempt from Dyl, who had done well to stay in the play.

Both hookers returned as Meninga prepared to complete yet another successful conversion to make it 4-25.

The onslaught was unrelenting and after every restart the Kangaroos looked capable of going the length of the pitch. Krilich collected it this time and was powerfully halted by Heron. Boyd again got involved and once more refused to go quietly even though he was well-held by Ward. This time Sterling spun it wide to Young who in turn released Pearce at full pelt. The second-rower exploded through what appeared to be an impossible gap between Norton and Nash. He was surrounded by Englishmen yet somehow managed to find a way to give Kenny a chance at a try. He should never have got past Drummond, who lamely made a timid reach-out with one arm, like a schoolboy playfully meeting a friend with a nudge to the shoulder. On a day when a lot went wrong for Great Britain the sight of the Leigh winger making one of the worst attempts at a tackle seen in an international match made for difficult watching.

'It's rather pathetic ... it's rather pathetic ...' screamed Mossop in the commentary box even before Kenny touched down, '... to see an England team disgrace themselves like this but how great are some of these young men in the green and gold?' On watching the replay Mossop could scarcely believe what he had seen.

'And look at that from Drummond, an international wing three quarter ... My God!'

With Meninga's kick it was 4-30 and there were still 20 minutes left. On the first two tackles subsequently the visitors were at least held at bay. But when the ball went wide on the next you could sense the trepidation enveloping Boothferry Park, especially when Price looked around after getting through another missed tackle – from Drummond – although the wingman recovered to snuff out the loose forward. Reddy drove hard again and then Pearce failed to take a misdirected Kenny pass. It was greeted with an ironic roar of approval. After what seemed like an age without it, the men in white had the ball.

Norton had first go and then Gorley piled forward but we had seen it all before. For the Australians, stopping this one-dimensional rugby was child's play.

Woods was again caught in possession on the next play when he had the chance to pass. It was getting embarrassing. As a working unit they were falling apart before our eyes. Next up the ball was moved slowly to the left where Dyl was cut off at the knee by Kenny and then Nash's kick was half charged down.

It felt as though, with every second, British rugby league was experiencing new and greater levels of humiliation. The manner in which Brentnall returned the ball with such pace and ease before sending the ball wide in the tackle from Ward to Boyd felt like another small dagger in the heart of British rugby. As the ball was eventually passed to Grothe all that was stopping him charging 60 metres to the line was the beleaguered Drummond. The stadium held its breath as the two men collided and this time there was some relief. The Aussie winger was pushed into touch but why Drummond continued to barge his opponents rather than tackle them with his arms would have been beyond the comprehension of many people watching.

At least Britain had the scrum, their one island of calm in a stormy ocean. Krilich was penalised and again Fairbairn kicked his country out of their half. Heaven knows what the score would have been if the penalty count had been more even.

On tackle one Grayshon took the ball in and as he twisted and found a team-mate in voice, cheering ironically, could be clearly heard. The Hull crowd were in a state of shock. Next up was Heron who made more good ground, and then came Woods, who again twisted and turned. Had anyone mapped his times in possession they would have made a good working model of spaghetti junction. Maybe the French referee was feeling sorry for his fellow Europeans as he awarded yet another penalty against Australia for not releasing the player in the tackle. It would have been an easy kick for two points but Nash beckoned his team-mates forward and Skerrett charged forward into the green wall without support.

Next up came Gorley who couldn't overpower Kenny and then, finally, some really nice stuff from the backs after a long pass from Norton. Woods stood up to his man and then drew another before releasing Dyl, who did well to get the ball to Hughes. But the veteran centre could not escape the clutches of Price. Drummond tried to slip away at dummy half but the Aussie loose forward was never going to let him go and finally, after Heron was stopped easily, Nash's kick was deflected and Brentnall beat one tackle to escape the in-goal area. Boustead also made more yards than he should have in taking his side out of the danger zone, but Reddy's attempt to do the same was much more muted and Great Britain had a good chance to finally force a clearing kick.

Captain Krilich ended those hopes the moment he squirmed away from Woods' inept attempt at a tackle and found Young with a brilliant one handed pass. As the prop kept Nash at arm's length inevitably it was Pearce in support and Young drew Fairbairn, laying it on a plate which allowed the second rower to cap a dream debut. Young ended the move on the floor as Fairbairn, whether in frustration or desperation, stiff armed the big prop a long time after the pass had been completed. The Scotsman would later recall that he was tying to get the ball. It didn't look good.

It looked even worse for all those concerned with the sport in the UK. In 11 extraordinary minutes the visitors ensured they would receive an elevated status for eternity, while their hosts would spend months coming to terms with what was being played out at a now slightly misty Boothferry Park.

The crowd applauded long and warmly as the players took their positions for Meninga's kick in front of the posts, while for those who had seen Britain demolished at Swinton two decades earlier, it must have been a case of deja vu. All that was left for this latest Australian incarnation was to break their greatest winning margin record of 38 points. There were still 16 minutes left and it was 4-35.

As Woods launched it deep to get the game back under way a section of the crowd roared their approval. You got the feeling that if a British player had tied their shoe laces properly it would have received a smattering of applause.

Boustead smiled at Skerrett as he got to his feet after returning the kick, and as Price took the ball forward without any frills the whole thing felt slightly more normal again. Boyd did likewise and then got annoyed, retaliating at some rough-house tactics post-tackle from the clearly frustrated Hughes. Strangely the French referee sided with the Widnes man and Fairbairn launched the ball deep into opposition territory. It was the 16th penalty Australia had conceded compared to six for Britain.

There was some good interplay from Nash and Heron without any actual ground being gained. The tackles were still being made with incredible ferocity as Australia made it exceptionally hard just to keep hold of the ball. Next, Gorley almost evaded a green shirt after crashing onto a short ball from Nash, before Grayshon ran straight at three defenders with a predictable outcome. The crowd groaned as Ward tried to pierce a gap straight from dummy half but he just did not have the legs to burst through Young and Sterling. The play was ended as Woods jinked back on the inside and Price was ideally placed to end the attack.

The contrast in the two sides was perhaps illustrated most accurately with what happened next. While Britain had plodded forward 20 metres from the goal-line with the dynamism of a rotating oil tanker, Australia exploded forward with the energy of a fire at a fireworks factory. After Sterling had gained vital metres to get his team away from their line, Reddy piled forward and did brilliantly to release Kenny, who threw an outrageous pass out of the tackle to Rogers, who somehow managed to eclipse the efforts of Kenny with a one-handed overhead pass that defied belief. Krilich stretched to reach it and as he was tumbling managed to get the ball out to Grothe and we were set for another race to the line with Drummond in pursuit. This time the Jamaica-born star used his arms properly to halt his man just three yards out and then Fairbairn showed his strength by stopping Meninga when the odds looked stacked against him.

Heron again was impressive as Britain ran out of danger but too many of his team-mates were out for the count and the set stagnated before Woods attempted a kick and chase. Sterling was aware of the danger and recovered possession.

Price got Australia going again by weaving his way to the halfway line but we were then treated to a rare mistake from Meninga, who clearly wasn't expecting Young to send him a long pass which missed out two others. As the centre finally picked up the ball he beat the ground in frustration. Maybe he felt he hadn't quite taken centre stage in the way many had expected. His opening try certainly seemed like a long time ago.

Australia's biggest obstacles had been the penalty count and the scrum and again they combined to send Britain back to their own line as the game entered the final eight minutes. Ward restarted and Skerrett trundled forward. Up and down the country a few more TVs must have been turned off. The lack of imagination in the British ranks was frightening. Did no one consider a cross-field kick for Evans to chase? Up against Boustead he had a considerable height advantage. The anonymity of the Hull player was one of the many truly shocking aspects of the whole affair. Next up was Gorley failing to break a tackle which had become such a feature of the afternoon. It was enough to make fans cancel their subscriptions to *Rugby Leaguer*. On tackle four we saw Evans but the problem was that Dyl didn't and the Leeds veteran was floored with his winger in space on his outside.

Back Britain came the other way with the ball going sideways at a decent lick, but with each pass the hosts were being pushed further and further back until Heron was clobbered. They were almost back to the halfway line when Woods straightened things up and made ten yards. Skerrett drove in on tackle five for little gain, before the move ended with the ball being swung to the right, finally providing a glimmer of a chance. Hughes did superbly to take out two men with a clever pass to Fairbairn but the Rovers full-back did not just have the legs to get past Reddy and Brentnall. It all got slightly chaotic for a while as Drummond jumped forward and over the line, losing the ball before landing. Was this tackle seven or eight? Nobody seemed very sure. No, there had been a penalty and the British had one more chance. Oh no it wasn't … Australia had the restart. It was the only really sticky moment for the French official.

The tourists looked to be just playing out time the way they went through the motions during the first three tackles, and then Reddy tried one too many passes out of the tackle to give

Sterling no chance. Nash stole back possession and the Aussies were penalised for offside on the first play.

Could there be a consolation try? That was all John's boys were playing for now. Grayshon kicked things off with a drive but his offloads out of the tackle had dried up. Skerrett was barely running when he took the ball forward on tackle two. Norton, again barely a factor in a British shirt, took a long pass and had no acceleration to trouble the defence. It was so easy to stop. Woods switched play – poor old Evans – in the direction of an isolated Drummond but his pass went straight through the legs of his clubmate. It was another moment to sum up the afternoon.

The home side were almost back on their halfway line although Fairbairn broke a tackle to restore some sense of normality to proceedings and then Hughes, who was starting to look like a man who knew what he was doing, linked well with Nash to create a half chance of a break but again the Kangaroos had too many men in the right place and it was time to hand the ball over.

There was then a rare moment of joy in the scrum for Krilich as Price picked up and left a few defenders in his wake on a 20-metre surge. Then it was Sterling's turn, making his least impressive run of the whole match as ground was lost. ut Australian fans, hungry for more, did not have long to wait. Young tore through a gap before releasing Kenny, who was held by Drummond and somehow Britain got the penalty with the Aussie stand-off fighting to get up to play a quick ball.

The visitors need not have worried. Skerrett lost the ball in the collision on tackle one. Wouldn't you just know it!

The Aussie props were still full of running as first Boyd and then Young bounded forward but the latter's first loose pass of the day proved a lucky one as it bounced straight into the arms of Grothe, who was hauled down at the first attempt by Hughes. Next, Young acted as the swingman and Reddy went on the runaround before finding Pearce, who almost punched through again. This time Heron just about clung on. Then Krilich had a go without much success before some neat interplay led to a break from Boyd, whose pass into traffic could not be held. The ever-willing prop recovered the situation and Boustead just waited for support in the shape of Meninga looping round on his outside. The wingman dummied a couple of times and a try for his fellow Queenslander looked assured but his pass could only find the touch-judge Mr Hill, whose catch raised plenty of smiles around the ground. As the gloom descended over the ground in more ways than one it was a much-needed moment of light relief. More chaos at the scrum ensued and this time Krilich's boys got the decision. As the forwards staggered to their feet, Pearce was announced as man of the match, setting off a ripple of applause.

With less than five metres to go, Sterling and his captain both had a little dart. Fairbairn flew out of the line on the third tackle in a desperate attempt to intercept but could only knock on and there was time for one final flourish. Monsieur Rascagneres was determined to get one decent scrum but despite putting considerable time and effort into getting it to form properly, the ball from Nash never really made it in and squirted out handily for Sterling, who wasted no time in unleashing the backs. Brentnall popped into the line and weaved his way back towards the posts, and, after being stopped at the third attempt, Sterling was waiting to collect his pass. The Australia scrum-half was standing still but, in the blink of an eye, he got rid of it to Reddy, who dived over for try number eight.

It was left to Meninga, with his eighth successful kick, to seal a 40-4 victory and before the ball landed in the building site the hooter blared.

As men who could quickly appreciate that they had just witnessed something out of the ordinary, the Great Britain management team were full of praise for their opponents. They may not have realised at the time but their battered and bruised troops, thanks to all those penalties, actually had more attacking opportunities.

'There is no answer to that,' said John. 'We just could not cope. They gave us an object lesson in everything. They were brilliant.'

Hutton added: 'On today's performance they were as good as any Australian team I've seen. They have mastered the basic skills to a high degree.'

'Their back three forwards (Reddy, Price and Pearce) were as quick as our backs,' recalled Ward. 'It was the pace that outstripped us.'

The Observer's Alex Murphy encapsulated the post-match feeling: 'The Australians were quicker, bigger, more athletic and, the final humiliation, far more deft and skilful, the one area in which Britain fancied that they might have had an advantage.'

Even the normally stoic Australian coach was taken aback by the extreme brilliance of what had just unfolded.

'We have seen something special today,' Stanton said in the post-match press conference. 'I've been involved in the game at the top level for 25 years and this was as satisfying a performance as I've seen, not only on attack but in defence. The rugby was good to watch and most of the crowd stayed right to the finish – that was our biggest reward.

'There is extraordinary ability in this team, but I'm not yet prepared to make comparisons with other sides,' he added. 'We've got to win the Ashes yet. It was a magic performance. They kept their cool, and were disciplined, just like we worked on.'

One Englishman was happy, at least. Cameraman Bob Jones, who was following the tourists around for a documentary, had put £20 on them to win by 20 points. However, as the victorious players emerged from their dressing room, it quickly became clear that he was not the only one.

In the minutes and hours that followed, the Australia squad encountered many British fans who were clearly smitten with their extraordinary visitors. One of the Aussie players was overheard telling a reporter: 'I've never seen so many people ecstatic after their team was thumped.'

The ripple effect even spread outside the game. Norman Harris, the noted rugby union writer, who was originally from New Zealand, said: 'Who would have thought that a team from rugby league would provide a lesson which promises to be the most profound ever experienced by rugby union football.'

Leading rugby league historian Professor Tony Collins called it, 'our Hungary moment'. He was referencing the famous soccer international back in 1953 when the magnificent Magyars won 6-3 at Wembley, and the iconic image of Ferenc Puskas leaving Billy Wright on his backside before hammering in another goal and leaving England supporters stunned.

Those types of thoughts were echoed by many a wise old sage among the journalistic ranks and within the RFL there was a deep sense of shock, as Howes recalled.

'It wasn't so much alarm bells going off as a nuclear event,' he said.

It would take years before the dust would truly settle but for now it was time to say an international goodbye to Nash, Dyl, Norton, Hughes, Ward and Gorley. In more ways than one it was time to start again.

Chapter Eight

Where Do We Go From Here?

T HE first tentative steps on the long road back for British rugby league were taken by Frank Stanton. Less than a week after the remarkable events at Boothferry Park, he dialled the home number of former Oldham centre Phil Larder.

Six months earlier the Saddleworth-based PE teacher had been given the role of overseeing the coaching strategy of the RFL and BARLA as the sport's first director of coaching. Previously, the RFL's National Coaching Scheme, which had been introduced by then League secretary Bill Fallowfield, had been run by former players Laurie Gant and Albert Fearnley, who focused primarily on helping spread the word in schools and with amateur clubs.

Although Larder's edict encompassed all levels of the sport he saw his role primarily as helping develop coaching at the very top. He retired from playing in 1980 and has seen at first-hand the coaching deficiencies that were prevalent even in the professional ranks.

'I played rugby union for four years and had 12 years playing rugby league and I had never ever been taught how to tackle or defend,' recalls Larder, who was bathing his two sons when his wife called up to say a man called Frank was on the phone. 'Frank who?' came the obvious response.

Just a few days into the tour Larder had spoken to the Australian management team to see if he could watch them train. Conscious that he might relay vital bits of information back to Whiteley and Hutton, the request was turned down with the caveat that once the Tests were over, the Australian establishment would help where they could.

The first Test gave rise to a serious rethink for senior rugby league officials down under and Stanton was instructed to open his doors to whoever the RFL wanted to send over. For Larder, Australia's display in Hull clarified his thinking after an unsteady first few months at the helm. It didn't help that the never-ending power struggle between BARLA and the RFL over who should control the top juniors was still rumbling on.

'I took this job and was sat there in my office and didn't have a clue what to do. I said to Maurice Oldroyd [BARLA chief executive] "What do I do?" He said go through your filing cabinet. But fortunately the 82 Kangaroos came on tour and it clarified my thinking. It inspired me and bang I went. I saw a vision of where rugby league in this country should be and realised it was my job to inspire that.'

Larder would spend two days with the Kangaroos – the Thursday and Friday before the Wigan Test – and he witnessed a well-oiled machine in action.

Stanton structured his training sessions so that four senior players (not Krilich or his deputy Lewis) each oversaw a pod of six others. With the captain and vice-captain they also formed a six-strong senior player delegation that would meet regularly with Stanton to discuss issues.

As Test matches drew near, specifics would be worked on. For example, ahead of the second Test, Stanton and Rogers came up with a plan for dealing with John Holmes, who had instigated a couple of moves in the Leeds match, involving Dave Heron and Les Dyl, that had exposed Rogers on his outside.

UK players did not train under match conditions because of concerns about picking up injuries. In contrast, Larder was amazed at the intensity of the Australians' sessions and struck by the continued use of video to plan attacking moves. He learned how Stanton had collated three months of tackle counts from all of Sydney's first-grade matches and averaged out a count for each position. This he made public in the team room, to encourage the squad to better their position.

'It was a real eye opener,' recalled Larder. 'We hadn't seen tackle shields before. It allowed Stanton to train more realistically than if unopposed. His ball players were driving into real opposition but the contact was not severe. And when ball-carriers were blocked, they were turning and offloading. Our players were playing tig and pass which encourages you to stand straight and shallow and doesn't encourage support play. Stanton told me: "Phil, train tig and pass, play tig and pass."'

The Australian coach had also made sure that each squad member had been psychoanalysed. Information gathered was used in different ways and played its part in deciding who would room with who. That meant the meticulous Steve Mortimer was paired with the slovenly Lewis, the intense Pearce shared with the laid-back Sterling and the outgoing Schubert was thrust together with the introvert Grothe.

Like Jack Gibson, Stanton was another coach who did not stir his team with rousing speeches. Rather, he found other ways to prod his players into raising their game. He instructed each one to make a note of any specific criticisms they heard about any member of the Australian squad. He used music to stir their souls and created a tour battle song, sung to the tune of 'The Fighting

Kangaroos'. That song became an anthem. He played the *Rocky III* and *Chariots of Fire* film soundtracks on the way to games.

Much of what Larder learned observing Stanton & Co would form the basis of a report that would start to oil the wheels of change in Britain. The shock of Australia's 40-4 win unquestionably proved to be the tipping point for important changes but not before the RFL dug their heels in over ending the ban on transfers between the two top nations. At a meeting in Leeds on 3 November 1982 only three voted for the motion – Hull, Barrow and Oldham. Twenty-seven voted against.

However, any changes the lawmakers might make were certainly going to come too late for this Ashes, with the visitors' superiority once again brutally proved by events later that evening at Hilton Park in Leigh, despite Colin Clarke, manager of the reigning English champions, striking a defiant note on the eve of his club's clash with the Kangaroos.

'I honestly believe we can become the first club side to beat the Aussies on this tour. We certainly have the ability in the backs to beat them but it is imperative that we play well when don't have the ball. If we move up quickly and tackle well then we could cause a few surprises.'

It meant a quick return to action for Drummond and also Woods, who captained the side, while only Meninga remained for the clearly-inspired Australians.

For Stanton, a return to watching his side play was a welcome distraction after all the extra interest in the Australia squad. The management had been fielding numerous requests to come along to training sessions, including some from rugby union clubs from as far afield as Nottingham.

If the rest of the country was buzzing after what they had seen at Boothferry Park so, clearly, were the rest of his squad at Leigh as they ran in 12 tries and played some extraordinary rugby. Their performance was capped by a try from Muggleton, who received a pass from Gene Miles which would have been remembered for the rest of their lives by every one of the 7,680 supporters who were lucky enough to see it properly. As the big centre ran sideways, with plenty of cover, he tried to stand up his marker. He then tried and failed to hand him off. The move looked dead as the players' feet tangled but as Miles started falling, and with the ball in his right hand – Muggleton was steaming up on his right hand side – he somehow managed to spin his body 180 degrees and, without looking, convert an over-the-shoulder pass to his team-mate with perfect pace and direction just a split second before crashing to the ground. It was a truly astonishing moment. Yes, the game was over and the tourists had licence to show off, but the manoeuvre remains arguably the greatest pass to be seen on a rugby field in England.

'It was the ambition,' recalled Leigh hooker Ray Tabern. 'We would never have thought to do it. The ambition they had to keep the ball moving and keep playing. Miles passes the ball but they did it a lot. They trusted each other so much. It was like he was saying, "Well, I know someone's going to be there and I'm just going to bob it up."'

Thankfully for Leigh, Meninga missed yet another conversion to keep the final score down to 44-4.

Second-rower McCabe had another stellar night. He scored three tries and his support play and efficiency with the ball in hand was on another level to anything the Leigh faithful had seen before. Had he been English he would have been the first name down on the British selectors' team-sheet. Quite who they were going to select in three days' time was anyone's guess but those Leigh players hoping to make an impression – Tabern and loose forward Ian Potter – must have wished they had stayed at home.

'They were fitter, stronger and ambitious and they overwhelmed us,' recalls Tabern. 'Every time you'd think you'd tackled them they would be up again and at you again and it was constant. That said, we were going well at half-time but it was just the relentlessness of it. They just kept coming and coming whereas we got tired.'

While holding a celebratory 'tinny' pitchside, McCabe was asked how he was dealing with not making the Test team.

'It is disappointing but every player in the Test team is playing well. There isn't a player out there tonight who couldn't replace them in the Test side. It is a great touring squad and all we can do is keep playing well. We are still playing for our country even though it is against the county sides but we've all got to give our best every week and you never know; you might just fling a Test spot.'

Wingers Chris Anderson and John Ribot also claimed hat-tricks while Wally Lewis helped himself to a late score with the home defence in disarray. Australia piled up 33 points during a second-half masterclass, the only blot for the tourists being the dismissal of Rod Morris. On 61 minutes the Aussie prop and Woods traded blows after a touchline altercation which triggered a mass brawl. Once the dust settled Leigh substitute Eddie Hunter was also given his marching orders.

Mortimer was at his usual diplomatic best on being questioned by the British press.

'Leigh really hit us hard in the first 40 minutes and almost knocked us off our game but we got things together in the second half.'

'With Bradford next to take on the 'impossible challenge' the timing of their showdown was perfect for any Northern players hoping to make the Test squad. Top of the list of maybes was full-back Keith Mumby, a renowned tackler who many seasoned watchers thought should have played in Hull.

His coach Peter Fox played him at centre for only the second time in his career.

'I wanted to take the pressure off,' the Bradford coach said after the game. 'Everybody's been getting onto the Mumby bandwagon recently and I knew he was going to be under the microscope. A lot of the press love having a go at me and I didn't want them to be doing so at Keith's expense. We had four centres out and I wanted tacklers in the middle. In Keith Mumby and John Green we have two full-backs better than most and I could have played either of them at centre but I opted for Keith.'

Loose forward Rathbone, who was something of a cult figure at Odsal, was another who had a great opportunity to stake a claim. He had made the summer training squad although his rather abrasive approach to following instructions meant he had not ingratiated himself with the British team management. Rathbone was famous for being something of a law unto himself. While at Leigh he told the then chairman Brian Bowman to 'shove that turkey up your arse'. Bowman had offered his loose forward some free poultry if he could avoid being sent off before Christmas. In the next game he was duly dismissed and Bowman was met with that coarse response after coming into the post-match dressing room to remind Rathbone that he had missed out.

Grayshon, one of the few to have done himself justice at Booth-ferry Park eight days earlier, captained a full-strength Northern against a slightly odd-looking Kangaroos line-up. Coach Stanton was certainly sticking to his mantra about there not being A and B teams by really mixing it up. Hancock returned from injury to pack down alongside Conescu, who got a rare start at hooker. Anderson, Miles, Muggleton and McCabe all played for the second time in four days and Murray and Kenny enjoyed a rare opportunity to link up at half-back.

With the rugby league grapevine alive with stories of Bradford struggling financially – twice in the previous three years they had been forced to turn to the RFL for financial help – it was a good opportunity for Fox to defy the odds and once again be something of a thorn in Australia's side. With a tour to Australia less than two years away and John Whiteley committed to leaving the post after the third Test at Headingley, the outspoken coach had to be in with a chance of replacing him. His Northern players did not let him down.

With Grayshon, Mumby and Rathbone all to the fore, the Odsal faithful roared them on. With eight minutes to go they were trailing by just one point only for scrum-half Alan Redfearn to miss two drop goal attempts. Tries from Brentnall and Miles then secured a 13-6 victory.

Writing two years later, Fox said: 'The Australians were worthy winners in the end but British teams still played some good rugby. I've got a video recording of the match in which Bradford Northern made the Aussies look like a second division team. They were stood around in numbers and I said to Frank Stanton: "Where's your supermen now?"

'I'll be happy to let anybody come and watch that recording to see how to match the Australians. I said at the time I thought the Aussies had one basic tactic that allowed them to make our sides look bad. They would have three men in a tackle, lying on, so you can't bring the ball back into play quickly. So we played that theory against them and we murdered them. I would have been pleased to advise anybody but nobody wanted to listen. But Frank Stanton wanted to listen to me – he always wants to improve his players.

'We had a young lad [Richard Davies] at centre playing only his third senior game and another lad on the wing [Steve Pullen] who was in junior football last season and we had several men out. But all the lads played with pride and did their tackling and showed what could be done.'

Mumby's replacement in the No 1 shirt was typical of the effort on display. Green made a series of incredible tackles to restrict their opponents to just one try before the break. That came after

23 minutes following a penalty award close to the Bradford line. Price had first go before Anderson weaved infield and popped up a perfectly timed pass to send McCabe through a gap in the otherwise watertight Northern defence.

Price had been getting some special treatment from Rathbone, who was clearly revelling in the opportunity to test himself against Australia's stellar No 13. There was also a display of the Bradford loose forward's short fuse as he flung an arm at Price in retaliation for some unnecessary roughing up of Mumby.

The hosts reduced the gap to 7-6 just after half-time and then Mumby, who had earlier reminded everyone of his tackling ability with a standout effort to halt Grothe in full flow, also showed there was attacking flair to his game. The closest Bradford came to a try followed his brilliant 60-metre break and the way he accelerated away from Grothe must have impressed the selectors. He managed to get his pass away to stand-off Bill Kells, but he was hauled down 10 metres out by a combination of Grothe and Brentnall.

It took another fantastic Miles pass out of the tackle to kill off the club side. Again the giant centre was horizontal and falling fast when he spun and found Brentnall, the full-back just hanging onto the ball by his boot straps before diving in to score.

The try clearly knocked the stuffing out of Bradford. Their standout tackling deserted them when Grothe recovered a deep kick and almost ran through the whole team. Only a contentious call for a forward pass denied Kenny Australia's third try.

However, they did not have to wait long to score it. The young Kangaroos' stand-off's pass bounced kindly for Miles and he strode over with ease just seconds before the final hooter.

Confirmation that Mumby had made it for the second Test came less than 24 hours later.

'Mumby is the type of full-back who can inspire confidence in the rest of his team with his tackling, much like a safe goalkeeper does for a soccer team,' his national coach said on the eve of the Test. However, his deserved call-up was overshadowed by another extraordinary twist in this rapidly developing tale. In their wisdom the British selectors had voted to make ten changes for the Wigan showdown in just under two weeks' time, with six making their GB debut. The selection of Hull KR second-rower Chris Burton came from nowhere, although he had looked good in that opening match of the Australian tour. Hooker John Dalgreen was plucked from the second division where Fulham were making a good start to the season. Warrington's Ken Kelly returned to the scrum-half position ten years after making his Britain debut. He would be partnered at half-back by Leeds veteran John Holmes, who had begun his international career a year before. Lee Crooks' knee injury was not as serious as first thought but he was only named as a travelling reserve.

The full team read: 1, Keith Mumby (Bradford); 2, Des Drummond (Leigh); 3, Mike Smith (Hull KR); 4, David Stephenson (Wigan); 5, Henderson Gill (Wigan); 6, John Holmes (Leeds); 7, Ken Kelly (Warrington); 8, Jeff Grayshon (Bradford N); 9, John Dalgreen (Fulham); 10, Trevor Skerrett (Hull); 11, Bob Eccles (Warrington); 12, Chris Burton (Hull KR); 13, Dave Heron (Leeds). Substitutes: 14, John Woods (Leigh); 15, Alan Rathbone (Bradford). Travelling reserves: 16, Lee Crooks (Hull); 17, Mike O'Neill (Widnes).

There was historical method in their apparent madness. After the Swinton annihilation by Australia in 1963 (GB's record 50-12 defeat), ten had also been dropped and the home side came back to win the third Test 16-5. It was a straw worth clutching. Certainly, the Great Britain manager still, outwardly, had high hopes.

'They're [Australia] not as happy when the ball is going out wide as when people are coming down the middle at them,'

Hutton told Australian reporters. 'I've seen breaks made out wide a number of times on tour. Britain are a faster side particularly around the scrum and in the three-quarter line and we are hoping that the creative ability of Holmes will enable us to a play a wider game.'

His coach could cling to relationships he had forged with the Under-24s as a basis to rebuild. He certainly knew plenty about Heron, Eccles, Smith, Stephenson, Mumby and Rathbone.

'We have been in crisis situations before and possess the capability to offer a stronger challenge this time,' said John. 'The Australians are a good side but as we saw at Bradford on Sunday they are not too happy when pressure is put on them. Two or three of their players are not all they have been cracked up to be.'

Quite which of Australia's Test side were off key was unclear. It did feel a little bit like the Black Knight in *Monty Phython's Holy Grail* film taunting King Arthur after having both his arms chopped off.

There was certainly more pace in the back row and Dalgreen had more zip than David Ward.

In the backs, if Stephenson was going to be a 'new Gasnier' as his Wigan coach had said two months earlier, then now was a good time to show it. Gill's considerable promise in previous internationals meant he made a welcome return, although it was tough on Steve Evans, who in the first Test had not had a chance to show what he could do. Making Grayshon captain also raised a few eyebrows.

It was only in May that he had led his Bradford team off the field against Hull KR in protest at the referee, although with Monsieur Rascagneres back in charge an irate and grizzled prop doing verbal battle in his thick Dewsbury accent with a Frenchman who could only muster broken English would have made for interesting viewing.

All the changes meant that 41 players had been used in just seven international games. Selector Hutton defended the wholesale changes.

'When a team is able to score 40 points against you, you have to be disappointed at the commitment shown by some of the players.' Yet those were players he had been lauding just a couple of weeks earlier.

In contrast, the SS *Australia* coasted serenely on. The five-day gap between the forthcoming matches against a Cumbrian representative XIII and Fulham meant there was a bit more time and space for the squad to prepare.

Possibly with memories of what happened in Barrow, Stanton named a strong side for the clash with Cumbria at Brunton Park in Carlisle. Ten of the men who had played their part in dismantling Britain were included, while Whitehaven coach Phil Kitchin, who was in charge of the county side, had a number of problems to deal with in the run-up to the Tuesday night showdown.

A planned get-together in Workington the previous week had to be called off while second-rower Les Gorley failed to shake off a knee problem he'd picked up in the Test at Hull. Consequently, the Cumbrians had just one session together the day before the fixture.

Kitchin told local reporters: 'Nobody is expecting us to win. I want the attitude of my players to be right. I want them to go out and do themselves justice and give the Aussies a hard game. And if everybody plays his heart out you can't ask for more.'

Gorley's brother Peter captained the side. Seven players from Barrow were selected, including the star of the show from the previous month, Derek Hadley, and the highly-rated young scrum-half Derek Cairns. There was also a run-out for Carlisle's 20-year-old Kiwi centre Dean Bell, who was enjoying his first season in England.

It would be a long night for the home side. Again, the Aussies suffered a 2:1 disadvantage in the penalty count and Oldham hooker Alan McCurrie won the scrums 15-6. But neither set-back stopped the tourists running in nine tries in a 41-2 victory. The result meant they had not conceded a try for nearly 400 minutes.

It had been 2-16 at half-time after the Cumbrian dam broke in the 15th minute when McKinnon barged his way over from close range after flying onto a Sterling pass. We had not seen the young Aussie scrum-half since Hull.

Five minutes later Sterling lit up affairs with a 30-metre run to the line after he had been sent clear by a stunning one-handed pass from Pearce out of the tackle.

Workington full-back Lynn Hopkins converted his second decent penalty attempt after Gorley got the treatment in the tackle, but that rare period of Cumbria pressure, midway through the half, was soon a distant memory as Ribot reminded everyone of his qualities with a clever run to the line on 28 minutes. The crowd were then on their feet soon after as a dizzying passage of support play from the Kangaroos culminated in the wingman touching down for his second try. The ball went through 16 pairs of hands before reaching Ribot. Incredible.

Rogers came on for Sterling, who had picked up a minor knock, at half-time and made an immediate impression, crashing over from short range after an excellent reverse pass from Muggleton.

Brentnall did all the hard work for the next try on 53 minutes. It appeared that his decision to dance into heavy traffic was an unwise one but just as he was stopped in his tracks, Ella arrived on his shoulder at full whack and the prolific centre was gone in a flash.

The home side had barely caught their breath when a moment of Lewis magic carved them open. His delicate chip over the top had the Cumbrian defence is disarray. When Meninga picked up he had the easiest task of drawing the last blue shirt and releasing Boustead, who had the freedom of Carlisle to coast over.

Ten minutes later it was all about Meninga as he broke two tackles inside his own half and outpaced the cover with only Hadley getting anywhere near him.

However, the home side refused to capitulate and, three minutes from time, Cairns came desperately close to touching down but dropped the ball in the act of diving over to score.

There was still time for Australia to remind everyone who was boss, with Pearce skipping past one and then gliding peerlessly for 80 metres to score under the posts. Meninga's kick took his points tally on the night to 17 points.

Ribot was asked afterwards about his chances of getting a run in the second Test but candidly explained how he effectively had missed his window of opportunity.

'I'm scoring tries now but had a pretty ordinary start to the tour. I wasn't used to the conditions and I paid the penalty and didn't play too well, and now it is just a matter of scoring tries and putting pressure on the players. It's definitely a game-to-game proposition over here and if I'm playing better than the guys in the Test then you've just got to be ready to play. At the end of the day there are 28 great players over here so it's a great thing just to play in the sides and be part of the Australian team and just go out and put pressure on the lads.

'Kerry is playing good football and Eric [Grothe] has been exceptional since he has come over here so it's just a matter of playing good football and keeping those blokes honest. And it's good for the team because if I am putting pressure on them then it makes them play better because I think pressure brings out the best in rugby league players.'

The efforts of the Kangaroos would bring them all kinds of records but the one everyone was focused on, ahead of their trip to the capital, was the longest winning run from a touring team. If they could overcome Fulham at Craven Cottage it would equal the efforts of the 1933 Australians who opened with 11 straight victories before losing their next three.

Only one Test player (Boyd) was picked for the Fulham game, reflecting Stanton's intentions ahead of the looming Hull showdown, which would take place just 48 hours later. Even though the clash with league leaders Hull was only four days before the second Test he was clearly going to play a very strong side at the Boulevard.

Fulham, who were formed in a blaze of publicity ahead of the 1980/81 season, justified the RFL's decision to take a tour match away from the sport's northern powerbase by attracting a crowd of 10,432. And the players, led brilliantly by Dalgreen, gave their supporters something to shout about, not least a first try against the Kangaroos in five matches. It was Moroccan winger Hussein M'Barki – who would become the subject of many a pub quiz question in the years that followed – who finally broke through the green and gold wall on 64 minutes. By then the result had been put beyond doubt, though, and the visitors would cross twice more late on to secure a record-equalling 22-5 victory.

Fulham, with their new Test hooker Dalgreen causing some discomfort to their illustrious visitors in the loose, actually took the lead via the boot of Eckersley after 100 seconds, maintaining their advantage for the next 11 minutes. During that time M'Barki pounced on a spilt pass and had the crowd on their feet as he set off down the line. As he made it past one despairing dive a length-of-the-field wonder-try looked possible, but Muggleton, once again, showed his exceptional speed to ankle tap the Moroccan and send him into touch. Some wonderful innovation from Schubert shattered the Fulham dreams. He juggled a high pass and spun past clearly-confused loose forward Joe Doherty to make the decisive break 20 metres out. Murray, playing out of position at stand-off, was supporting well and ran in unopposed.

The tourists had to wait until two minutes before half-time to cross again. Lewis, again playing in the centre, bobbed and weaved to good effect before finding Reddy with a sublime lofted pass. The big second-rower quickly handed on to McCabe, who just managed to get the ball away to Ella, who once again showed his extraordinary ability to pop up in support at full pace. The race to the line was no contest.

Ella played his part in Australia's third try of the afternoon, this time turning provider for McCabe on 46 minutes. Mortimer's burst and shimmy set the ball rolling and he then fed McKinnon who leapt into a two-man tackle to free his arms near the Fulham line. Muggleton was on hand to collect the inevitable perfect pass that followed and dive over to extinguish any lingering hopes for the home side.

However, Fulham would have their moment and once again it was a kick ahead that created the opportunity. With Australia rushing up on the halfway line the London side appeared to be in trouble but after John Crossley got a toe on the ball full-back Eckersley got an even bigger boot to it to set up a race to the line. As Ella came across there appeared to be little prospect of a score but the Aussie full-back slipped at the critical moment and the man from Morocco dived over him and onto the ball.

In the last five minutes McKinnon just held on to a Steve Ella pass to score. Ribot rounded things off after Crossley dropped the ball on his own line, enabling Lewis to collect. He found Miles, who spread it wide to his winger five metres out.

'I don't know how they're not a first division side,' said Mortimer, slightly in a daze as he was interviewed for TV. 'They certainly tested us. Conditions were difficult but we've come to expect that over here. We've got to combat that by making sure of our handling and passing of the ball. It was typical today of what we're expecting and we've just got to cut our mistake rate down.'

The Canterbury playmaker was also asked whether the players were thinking about Test places, although he must have known that a 17-point margin over a second tier outfit was not going to alter the selectors' thinking unless the injury to Sterling was more serious than had been disclosed. However, the look on his face, as he was interviewed by John Helm, suggested there would be no changes in the half-back positions for the next Test.

'The competition in all the positions is very intense and there is no second string side as such because everyone is playing for a Test position and that competition brings out the best in everyone. I think Australia has two very capable Test sides and we are all trying to get into that first XIII. The fellow ahead of me, Peter Sterling, is a very fine half-back and, in fact, with Mark Murray as well, it is nice to be one of the best three. Peter's there and I have got to chase him now and I'll be doing my best in the future games.'

Australia's win at Craven Cottage meant there was just one team standing between them and a new match-winning record: Hull FC.

Arthur Bunting's outfit would go on to take the 1982/83 title. He had assembled a formidable-looking outfit with recent Kiwi arrivals James Leuluai, Dane O'Hara and Gary Kemble injecting pace and craft into the back division.

Such was the interest in their impending meeting with the Kangaroos that an anonymous phone call to the club tipped them off that forged tickets were being sold in Hull city centre. Fans who had purchased theirs legally received assurances that the forgeries were easy to spot.

Stanton laid down a marker by selecting the same side that had played in the first Test just half a mile down the road 17 days earlier and conceded that the prospect of becoming the first Ashes tourists to win every game was starting to have a bearing.

'Obviously the players are aware of the record targets and it does add a little extra incentive to each game, but we don't discuss it. Our prime objective is still to win the next Test.

'There is obviously a risk of injury and I suppose Hull could go out bent on damaging our players before the Test but I don't think that will happen. The fact we have picked our first Test side is testimony to Hull's challenge as league leaders. If they are prepared to join us in playing football we should see a great game.'

With 16,000 packed into the Boulevard, the Australia coach got his wish. Lee Crooks was among those walking out into a cauldron of noise that clear Tuesday night, his appearance taking quite a few people by surprise. Just 24 hours earlier he had informed the international team doctor he wasn't fit to play against Australia the following Saturday. It was a huge gamble from the 19-year-old, who clearly had a long-term international future.

Crooks recalled: 'They picked me on the bench for the second Test and I had tweaked my knee and we [Hull] were due to play them on the Tuesday before the second Test. Arthur [Bunting] said to me: "I can't understand why they have put you on the bench. We want you to play for us. You will get more out of it." They wouldn't let you play for your club the week before the Test so the only way I could was to withdraw. So I went to international training on the Monday and told the club doctor about my knee. There was no comeback from GB because they picked me to play in the third Test.'

With Skerrett unavailable because of Great Britain commitments and Charlie Stone injured, Bunting turned to 36-year-old Mick Harrison for a rare start. Back for one last season after eight years with Leeds, the Hull-born prop came in for his first start of the season. It was his 521st senior game of rugby league, more than 18 years after he made his debut for the Airlie Birds against their cross-city rivals.

'There was a lot of confidence in the side [Hull],' recalled Harrison. 'Over the years Hull had always pushed the Australians close and at that time, in 1982, we were all playing so well.'

Norton had also failed to recover in time from a badly bruised hip so Mick Crane grabbed the No 13 shirt, but the side was still full ofexperience, with with prop Paul Rose, scrum-half Tony Dean and the mercurial playmaker and captain David Topliss all set to play major parts in a five-star blockbuster.

For the first 40 minutes the Kangaroos were hustled and harried and in many respects were lucky to be trailing just 7-0 at the interval. With a little bit more composure Hull could have been out of sight.

The inspired home side clung on to their lead well into the second half and were denied what appeared to be a legitimate try for O'Hara. Eventually, the visitors once again showed how clinical they were, running out 13-7 winners.

Ironically, having been hammered by referees in the penalty count in all their previous tour matches, on this night the Kangaroos finally achieved parity (14-14).

Mal Meninga said: 'We came here tonight expecting a hard one and we got one. We were always worried, especially going in 7-0 down at half-time, but we were playing well and they were playing a little bit better. We came out fired up for the second half and got the result, which is the main thing.

'There were really harsh words at half-time because we were playing fairly well. We just didn't have much possession in the first half because Hull had us camped on our line all the time and put in a very clever chip kick to score the try. But we came back, which proves our character and we can keep on winning.'

From the very first set the home side set the tone for the night. After three fairly predictable one-up charges by the forwards, Crane chipped ahead to the delight of the supporters. With the tourists flying out of the line in typical fashion, he just had enough of a lead to beat Kenny to the ball. Rogers was on hand to delay the next play. It didn't matter too much as the tourists were penalised for not retreating in time. Coach Bunting must have dreamt the first minute or so would pan out like this.

With Rose and Harrison flying onto the ball on the next two plays Hull were just 15 metres out when Bridges' disguised pass out of dummy half really caught the Aussies on the hop. With a man over, Crooks had a huge gap waiting for him to fly through but he just couldn't take a difficult pass from Crane, who had done well to get the ball away in the tackle. Krilich was able to fall on the ball.

On the second tackle Leuluai was caught offside but Brentnall's subsequent kick failed to find touch. Evans fielded well and fed Kemble, who beat the first man and made it back over the halfway line.

The Australians were rattled and Boyd took umbrage with scrum-half Dean after a fairly innocuous-looking tackle. The prop was still complaining as Hull got on with it and again Crane was to the fore. This time it was Young who was penalised for not letting Crooks get up, with the teenage second-rower just within range. Topliss instructed Welsh winger Paul Prendiville to find touch. It was such a bold decision.

So was Crane's attempt at a kick through on the third tackle. It didn't make it over Pearce but the ball ricocheted straight into the hands of Dean. Six more tackles to come! The crowd kept roaring.

Dean ran it himself and chipped towards the line. For what seemed like an age the ball tiptoed towards the whitewash but Kenny appeared from nowhere to deny the Hull scrum-half, who was then penalised for refusing to let his opposing half-back get to his feet. This time Brentnall found the stands and Grothe had a go. It was not a good idea. He ran straight at Harrison, who not only stopped the winger but pushed him back five yards. To those who had played against the veteran prop this was no big surprise.

'Mick Harrison was the strongest man I ever played against,' said his fellow forward Chris Burton. 'When you ran into him it was like running into a brick wall.'

Another penalty allowed the visitors to finally escape their own half but again Grothe was pushed back five yards in the first tackle. Hull were putting three into the collision point and had clearly learned from their opponents by doing everything they could to delay the restart for as long as they dare. It did irk referee John Holdsworth when Bridges made no secret of his desire to pummel the ball out of Boyd's hands after a tackle, and finally the Green and Golds had the ideal position to mount a try-scoring attack. Captain Krilich beckoned Meninga over for a difficult attempt near the left touchline which went well wide.

On the next attack Evans took it upon himself to give Pearce a bit of what for and the young centre conceded a penalty with the touch-judge furiously waving his red flag. Everyone was clearly pumped up. On the next attack Meninga had a chance to go close but was sent flying ten yards out, Kemble demonstrating the perfect way of stopping him: cut him off at the knees. With Hull also racing out of their line, two plays later Young decided to kick ahead but his bomb sailed over the dead-ball line. It was an odd move from a prop and a bit more evidence that the tourists, with that record in sight, were no longer in their comfort zone.

By the second both sides were getting more wound up, and on ten minutes Boyd, who was clearly rattled by Hull's lack of deference, couldn't resist going high on Crooks after the ball had gone. There was only one thing that could happen now. The two players took it in turns to throw right handers and referee Holdsworth showed bravery by forcing himself between them as the rest of the players charged towards the melee. Once the dust had settled the captains were given a stern lecture by Holdsworth, who ordered the first scrum of the night. Dean did not get the chance to feed it as Hull were awarded a penalty, with the scrum, rotating like a spinning top making its final two or three turns.

Prendiville booted his side out of their half and Rose took the ball on the first, flinging a stiff left arm in the direction of Reddy as he got to his feet. Once again the touch judge entered the fray for a quick chat with his fellow official. Penalty to Australia and Price got the game under way but as the set reached the second tackle more punches were being thrown off the ball. This was like 1978 all over again. Crane was picked out for admonishment and with just 12 minutes gone Australia had already been awarded six penalties, one less than they won in the whole of the first Test.

After rampaging into the Hull line on the next tackle Boyd got to his feet and was pushed back by Harrison. For a split second it looked like the young Aussie was going to fling another right hand but he perhaps realised that the veteran forward was the wrong man to pick a fight with. The smile on his face provided a rare light-hearted moment. Pearce injected some exceptional pace into the attack and made a half-break, and on the next tackle the ball was flung wide where Meninga was met with a sea of black and white shirts. From just five yards out Sterling attempted a little grubber but the ball bounced off the upright and a grateful Prohm clasped the ball to his chest with all the intensity of a mother trying to shelter her baby in a storm. Price and Kenny had been queuing up to collect it.

Australia levelled up the penalty count to let their opponents off the hook as the home side struggled to clear their lines. Rose then took the ball up on the third tackle but was accidentally caught on the head by an opponent's knee. After staggering to his feet he did a great impression of an aggressive drunk by flailing wildly in the direction of Price. The players rushed towards the flashpoint and Holdsworth indicated it would be Australia's ball.

Thirty seconds later Steve Rogers touched down after some brilliant interplay between Sterling, Kenny and Pearce, but the final pass was deemed forward. Australia were finally starting to assert themselves and for the first time forced their opponents to kick long on the sixth tackle. It would be returned with interest and, luckily for Hull, Grothe slipped just as he was threatening to cause real problems.

Topliss came close to intercepting on the third tackle. From the scrum Sterling darted and probed but turned straight into Dean, who picked his proverbial pocket in impressive fashion. It proved to be a pivotal moment. Australia's momentum had been checked.

With a quarter of the game gone the Boulevard was on its feet. Topliss dummied one way and slipped his marker before finding Evans, who clearly had the legs on nearly everyone … except Kenny, who made a brilliant sliding tackle. The home side had advanced 60 metres and some skulduggery from Brentnall was spotted by the touch judge. The inspired Crane almost got through as Hull piled forward with renewed gusto but he did not have the support when he looked to pass out of the tackle. Arguably his efforts in the first half of this epic encounter earned him selection for the third Test. What made him stand out even more was that his opposite number Price had been wholly anonymous.

Dean tried a one-pointer but again fortune favoured the kick as he collected the rebound and the tackle count was reset. Hull then came pretty close as Leuluai and Rose worked an opening but the big Hull prop just couldn't find the required pass.

The crowd sang their appreciation as the Kangaroos took possession after another messy scrum. They wasted little time in giving the ball air only for the normally unflappable Rogers to lose it in flight, the ball smashing off his head and shooting backwards. Sterling was one Aussie who did not appeared fazed and his wonderful runaround and pass almost sent Boyd clear. These fans would see plenty more of his half-back wizardry in the years that followed.

With Crooks prostrate after more of Boyd's post-tackle shenanigans, Australia shifted right. Pearce finally showed he was human by trying a reverse pass out of the tackle straight into the hands of Dean, who wasted no time in setting off in the opposite direction. Brentnall brought him down 30 metres out and was penalised for holding on. The Green and Golds stood firm as the home side tried another grubber on the last tackle but Rogers' goal-line dropout barely travelled ten metres forward and some wonderful quick handling, with Crane looping round, created a fine opportunity for Prendiville. Unfortunately for the screaming hoards he was held up inches short. However, the referee pulled play back which meant an easy two points for Crooks, due reward for what had just transpired.

After a breathless 28 minutes, Hull led 2-0 and they did not relent. From deep inside their own territory, Crane kicked ahead and his deflected effort fell nicely for Leuluai who rolled towards the halfway line. Bunting's men were clicking all over the pitch and second-rower Wayne Proctor did his best impression of team-mate Evans with a long-striding charge, dummy and half-break. Meninga was on hand to remind everyone that this Australian team were fairly handy as he flattened Leuluai and Hull's momentum was temporarily halted. The tourists were awarded a penalty for a stamp. It appeared as if Krilich was debating with half of his team-mates whether Meninga should kick at goal and after what felt like an age the big centre's 45-metre effort drifted to the right of the uprights on 34 minutes.

It set the scene for one of the great Boulevard moments; the roar must have been heard halfway to Norway. An obstruction dented

215

Australia's hopes of turning around in the lead. Two minutes later they were 7-0 down. More creative mastery from Crane broke things open with Prohm offering good support. He then linked brilliantly with his winger O'Hara, who was brought down two metres short. Hull were unrelenting and after they had been awarded six more tackles the New Zealand winger did well to keep things going when a wild, long pass missed out everybody. There was a momentary lull as the forwards packed down three times in quick succession but the game exploded into life when Dean emerged from the collapsing scrum with the ball and Leuluai went close on the left-hand side. Four uneventful plays later Topliss's exquisite, delicate chip floated into the in-goal area like a golfer flicking a lob wedge from the side of the green. It only travelled five metres but it did the trick and he won the race to touch down. Crooks' kick was followed by the sounding of the hooter. Australia were in trouble. Big trouble.

The second half opened to a resounding chorus of 'C'mon you Hull' and the fans were cheering as magic-man Crane fell on the ball after a terrible play-the-ball involving Pearce and Krilich. Hull were still throwing the ball around well but could not create the break and Crooks' towering kick on the sixth tackle was well fielded by Brentnall. The tourists were struggling to make ground so a penalty against Harrison for interfering around the ruck came at just the right time. Five plays later Australia finally registered some points with Boustead crossing in the corner. Firstly, Rogers had weaved his way past a couple of tackles which caused enough panic to allow Sterling to exploit a rare gap. He needed no second invitation and timed the final pass to the Queensland winger perfectly.

The score was met with almost stunned silence and perhaps a good dollop of anxiety. No conversion was a welcome caveat for the home fans who must have known that their four-point advantage was unlikely to be enough to see out the remaining 35 minutes.

There was no let-up following the restart. Pearce, Krilich and Boyd punched huge holes in the black and white wall before a fine tackle from O'Hara brought a swift end to the set. Australia then enjoyed some rare joy at the scrum only for a Price misdemeanour to halt them in full flow – he kicked out at Crane and again the sides squared up. The stupidity of the action led to the usually ice-cool Sterling to give his older team-mate a bit of a talking to as Hull restarted matters via the boot of Prendiville. The hosts made good ground in response but got a bit stuck towards the end of the set and a wonderful piece of improvisation from Crooks put the ball out of play just eight metres from the Australia line. Hull kept pushing from the scrum and the ball squirmed out on their side. Dean and Topliss were in a hurry to press home the advantage. Hitting back straight away to counter the green and gold onslaught would have represented a huge psychological blow. It wasn't to be though as Crooks' chip ahead was collected by Brentnall and he was held in touch by Evans.

Rogers once again fluffed the goal-line dropout. It hit the referee and Hull had the ball back just 15 metres out. Some wonderful stuff involving the three Kiwis had O'Hara just falling short. The winger took the tap himself and appeared to have successfully flopped over the line but the referee decided he had dropped the ball. It was a decision that has riled Airlie Birds players and supporters alike ever since.

Harrison recalled the moment well 37 years later.

'We gave them more than they gave us and I think it knocked them off balance a bit. We were getting on top when O'Hara's try was disallowed in the corner and I think it would have been a different story had we got those three points. After that they seemed to raise it a bit.'

Brentnall kicked the ball into touch with boos ringing all around the Boulevard. It is a shame that, with just one camera filming the clash, we can't review the incident properly because O'Hara's 'grounding' was hidden from view.

However, Hull quickly won the ball back and there was no chance of lying down. Rose's kick to the corner was judged beautifully and Brentnall passed the ball forward in a desperate and needless attempt to keep the ball alive, having made so much ground on the first tackle. Kenny's alertness as Hull's next attack broke down gave the visitors possession.

There was still more than a quarter of the game to go but both sides were playing as if there were two minutes left and the scores were level. However, Stanton's side were accustomed to playing this high-risk stuff and cut the gap to a point with a typically flamboyant 70-metre effort. Not for the first time Pearce, who appeared to have one more gear than anyone else on the pitch, flew onto a pass and scythed his way past a despairing O'Hara. Meninga collected his pass only for Prohm to stop him with a staggering effort. Equally good was the centre's pass out of the tackle to Grothe in support enabling the big winger to coast in. Rogers took over the goalkicking with his centre partner still catching his breath. Meanwhile Leuluai was out of the picture with what turned out to be a broken jaw. The versatile Barry Banks replaced him.

Rogers was nowhere near with the conversion attempt, the fourth bad miss of the night for the tourists, but they were scenting blood and Meninga was quickly off again down the touchline. This time he kicked ahead with Prohm hacking the ball into touch. Hull won the subsequent scrum but it was noticeable that the likes of Harrison and Crooks were not attacking the line with the same intensity and Dean was forced to kick from deep inside his own line. Boustead coasted back into enemy territory.

The metronomic Pearce made his usual break to set up another chance and Hull hearts sank as Bridges' attempts to nick back possession only led to him giving away another set of six. Reddy piled through a massive hole on the first tackle. Hull's defence was creaking desperately and Brentnall was held up inches short. A scrum was welcome relief for those watching. Bridges could not ease the pressure as he was held over the line. The good news for Hull was that Crooks was a far better drop kicker than Rogers and his effort forced a mistake from Pearce. But with the ball going backwards Grothe smothered it, surrounded by black and white shirts. The pace was unrelenting and Boustead almost made it over on the last tackle.

Hull were on the ropes but some quick thinking from Dean relieved the pressure as he somehow managed to scramble to the ball first even though it had come out of the scrum on the Australian side. As the forwards eased their side clear of danger another chorus of 'C'mon you Hull' cascaded from the stands and Crane's sixth sense for the right path to take from a restart took his side close to the halfway line on the fifth tackle.

In response Rogers knocked the ball forward after failing to take a Price pass. The home fans must have been counting down the seconds. The sense of anxiety was palpable and was clearly affecting some of the men in green. Rogers, particularly, was having an evening to forget.

However, the way in which Bunting's side finally lost their lead with 16 minutes left remains a source of much frustration after all the toil. Harrison kicked the ball away to give the Kangaroos an extra ten yards from a penalty, making it a much easier kick at goal for Meninga who must have been swallowing hard as the ball hit the left-hand upright and cannoned over.

Hull were not going down without a fight and a good deal of innovation. Evans charged forward to the halfway line and took a quick restart. It worked a treat. He got to the ball first, kicked ahead and the supporting Topliss dived on the ball just 25 metres from the Australia line. They couldn't could they? Crooks took the tap to himself on the second tackle and sent through a teasing grubber kick which Brentnall smothered well. Not this time.

It was critical for Hull to pin the visitors back on the next set but Sterling's mazy surge initially ended those hopes. Once again the little playmaker was putting on a scrum-half masterclass but not even he could do anything about his forwards' inability to exert any sort of control in the scrums and a penalty from just 35 metres out appeared to have given Crooks the chance to kick his side back into the lead. Quite why Prendiville was asked to find touch will always remain a mystery.

The Welshman's spiralling kick meant that at least Hull started their next assault just five yards out, but with each play the hosts were nudged backwards and when Evans dropped the ball on the fifth tackle he was nearer halfway. Seconds later Crooks was stopped dead in his tracks.

With the scrum taking forever to form properly there was time for a breather heading into the final ten minutes. Hull were handed a golden chance to take the lead again when referee Holdsworth indicated that Sterling was feeding the scrum. But before Topliss had time to consider his options, he inexplicably took a tap quickly and fed Evans. It was right in front of the posts from 25 metres out.

On the second tackle the crowd roared as Topliss wrong-footed two defenders but didn't have the pace to exploit the gap before the cover arrived. Regardless, it was magnificent stuff from the 32-year-old. With ten metres to go the desperate home side just ran out of ideas and there was a huge sense of anti-climax as Paul Rose's drop goal attempt sailed wide.

Wally Lewis replaced Greg Brentnall and Australia again surged forward with Pearce to the fore. He broke two tackles and fed Reddy, who did brilliantly to keep the ball alive as the ball was switched back the other way with Price finally being scragged just over the halfway line. Reddy followed it up with another break, ably assisted by his captain, who took it to the 20-metre line. Lewis and Sterling linked superbly on the next tackle before the substitute jinked his way past a couple more. It was top-class stuff and thankfully for the Challenge Cup holders Reddy was caught in two minds on the sixth for just long enough for two defenders to pounce.

Hull had to win the scrum but thankfully it was even better than that as Holdsworth gave them a penalty and Prendiville boomed a kick 30 metres up the pitch. Rose, Crane and Harrison all ran with plenty of purpose to get their side into opposition territory but as the ball was flung wide Meninga emerged with it after a particularly heavy collision and the huge centre took a quick tap and sent bodies sprawling as he trundled forward to great effect. Next came Sterling and it was fitting that another of his weaving forays set up the clinching try. Krilich powered ahead and found Reddy, who beat one man with a lovely step, dart and pass out of the tackle to Rogers, who quickly fed Grothe. O'Hara looked to have the danger covered but the Aussie wingman ran straight through him and that was that with just six minutes to go.

As Krilich walked back he goaded home fans in the main stand. The relief was clear. This time Meninga did convert to clinch it. Applause could be heard from all quarters of the Boulevard as the Hull players trudged back to their marks. The extraordinary effort was warmly appreciated.

The game fizzled out despite another half-break from the peerless Pearce. The critical twelfth straight victory had been achieved in the most remarkable circumstances and Meninga was a picture of relief as he was asked about breaking the record.

'It's a tremendous thing to be part of. We got a lot of criticism when the team was first picked over in Australia and we are very pleased we did set the record and just hope we can set a new record and win all the games over here in England.'

For Hull, loose forward Crane had been dazzling for 50 minutes and he was asked about the challenge of taking on the undisputed best team on the planet.

'It was definitely hard. We set out in the first 20 minutes to hit them with everything we had and try and put them off their game. When we got the ball we put a few chips over the top and tried to stop them rushing up at us all the time. I think it worked. I think it is the only way you could have beat them.'

Asked about the Australians' ability to train more professionally, Crane, who was visibly overweight and would smoke before matches and at half-time, added: 'The fitness. That's where they've got it over us. We train twice a week, two hours on a Tuesday and Thursday … pouring with rain. Snow. They train in the sunshine … they've got no jobs and are all sponsored. Until we do that over here I don't think we have got a chance against them.'

While the Hull hero clearly had a point, the irony that it was he who should so starkly identify the main reason for British players' uphill battle in that era would not have been lost on anyone who had followed his career. Now nearing its end, he was finally playing at a level that matched his ability. The fact remains that had he possessed half the dedication of someone like Pearce he would have been the Mal Reilly of his generation.

Chapter Nine

Invincible

O N the eve of the second Test at Central Park a group of rugby league delegates from all over the world met in Wakefield to discuss some pretty hefty topics. Proposed rule changes, which would have far-reaching effects on the game, were top of the agenda.

With the RFL having already voted against lifting the international transfer ban the Australia delegate, with no strong feelings either way, agreed to back whatever the British wanted and the proposal was unanimously voted down.

RFL Secretary David Oxley had also been instructed to vote against increasing the value of a try to four points. But this motion was passed because the other four Test-playing nations – Australia, New Zealand, France and the recently admitted PNG – supported it. The change would come into effect from the start of the 1983/84 season.

Australia's proposal that the defending team should automatically restart the game after the handover was passed and delegates also agreed to change the method of feeding the scrum. From now on scrum-halves would have to roll the ball in with two hands rather than the fast-feeding, upward motion which often made for chaotic restarts. Those who had seen Hull disrupting the Kangaroos' flow 24 hours earlier would have known exactly why the Aussies were so keen to make these alterations. In addition, timekeepers would now have to stop clocks when a penalty was awarded and restart it once the kicker began his run, and there was an instruction to referees to clamp down on players slowing down the play of the ball. It was estimated these two changes would give an average game five more minutes' playing time.

If the touring Kangaroos had been playing under these new conditions, goodness knows what they would have done to some teams.

The news of no change to the international transfer ban came as something of a shock to the Rugby League Professional Players Association (RLPPA), which had made its case to the RL Council back in June and had come away believing the restriction, which had been in operation since 1977, would be removed.

'We are confident that the board's decision is not only irrational and damaging to the game but it is also of questionable legality,' said spokesman Alex Gerlis.

The RLPPA claimed they were going to advise their members to ignore the ruling.

Gerlis added: 'We will back them in the courts if either the British or the Australian Rugby League try to prevent them from playing.'

The RFL would not be able to hold back the will of their players' association for much longer and the following year the ban was abolished, paving the way for a wave of Australian stars to head north. Many of those who would go on to light up the game in England in the mid-80s would, before then, give the fans of Hull, Wigan, St Helens and Leeds another taste of their excellence in the second Test. Stanton was able to name an unchanged side for the match despite Australia's bruising encounter at the Boulevard, although a neck problem for Krilich meant Brown came in as a substitute for Muggleton, while a newly motivated Lewis replaced Ella in the No 14 jersey.

This was no time for over confidence. For the Australian coach the encounter with Hull was were an ideally timed reminder that they could not expect to steamroll everybody.

'We are well aware of how Britain have come back after a defeat in the past and will be prepared for a spirited performance from them again. Despite winning all our games I am also looking for an improvement on our recent performances.'

As the two sides made their final preparations the RFL announced a revised international structure, leading up to the 1988 World Cup in Australia. Britain would tour Australia in the summer of 1984, with the Kangaroos returning two years later.

With Stanton's side re-energising interest in international football, the wheels were set in motion for a decade of increasingly high-profile Ashes meetings, starting at Central Park on Saturday 20 November. Such were the reverberations still emanating from the first Test that demand for press passes surged and some slightly less well-known journalistic faces appeared among the more seasoned rugby league hacks.

Quite how Britain's much-changed side would cope against a seriously well-oiled machine was the subject of much debate. For someone like second-rower Chris Burton, who had not even been to any of the summer training sessions, there were just ten days to familiarise himself with his new team-mates.

'We didn't have time to prepare much and there were no set patterns of play as such,' recalled Burton. 'We just went through the general defensive structure and organised a few set moves.'

There was also a lot of last-minute homework to be done for the BBC commentator Ray French. 'They were picking players I had never seen before,' recalled Ray.

Central Park was packed as Rogers kicked off in hazy sunshine, and it was full-back Mumby who got straight into the action with a solid kick return.

As Britain were awarded their first penalty for offside on the very next play, Alex Murphy predicted it would be closer than last time.

'British pride is at stake after the miserable performance in the first Test and I think the game will be in the balance until a lot later. But I still fancy the Australians ... but not by a lot.'

The Wigan coach was right in that the final score would be a lot closer (27-6) but with Boyd being dismissed before half-time the home side had an opportunity to at least negate their deficiencies in strength and fitness in the second half. The problem was that you would never have known.

Unlike the first Test the Kangaroos dominated the early exchanges, aided by four successive penalties. In the final reckoning they finally finish on the right side of the penalty count (17-13).

'We didn't have any ball,' recalls Burton. 'I didn't think we got the rub from the referee and don't think we had the ball for the first ten or 15 minutes, which is tough.'

The Rovers second-rower's tricky start was compounded by collecting a shoulder injury early on during a collision with Rogers. He battled through the pain until the 72nd minute, coming off just as Meninga was kicking his sixth goal to round off the scoring.

'After five minutes I was absolutely knackered but essentially they were so good for two reasons,' added Burton. 'Defensively, even around the ruck, you would be in two minds. Normally you would know a prop would take it up and then another prop but they always seemed to have a little play or you didn't know who was going to get the ball because there were runners coming from all directions so you couldn't set yourself for a big hit.

'It was totally different from playing a club game. And then when they did go wide, it could be anyone, the prop forward, the second row, anyone flying out down and offering a really good pass to the wingman. And in positions where you wouldn't risk the pass they just seemed to be offloading it all the time. And nine times out of ten it came off.'

There was plenty of offloading during a move midway through the second half, which left the crowd roaring their approval. The ball successfully changed hands 12 times via the following players: Krilich, Lewis, Sterling, Rogers, Reddy, Boustead, Sterling (again), Reddy, Pearce, Lewis (again), Brentnall, Lewis (again) and Price.

Mumby's heroics at full-back went a long way towards preventing another cricket score, while his Bradford team-mate and captain Grayshon led from the front. In the very first set the veteran prop indicated Britain's desire to be more expansive with a risky offload in the tackle. But on the next play Kelly's attempted kick to the corner was skewed horribly and Boustead was given an early chance to show what a dangerous broken field runner he was. As the winger finally got to his feet referee Rascagneres awarded a penalty for lying on. This provided a platform for a sustained assault on Britain's try line. Mumby raised a cheer with a scything tackle on Young just five metres out which halted what seemed like a certain score. His team-mates followed his lead and Les Boyd was never in danger of crossing when he was halted on the sixth tackle.

But Britain could not release the early pressure. A loose arm in the scrum handed the ball back to their opponents and after Sterling probed a couple of times the hosts were penalised for offside just after regaining Reddy's spilt attempt at a risky pass.

With just seven minutes gone Australia were 2-0 up but their next play came to nothing and on 11 minutes it was 2-2 with

Rogers being warned after being caught offside again. Mumby found the target from 25 metres out.

One of the biggest roars of the day followed on the next set as Boyd was held well in the tackle and then pushed back almost ten metres by Grayshon, who was clearly revelling in the captaincy role. However, on the following play Meninga's presence drew an extra attacker and he released Grothe, who charged down the touchline. As home fans took a deep breath, the sight of Mumby felling his man with a textbook effort offered some much-needed comfort.

The home side were doing much better job of going low in these opening exchanges but as Britain swept forward in response Kelly was poleaxed by Young, who hit him man and ball. It demonstrated the Aussies' ability to stop the opposition dramatically. At first the Warrington scrum-half appeared to be in a lot of trouble, his right arm waving disconcertingly. British anxiety was compounded when the French whistler indicated a penalty to Australia for obstruction. Thankfully, Kelly was able to continue but not before Australia grabbed their first try when Price drove over from a metre out after Sterling had gone close. A difficult conversion from Meninga made it 2-7.

The signs were ominous for John's boys especially as little things, largely out of their control, appeared to be going the Kangaroos' way. The home side were hanging on for dear life and just five minutes later Sterling held off the attentions of Drummond to cross after a wonderful flowing effort. Grothe's ability to adjust his hands and get the ball away to his scrum-half while being tackled was testament to the abilities flowing through his side.

From the restart Britain were under pressure and once again it was Pearce who made the decisive play with a typical and perfectly timed run onto a pass from deep. He was in top gear as he danced past two defenders, leaving them sprawling, and then found Kenny who was caught well. Pearce wasn't done, though, and he looped round to collect the pass, draw his marker and free Grothe, who trampled all over Eccles and then crashed through Kelly to score in the corner and give his side a 15-2 lead with just 25 minutes gone. The big winger struggled to get to his feet and was replaced at half-time by Lewis; Meninga moved out wide and the substitute took his place among the centres.

Mumby's penalty on 30 minutes came after centre Smith was the subject of some undue roughness. The Hull KR player had already managed to get in a sly dig on perpetrator Kenny and for a while Stanton's side lost their way, possibly as they worked out how they were going to manage without Boyd who had been dismissed on 34 minutes for a retaliatory kick on the prostrate Dalgreen. With Mumby adding two more points before half-time, hopes of an extraordinary comeback were raised a couple of notches.

Meninga kicked Australia 17-6 ahead two minutes after the restart and the home side were let off the hook shortly afterwards when Sterling's teasing grubber was collected over the line by Rogers, who was incorrectly penalised for being offside.

Whiteley's boys just could not sustain any kind of pressure and once again it was Mumby to the rescue after Kenny had slipped his man with an audacious dummy and thrilling surge. The Aussie stand-off tried another shimmy but the full-back was not buying it and Kenny was felled ten metres out.

Two plays later Lewis left the crowd gasping as his 25-metre pass sailed over the heads of three British players to his left and dropped into the hands of Meninga who strode over. Cue more spontaneous applause. As Lewis jogged back he looked up and appeared to be in a slight daze. That reaction was later explained by his biographer Adrian McGregor.

'After the great pass for the Meninga try in the second Test he heard a shout of "Wally" from the bench and saw Stanton clasping his hands in admiration. Wally said: "I didn't know whether to say, 'get rooted' or 'thanks' so I just nodded my head and kept going.'"

John Woods replaced Holmes with a quarter of the match left, after Holmes had failed to make any impact. The Leigh man just made it on in time to see first-hand one of the great passages of play. In the commentary box Ray French could not hide his admiration: 'Awwww. This is unstoppable.'

Krilich got the ball rolling, if not literally, by taking it from dummy-half and sending a long pass to Lewis, who found Sterling with a piercing ball. The scrum-half kept it swinging wide and Rogers did well to hang on before drawing his man and shuffling it on to Reddy, who faced up to Drummond and sent Boustead in on his inside. The winger waited for Sterling, coming on the opposite angle and the move started to have an exhibition feel as the little scrum-half reversed the play again. Reddy did well to wrestle free and float a reverse handed pass over the top to Pearce, who injected considerable pace into the attack and made 20 metres before finding Lewis who in turn passed along the line to Brentnall. The full-back gave something of a hospital pass back to Lewis but the master of the unexpected collected the ball and flicked it backwards to Price, who was finally held after dancing past an opponent. Unforgettable stuff.

As the applause died down Murphy, a man well known for appreciating great rugby, gave the moment extra relevance by saying: 'I cannot believe this side was actually criticised in Australia for not being good enough.'

Rogers crashed over for Australia's fifth and final try nine minutes from time just to further emphasise the point. Clearly the gap between the two sides was as wide as ever, even though the 6-27 scoreline was a marked improvement. Better tackling kept things more respectable but the sad fact was that the home side had barely got a sniff of a try, never mind scored one.

The feats of Stanton's heroes were beginning to resonate outside rugby league. After watching events at Central Park, Clem Thomas, *The Observer*'s chief rugby union correspondent of 35 years, said: 'There can be little doubt that these Australians are one of the greatest rugby teams ever to visit our shores ... their professionalism is such that with two extra men they would convincingly beat any of the four home nations at the rugby union game.'

The fact the series was lost was submerged by the bigger picture, and with the final Test taking place the following Saturday there was precious little time to magic up an effective Plan C. The eight selectors would be sitting down to consider their options in less than 48 hours but it did not really matter who was selected. Britain did not possess the players to threaten the Kangaroos' dominance.

Clearly, Hull's efforts from the previous week had an effect as Crane and Topliss were called up, although the selectors appeared unaware that the latter was on a plane to Spain while they were in their meeting. This was despite the fact that Hull board member Dick Gemmell was one of those choosing the team.

'I know it makes me look like a fool for not mentioning that Topliss was on holiday but I knew nothing about it,' said Gemmell. 'I was talking to him on Sunday after the match at Leigh and he never mentioned the holiday.'

With the squad due to assemble on the Wednesday before the Headingley showdown, the RFL looked set to choose between Woods and Holmes as a replacement for Topliss, but after Hull coach Arthur Bunting took it upon himself to contact his captain and let him know what was happening, Topliss informed the Great Britain management that he was happy to fly straight back home.

'Topliss says he is delighted with his selection for Britain,' said RFL spokesman Howes. 'We are quite prepared to await final confirmation of his movements before making a firm decision about the position.'

Ahead of his final match in charge, the GB coach added: 'I'm happy to see if Topliss can get back by Wednesday. I know I would swim back from Australia to get the chance of leading Britain.'

There was also a good deal of confusion over Skerrett's availability. His coach heard indirectly that a specialist had told the Hull prop that he needed a cartilage operation on his knee, which would keep him out of action until after Christmas. This meant that Skerrett was quickly replaced by Warrington's Neil Courtney after initially being named in the XIII.

Grayshon's unavailability because of illness left Drummond the only British player to play in all three Tests. In the forwards there was a debut for Bradford's combative hooker Brian Noble, who had been a first-team regular for less than three months. Grayshon's replacement was the Widnes youngster Mike O'Neill. The back row was also completely overhauled with Crane being joined by his clubmate Crooks and 27-year-old Featherstone second-rower Peter Smith. The presence of O'Neill and Smith certainly gave the pack a more mobile look.

'We do not want to throw people in at the deep end at this stage,' manager Hutton told British reporters. 'The side has been picked purely with the intention of trying to win the final Test. What we have tried to do is bring in players with the ability to do something out of the ordinary. There is no way you can break down the Australian defence with orthodox British tactics.

'There has got to be an acceptance that things will change in this country but first a lot of clubs with influential coaches are going to have to change their attitudes with regards to playing and training techniques.'

While Britain was in disarray, the Kangaroos had what constituted a mini crisis for them. Coach Stanton finally had a few injury problems of his own to sort out, with Price ruled out with a broken thumb and Grothe also struggling. Boyd faced an appeal against his two-game suspension just two days before the match, which meant Stanton would not be able to name his team until the Thursday night, and before that there was the small matter of Widnes to deal with. Doug Laughton's outfit had been the last English club side to beat Australia four years earlier and the hero of that night, the then teenage Mick Burke, was back in the side alongside a host of young and hungry team-mates. Scrum-half Andy Gregory would get his first go at players who would become familiar foes. He would only have to wait five days for his second chance, with Kelly set to be ruled out for the third Test because of concussion.

For Widnes, Gregory played stand-off alongside David Hulme, and teenage centre sensation Joe Lydon was made the hub of an exciting young backs division which also included wingers John Basnett and Chris Camilleri, who had both been on the fringes of the international set-up for the previous two years.

Kiwi prop Kevin Tamati was sure to be relishing the opportunity to pile into a few green and gold shirts and 22-year-old Tony Myler would captain the team from stand-off. With no Les Gorley or Mick Adams (both injured) and Mike O'Neill out of the picture because of his international call-up, Laughton had to pick a few youngsters.

Stanton made nine changes from the previous Saturday with Meninga, Rogers, Boyd and Young set to play three times in eight days. Schubert made his first appearance in the No 13 shirt while Boyd moved into his more familiar second-row position. It would be something of a special night for Anderson, who spent a season at Widnes in the 1974/75 season. However, he surprisingly failed to mark his return with a try as the tourists racked up win number 14 with a 19-6 victory. The scoreline did not reflect their dominance. Meninga put in a poor kicking display and, on an evening of non-stop rain, the tourists left something of a sour taste when Muggleton laid out Hulme with a terrible, high, off-the-ball swipe 13 minutes from time. The Aussie second-rower was sent off.

After Burke kicked Widnes into an early lead from one of their 21 penalties, Mortimer kick-started things in response, wrong-footing prop Steve O'Neill five metres out, after a quick play-the-ball, and diving over for the first of two tries.

The towering McCabe was next to cross on 27 minutes after an elaborate training ground restart orchestrated by Mortimer. The move worked a treat as the second-rower stormed onto the ball, slipped two poor attempts at high tackles and just had the legs on Myler.

A scrambled effort from Mortimer completed the first-half scoring to make it 2-11 but Widnes came out fighting and two Burke penalties, both coming after obstructions, trimmed the gap to five points. Any hopes of the home side repeating their 1978 heroics were extinguished, however, on 58 minutes when Ribot collected Mortimer's bullet pass just five metres out, feigned to go inside and then cut back for the corner with the defence stretched to breaking point.

With Muggleton off, Widnes were still not able to threaten and it was Rogers who rounded things off seven minutes from time with a brilliant run, combining wonderful balance, quick feet and considerable strength in eluding five Widnes players in quick succession.

For Anderson it proved an enjoyable return, although he was disappointed with the quality of the opposition.

'I don't think they're as good a side as they used to be and we had the measure of them. It was too slippery to throw the ball around too much. It would have been nice to get on the scoresheet but those are the breaks.'

The wingman was also asked about the tantalising prospect of that 15th and final historic win in four days' time.

'The boys are very keen to win the final Test and it will be tremendous to be part of it. I don't think the football over here is as good as it was in 78, plus the boys have played some real good football. But I don't think the English side is as strong as they used to be.'

Exactly what the home side would be for the Headingley showdown was not clear until the Thursday night.

As the Australia squad made their way back to Leeds from north Cheshire, Topliss was heading north from Gatwick Airport having paid his own way back from Spain, where he had been contacted by *Yorkshire Post* scribe Raymond Fletcher.

'I am delighted to have been given the Great Britain captaincy,' said Topliss. 'I thought I would have got in the second Test and I was disappointed at not being selected. This time I thought the selectors would go for youth and although I had it in the back of my mind that I might get back in I didn't really think I would.'

Topliss met up with the rest of the squad the following morning at Headingley before they moved on to Harrogate for three days of final preparations. He was joined by his Hull team-mate Evans, called in for Gill, who just couldn't shake off a slight niggle.

After a couple of sessions with the 17-man squad, the Great Britain management announced that there would be more changes. Ahead of his final match as a coach, John Whiteley initiated the ending of the era of selecting British international teams by committee and had the final say on the make-up of *his* team. The fiasco over Topliss had been the final straw for a man who had kicked out against the committee system for much of his coaching life and he wasn't going to pass up this opportunity to lever more control, even if it was his swansong.

The British coach decided that Warrington prop Courtney was going to start from the bench rather than '17th man' Rose.

'The decision was made after seeing all the forwards in training this week,' John told a press conference on the Thursday night. 'Rose has gone well in training and looks the best man for the job.

'Also, we now have three Hull forwards in the pack and with the limited time left they gave us a solid combination, especially as we also have their club captain Topliss leading Britain at stand-off.'

The late switches meant Britain had a completely new pack. In total there were ten changes: 1, Fairbairn (Hull KR); 2, Drummond (Leigh); 3, Stephenson (Wigan); 4, Smith (Hull KR); 5, Evans (Hull); 6, Topliss (Hull); 7, Gregory (Widnes); 8, O'Neill (Widnes); 9, Noble (Bradford); 10, Rose (Hull); 11, Smith (Featherstone); 12, Crooks (Hull); 13, Crane (Hull). Subs: 14, Woods (Leigh); 15, Courtney (Warrington).

Unusually, coach Stanton identified one player for special mention when he was asked for his views on the British line-up.

'I am not surprised at the introduction of Rose, who I believe has been brought in to create a little havoc. In fact I think the theme of Britain's side is to try to unsettle us.'

Stanton was clearly referring to what had happened at the Boulevard when the likes of Crooks, Rose and Crane had all taken it in turns to fling a few punches in his side's direction in the opening 20 minutes.

The Australians, however, would be able to call upon their own man of mischief for Sunday's showdown but not before a real scare. Boyd was given a two-match ban for his second Test sending-off at the disciplinary hearing in Leeds. Manager Farrington appealed straight away and the review was held 24 hours later. This time the Aussies got the decision they wanted with the fiery forward fined £500 instead. His ban was suspended. It was successfully argued that the sending off was his first in 15 Tests; that he was provoked by Dalgreen, who had kicked out while on the floor: and that the ban was inconsistent with previous examples of disciplinary action taken after international matches.

It meant Australia would line up at Headingley on Sunday with three changes from the Wigan encounter; Young had also been ruled out after collecting a knock in the Widnes game.

Morris came in at prop, Ribot replaced Grothe on the wing and McCabe partnered Reddy in the second row. Pearce shuffled back to his more normal No 13 position with Price nursing a broken thumb.

Stanton's side rocked up at Headingley with a host of records in their sights but their coach was refusing to let anybody get carried away.

'I will be happy to win by one point. That would be enough to complete the tour unbeaten and it is the main record I want to take with us to France. But each Test has been that little bit harder and this should be the toughest of the three.'

Stanton's prediction that Britain were not going to go down without a fight – literally – proved eerily accurate and unsurprisingly Crooks and Boyd featured in the trials of pugilism as well as in the rugby.

An all-in brawl brought a bruising first half to an end after Boyd had crash-tackled Topliss. Following the restart the Aussie was sinbinned along with Crane, and 13 minutes later Crooks was given his marching orders after going in too heavy on the Aussie captain as he was about to score his team's second try of the afternoon. As the teenage forward made his way off he was met by his first Test nemesis Price, who was bringing on the sand for Meninga. Words were exchanged and Crooks recalled having to be restrained from doing yet more talking with his fists.

'I'd had a bit of a go with Ray Price in the first Test – I had a bit of a go with everyone in the first Test to be honest – but then Max

Krilich scored under the posts and I came in late and gave him a clip and the French referee sent me off. Ray Price came on with a sand bucket and he was giving it all this and I had to be pulled back. Nowt came of it.'

Five minutes later Rose justified Stanton's pre-match comments by engaging in a bout of fisticuffs with Brentnall and both were sent off for ten minutes to cool down.

With one man fewer the wheels started to come off for Topliss & Co but not before they finally scored a try. The sight of Evans crashing over must have been a huge relief for a lot of people. At this point in time even this represented something of a small victory for the British game. It was the seventh try Australia had conceded in 15 matches.

Any hopes that it would kickstart something even better were swept aside as the Kangaroos ran riot in the final ten minutes with four tries straight out of the top drawer. It was fitting that they should end with such a flourish.

'That was a true Test match,' said Stanton. 'The score does not reflect how close the game really was. Great Britain can feel justifiably proud of their efforts.'

Britain, with Topliss and Crane testing out their opponents with a number of kicks, got to half-time trailing 6-4 and without their line being breached.

However, they could not sustain concerted early pressure against a side who once again set new standards in keeping a team out. On three minutes Meninga missed a good penalty chance and in those opening exchanges the men in white were bolstered by a succession of favourable penalty awards, although Fairbairn struggled to make much ground such was the strength of the wind in his face.

Inside the opening ten minutes McCabe barged past two, creating a great platform for an attack, but there was relief for the crowd as Sterling's grubber kick, with Rogers poised to pounce, was just too heavy and Evans held on for dear life just inches from the line.

The response electrified the home crowd. After easing their way out of danger the ball was spread wide on the fifth tackle. Topliss sold a great dummy to Kenny. He delayed his pass for what seemed like an age before feeding a fantastic, round-the-corner ball to Mike Smith on the burst. The home side had a two-on-one with Meninga, who knew not whether to stick or twist. Stephenson drew the big centre and released Drummond, who just couldn't quite get around the covering Ribot. It was almost like watching the Green and Golds in full flow. The home side couldn't quite follow it up and on the next set Australia took the lead with a long kick from Meninga, who used the favourable wind to considerable advantage.

They would not hold it for long. A short tap restart was gathered by Australia but Krilich was penalised for blocking off Noble and Crooks was on the spot with a long-range effort to make it 2-2.

Australia kept coming and it took a heroic piece of defending to keep them out. The sight of the diminutive Gregory jumping into a tackle on Meninga five metres out out was definitely something. The commitment was certainly being appreciated and from the resultant scrum Britain won back possession with Mike Smith making a critical few yards before Drummond took a quick ball. Krilich was half asleep and was not even facing the right way as the spring-heeled winger tore past him to the delight of the crowd. He made it all the way to the halfway line where Brentnall's presence made him look around. That gave Rogers just enough time to bring him down. It was great stuff and again the decibel levels surged as Crooks and Gregory kept passing out of the tackle but Peter Smith just could not hold on to a difficult pass and the chance was gone.

Another long-range effort from Meninga on 25 minutes kept things tight but this was definitely much more like it. Rose and Noble both featured as the hosts managed to get out of their half well and the Bradford hooker followed it up with a tigerish bit of defending after Crooks' kick on the sixth tackle had been easily diffused. The manner in which the young English hooker dealt with Sterling caused a few wry smiles as he swung a right in the tackle which fortunately for him, and the Aussie scrum-half, did not connect.

'Well, I think had Brian Noble connected then Sterling's head would have been over the Pennines,' chuckled commentator French.

Twenty seconds later Australia were one pass away from scoring one of the game's great tries as Boustead, Rogers, Kenny and Reddy combined to thrilling effect on a 75-metre assault. Ribot grounded the critical pass to the dismay of his team-mates. You just could not give them an inch.

With that in mind it was something of a minor achievement for the underdogs to get to half-time without conceding a three-pointer; Meninga and Crooks had exchanged further penalties to leave Australia just two points ahead.

On the last play before half-time Boyd piled into Topliss, who kicked out. The Aussie prop then tried to punch the Britain captain on the floor. Fortunately for all concerned Reddy was able to drag him back. It did not stop all hell breaking lose, though, and there was a furious exchange of blows involving Pearce and O'Neill; Drummond and Ribot were having their own wrestling match. As the hooter blared other scuffles broke out and Crane and Pearce squared up while others pushed and shoved. The presence of Meninga seemed to diffuse matters somewhat. Nobody in white was prepared to question the authority of the Queensland policeman.

The second half opened with a stern lecture for both captains from the referee, who left Topliss and Krilich to do the dirty work and inform Crane and Boyd that they could enjoy an extra-long break. After a good deal of confusion the Hull loose forward eventually jogged off to the sinbin but any number of players could have been penalised.

Noble's excellent foray gave the home side renewed hope as the game was finally restarted and Gregory's superb kick to touch on the last was met with plenty of appreciation. Coupled with British dominance in the scrums an orchestrated and well-executed strategy of kicking would have gone a long way towards blunting all of Australia's other advantages. It was just a shame that it took this long to realise it. In the first Test they barely put boot to ball in open play.

Once again the home side came out on top after a messy scrum and Sterling was caught offside. Crooks grabbed the ball and immediately indicated a kick at goal but was overruled by his captain. Fairbairn found touch just ten metres out. O'Neill had first go and then Noble had a dart but was put on his back by McCabe. Tackle three and Mike Smith took the ball in on the reverse from Gregory. It was determined stuff but more invention and skill were required. Evans delayed from the restart and, as the Kangaroos rushed out of the line, Crooks was met man-and-ball by Sterling. Ten metres of ground had been lost and back they went again as Peter Smith took the ball standing still and was flattened before. Topliss and Gregory just couldn't quite work the opening to end the set. At that moment a try looked further away than ever before. It was clear the Kangaroos were desperate to maintain their remarkable record in the series.

But the men in white would not relent and some good drives from Rose and O'Neill put Crooks within range. The gap became one point as he landed a superb drop goal on 46 minutes.

However, crucially, his work was almost done for the day and seven minutes later he was sent off. Before that Ribot just squeezed in at the corner after Pearce finally broke his man to leave the home defence floundering.

It wasn't long before Stanton's men established clear blue water with Pearce setting the wheels in motion by bursting away from Crooks and finding Rogers on his shoulder. He found Krilich on his inside with the perfect square pass and the captain had the legs to make it under the posts from 30 metres out.

With Crooks sent offfor perceived foul play on Krilich many in the ground must have feared an onslaught – and they were right, although it didn't come as quickly as they might have expected. Firstly, there was the small matter of Evans' try on 65 minutes. It followed the best passage of play from Great Britain in the whole series with Peter Smith, Gregory and Topliss to the fore. Meninga made a mess of the GB skipper's shallow kick on the last, which had been meant for Drummond. With Mike Smith defying the odds to recover the ball they had six more tackles and the Hull KR centre almost made it over after some clever work from Crane and Gregory. Then Drummond came agonisingly close as he scurried and scrambled his way to within a few feet of glory. We had not seen the Aussies creaking like this before.

With another penalty and another six tackles the crowd were screaming and Alex Murphy responded to his co-commentator's joke that the Aussie line 'was booby trapped' by saying, 'Well I think we will score a try … believe it or not!' He would not have to wait long to be proved right.

Crane and Stephenson both did brilliantly to get the ball away under intense pressure, opening the way for Evans, who raced the final 15 metres to his own little piece of history. There was still a split-second wait as he was momentarily halted by Kenny but the rangy Hull player reached over the top and plonked the ball down. It was barely six inches over the line but sometimes six inches can make a big difference in someone's life.

It would be the high point of the series for the British but they did not have long to enjoy the moment.

First came a try for Boustead on 70 minutes with Rogers coolly paving the way with a clever give-and-go link-up with Lewis and Kenny, who were both now playing among the centres. Fairbairn had no chance of stopping him finding the winger, who touched down in the corner.

Four minutes later the score was 8-22. A shuddering tackle on Rose from McCabe saw the ball pop up nicely for Sterling. With 20 metres to go they didn't need the second tackle. It was already exhibition stuff as Kenny sucked in two players and provided a delicious, back-of-the-hand offload to Boustead. He, in turn, was well tackled by Mike Smith but Rogers was ideally placed to take the pass and he powered in from ten metres. Sterling leapt in delight as if the realisation of history being made dawned on him. There was also, undoubtedly, plenty of relief in his reaction. Meninga's conversion was a formality.

With the result beyond doubt it was time to show off. Lewis's sent an outrageous 35-metre pass to Kenny, who weaved past a couple of players before setting Meninga off on an extraordinary run. First he barged over Drummond, wrong-footed Stephenson and handed off Drummond and Rose in quick succession and with such force that they looked like they had just been hit by an upper cut from George Foreman. Ironically it was Gregory, the smallest player on the pitch, who brought him down by hitting him at his knees. On the next play Lewis sent another raking pass to Kenny. Pearce was next in line to collect the ball and surge through a giant hole for try number four.

From the restart, Lewis sliced through another gaping gap as many of Britain's players waited for a knock-on to be awarded. The substitute kept going and handed over to Kenny who, in one of rugby league's most iconic moments, surged one way and then the next to wrong-foot Mike Smith and dive in between the posts. Meninga kicked his 50th goal of the tour. It was all over.

The legend of the Invincibles was well and truly born and the records set were breathtaking:

- The first Australian team to win a series in Britain 3-0.

- The first to win all their matches.

- Their total of 99 points in a series was the most by either country.

- It was their 13th consecutive Test match win and in the six most recent clashes between the two sides the aggregate score was 186-36.

England's rugby union coach Dick Greenwood said: 'The videos of the three rugby league Tests should be compulsory viewing for every serious rugby union player.'

As the teams walked off many of the young fans who ran onto the pitch headed straight for Meninga. He was quickly surrounded by boys of all ages. A couple of them dared even to reach for his arm. Alex Murphy had famously said that this Australian team were 'men from another planet'. For these young fans it was their one chance to meet Superman and the Hulk rolled into one bulging No 3 shirt.

How could any young player, regardless of where they came from, not have been inspired? The Aussies lit up the gloom that had infested the northern heartlands in the autumn of 1982. We had seen the same happen the year before when Botham set the cricket world alight at a time when Toxteth was burning. At the end of November 1982 Britain's unemployment rate was about to peak at 11 per cent. In the rapidly de-industrialising towns of Halifax, Dewsbury, Bradford, Wakefield, Wigan and Hull, the rate was much higher. But great sport has an almost unique way of offering solace from the rigours of the crap that life can throw at you and my, how the 181,474, who came to watch the Kangaroos over the previous seven weeks must have appreciated it.

One non-paying spectator certainly did, although for Britain's coach it was a sad farewell.

'It would have been nice to finish as Britain's coach with a victory but there was a lot in today's performance which gave me satisfaction,' said Gentleman John. It would be the last professional team he ever coached.

His opposite number had been worried at half-time and was concerned his players had been distracted by some of the niggling play.

'I thought it was a great performance. I think the English challenge was much greater than it has been and at half-time we were in quite a bit of trouble. But our fellows stuck to their guns and showed a lot of maturity for their age.'

While Stanton was heralded for his achievements, his tough-love approach proved to be universally respected even though he was someone the players would not love.

Ray Price, writing five years later, said: 'Stanton has to take a lot of credit for the success of the 1978 and 82 Kangaroos. With so many great players in those sides, probably anyone could have coached us to victory when it came to on-field tactics; we didn't need any revolutionary moves and we were a class above the Poms by then in speed, strength and fitness. But the biggest danger on the tour was to let it become a social outing like at least one English side had treated its trip to Australia. Frank Stanton proved a master of keeping us fit, united and hungry.

'Plenty of Test players, who came under him reckoned he did it in an impersonal way and in many ways he could be vindictive, but as long as you trained hard and did the right thing under his many rules, he was alright.

'He became Test coach at the same time I became a Test player. He retired as Test coach the same time I retired as a Test player. In my 22 Tests for Australia, Stanton was coach for 20 of them. We saw a lot of each other through football, but we would never regard ourselves as great friends. Nor enemies. We were just player and coach.

'Frank Stanton was a hard man, a disciplinarian. When we went on a Kangaroo tour for three months he didn't want us slackening, which could be easy to do when 28 players are together overseas. He kept us on our toes and he didn't try to gain any friends along the way.

'I didn't mind hard training and, like Biscuits [Stanton], I went away to win, but plenty of Kangaroos saw him as unapproachable, unbending and some even thought he was unfair. We'd train twice a day and began every morning at about 7am with a brisk walk through our tour-base neighbourhood of Leeds. It was never any different; from one to the last. He was unrelenting.

'Mind you we had plenty of enjoyable times on that tour (1978), too, as we did when we returned in 1982 and became tagged as the Invincibles. Some of the new players in the Australian team could not believe how tough Stanton was in 1982, nor would they believe it when we told them he had mellowed incredibly in four years.

'Stanton's biggest problem was he was abrupt with people. And he was worse when he'd had a few beers. He coached Manly to a Premiership in 1976 and 78. In 76 they beat Parramatta and in 1978 they won amid plenty of complaints from us, particularly over the refereeing of Greg Hartley. I don't think Stanton had much time for Parramatta and after he had had a few beers he left little doubt ...

'John Monie called him a coach of consistency. He said he wasn't into trick players or magical cures and that it was up to him and his players to perform consistently under pressure. That, he thought, was the sign of a good team.

'Those words really summed up his attitude and how he regarded himself as one of the team rather than a level above his players. That was always how I saw him, although I knew that he was the boss and it was his head that was on the chopping block when things went wrong. Like Gibson, he wanted to be in control of his own destiny so he relied on his own instincts and his intimate knowledge of the players.'

Peter Sterling added: 'Stanton did an outstanding job. Sometimes I'm sure we all called him a bastard under our breath, but when we did it, it was out of respect. He set out to build toughness and intensity and collective will into his Kangaroos. And he did it.'

On the evening of Sunday 28 November, Price, Sterling, Stanton and the rest of the Australian party would celebrate long into the night along with assorted guests including the likes of *Chariots of Fire* producer and renowned rugby league fan Colin Welland. Krilich was clearly emotional as he opened the champagne and was asked about leading the side to new heights.

'I am quite elated to say the least. It has been a magnificent tour for myself personally and the rest of the players. Something that you dream and it has really happened to me.'

Krilich was also asked whether he thought his team were the best ever.

'I can't really comment about this. I can only comment about this side and the last side and I think it is a better side than the last side. It is very complimented and each player looks after each other. It is a great team.'

One man more qualified to assess their relative merits was Arthur Clews, who played in England and Australia and gave great service to Leeds.

He said: 'I think they could have put the second team in and killed them. I think this is one of the finest sides I have ever seen. I've watched every team since 1948 – I played for Leeds in 1947 – but they [the 1982 Kangaroos] were tremendous and I don't think I've seen a finer side in my life.'

For Australian rugby chief Kevin Humphreys the pride in his side's achievements was obvious as he was asked about the rapport between the Kangaroos and the British public.

'This is not a team of 13, this is a team of 33 with 28 players and a management of five. They have all been part of something which has been a wonderful experience for me. I have been on a lot of football trips and this is the greatest bunch of Australian sportsman I have been with in my life.'

While there was time to celebrate for the Kangaroos there were still seven matches left, culminating with a second Test match against France in Narbonne on 18 December. The Australia coach would have one more press conference with British journalists before flying to France.

'When we first arrived in England there was a press conference and a lot of the English journalists were saying to me, "You've got a young team, based on defence and you are going to try and defend your way out of it, etc., etc. Will you have a sufficient attack to worry the Englishman?" It got under my skin a bit but I let it go. However, at the end of the tour we had another press conference and I recall repeating what had happened earlier when I was asked whether we were going to score tries. I rested my case in terms of the stats. We could attack as well as defend.'

In the first Test in Avignon, Lewis dislocated his shoulder as the Aussies ran out 15-4 winners, and two weeks later Grothe scored two more tries in a 23-9 victory. Between the two Tests the Kangaroos won four club matches, conceding just seven points while piling up 188 at the other end. Was there any point, especially in front of crowds of 1,000 at Pamiers and 2,000 in Toulouse?

'There is no need for lengthy tours now that we have a faster mode of transport,' Stanton told Australian journalists. 'There should be more concentrated tours of about six weeks' duration. It would be better all round for players, costs and organisation.'

Four years earlier the tourists had wanted to play just the Tests but that notion was rejected by the French federation.

While the Australians were trampling their way across the harder grounds of south-west France, talk in England turned to who would lead the international team. It would be a critical appointment in more ways than one. The following year the rules were changed to enable the coach and manager to pick their teams, although the international selection committee retained power of ratification. The RFL's first job was to replace Hutton. The new manager would take the team through to the end of the 1984 Australia tour. At a 16-man meeting of the international committee in Leeds, led by chairman Bill Oxley, two candidates emerged: Hull's Dick Gemmell and Salford's Les Bettinson.

Gemmell, who had been in charge of finances during the disastrously unprofitable 1979 adventure, was voted in to the dismay of his chief rival.

Writing almost ten years later, Bettinson gave his account of what happened: 'Bill asked Dick and me to leave the room. Reg [Parker] suggested that we should be invited to make a statement. "Not necessary," said the chairman. "Everyone knows Dick and Les well enough – it would be a waste of time."'

'I left the room in a state of incredulity. I could not believe that such a charade was actually happening and that I was part of it. Dick and I indulged in small talk as we waited for the vote. He told me that he had not lobbied anyone, which seemed odd under the circumstances, an odd thing to say. When we returned, the chairman announced that Dick had won the vote and was duly elected Great Britain manager.

'Dick Gemmell was a former international who had served on the 1979 tour as business manager. When asked on his return to present his financial report, Dick said that there were a few accounts to be settled but he was confident that there would be a profit of £100,000. The tour in fact, declared a loss of £30,000.

'Dick was obviously not a man for fine detail, and such inaccurate accounting hardly recommended him to be appointed tour manager. Yet appointed he was, by a shambles of a system that exemplified why the international team was in such a parlous state.'

Two days later the same committee would decide on John Whiteley's replacement. In the frame were Alex Murphy (Wigan), Malcolm Reilly (Castleford), Peter Fox (Bradford), Roger Millward (Hull KR) and Frank Myler (Oldham). After voting for Gemmell as manager they began to debate the merits of the five candidates for the coaching position before deciding on a final two. Myler and Reilly were invited in the next day to field questions and to ask some of their own.

The vote was tight but the 44-year-old Oldham boss just edged it. He was awarded the job until the end of the season – when the situation would be reviewed ahead of the 1984 tour of Australia – and, critically, he would pick the squads and the team. The much derided international selection committee was no more.

Myler, a former Great Britain captain, would continue to coach at the Watersheddings while preparing the squad for two games against France on 20 February (away) and at the Boulevard on 6 March. He would go full-time with Britain at the end of the 1982/83 campaign.

'We don't have much time to get things right for the French games but, hopefully, we can only go better,' said Myler on the day of his appointment. 'My head is on the block. I know that in many ways I am taking a risk.'

Later in the week he told journalists: 'Our entire approach to the game needs looking at and we need the help of both players and club coaches. We must find a pattern of play which suits all and stick to it. The doubt about fitness is ludicrous. Players should be 100 per cent fit. Any young players who we believe have the potential to play at full international level will be given a chance. Sticking to the older players is not the answer.'

Myler's thoughts echoed so much of what his predecessor had said and he also would face the same problems with club co-operation and player commitment. Once again the RFL was still essentially relying on Britain's top players doing extra work for no financial gain.

Thankfully, though, a golden generation of exciting new talent was just bursting to the surface but it came too late for Myler. The man he beat to the top job would ultimately be the one to get enough out of Britain's leading players to restore pride in the Lions.

Chapter Ten

The Long Road Back

'Gregory, has he got the legs?

'Down he goes.

'He'll get there.

'Mike Gregory has done it for Great Britain.

'Under the posts.

'Oh boy, oh boy.'

The frenzied exhortations of commentator Darrell Eastlake in describing the moment Great Britain finally secured a victory over Australia after a wait of nearly ten years were special and poignant in the same breath.

The excitement in his voice did justice to the significance of a 24-year-old Warrington forward running from inside his own half to score a try in the 72nd minute.

Chasing Gregory all the way to the line was Wayne Pearce. Six years earlier nobody in the British game seemed capable of halting the Aussie star in full flow and the gap between the two sides appeared insurmountable. It was a measure of how far Britain's top players had come that the No 11 in red, white and blue could run 70 metres with the Kangaroos' all-action hero unable to close the gap, never mind tackle him.

Lions coach Malcolm Reilly had found a formula and a group of players that gave Australia problems ... not just for 20 minutes or even a half but for the whole of the match.

It was only one victory (26-12), with the home side having already retained the Ashes, but critically its relevance and the profile of rugby league at that time in the UK was reflected in the reaction in the English media. On 9 July 1988 the main evening news bulletins opened with the victory and flashed up images of Henderson Gill 'doing a bit of a boogie' – the Wigan winger had made it 20-12 with a stunning try set up by Paul Loughlin's dazzling break and had celebrated with his iconic hip swivel. On that bright evening in Sydney, fans dressed in the shirts of Wigan, Widnes, Castleford, Hull, Bradford and Leeds danced in the stands. The contrast between their last victory on a cold, autumn day on a muddy Odsal pitch back in 1978 could not have been more stark. Reilly's side had not ground their way to glory ... they had beaten Australia at their own game and in doing so earned the respect of their hosts.

Former Kangaroos' scrum-half Tom Raudonikis summed it up best when he said: 'They have done the game at international level a service. No-one can say they didn't play well, didn't deserve to win. They flogged us ... now there's something to look forward to.'

What all rugby league fans would enjoy was a return to knife-edge Ashes battles. After 1988 and up until the 1995 World Cup, it was very much like the old days: Australia were generally favourites but not by much. The days of horror shows for British fans was over and they could watch their boys do battle from the comfort of their sofas rather than from behind them. But getting to that point was not straightforward. It took nearly six years to exorcise the demons of the Invincibles.

A lot of things had to change.

Back in 1982, while Stanton's Kangaroos were preparing for their final match in France, the GB inquest began in earnest. On 15

December the RFL's coaching committee chaired by Les Bettinson held a four-hour meeting in Leeds. It would be the first of three 'where do we go from here' discussions held in quick succession. The second was during RL Council meeting on 26 January; there would be a get-together of club coaches on 5 February.

National coaching director Phil Larder was at all three meetings. Encouraged to start with a blank piece of paper, Larder struck a positive note by outlining how dramatic improvements could be made in a relatively short space of time if the National Coaching Scheme received more support. At the end of his presentation he handed out details of his intended changes. Most pressing was an updated and more detailed coaching qualification scheme.

RFL spokesman David Howes's statement before the Council meeting emphasised the seriousness of the situation: 'The time has come when we must look at every level of the game. It is not just about sacking the selection committee and appointing a new manager. They are merely cosmetic changes. We have to look at many other areas where our game can be improved upon, including such things as coaching clinics and special coaching schools for our better-class players.'

Larder also set about explaining how the Australian Coaching Scheme, which had been running for nearly 20 years, had been a huge success. They had 7,000 qualified coaches. He showed the 30 British club representatives video clips from various tour matches to emphasise what everybody in the room already knew: Australia were playing a different game. The only common denominator was that both sides had 13 players and were on the grass at the same time.

Also at the second meeting was fitness guru Rod McKenzie, who had had limited time with some of the players for the previous 18 months. He took the opportunity to lecture, not only about fitness, but on a range of related topics. He took those watching by surprise by explaining how rugby league was competing for people's time with other leisure pursuits and even outlined how the changing make-up of society – the breakdown of the traditional family, for example – was making it important to target women. He claimed there were already more one-parent families in the UK than those headed by mum and dad.

The Carnegie College lecturer said that although most club coaches had been top players they had no formal coaching qualifications and that their backgrounds were not necessarily suited to the job description.

In terms of fitness he said most clubs lacked professionalism compared with Australian players, who were 'rugby athletes'. Too many of the British players were overweight and lacked speed, endurance, strength and skills. McKenzie did praise those who came to the summer training camps but conceded it was just too little, too late.

Both speeches were met with a positive response and, clearly inspired by the positive wind of change, a number of the clubs took it upon themselves to write letters to the RFL outlining how its own decision-making processes could be streamlined to meet the faster-pace of the modern world.

With the addition of Cardiff City, Carlisle and Fulham, the 1982/83 season involved 33 teams, all of whom nominated one person to sit on the RFL Council. The delegates were split into two other main committees – finance and international matters. The full council only met quarterly so great affairs of state took a long time to sort out once the politics had been taken care of.

A less unwieldy solution was proposed and discussed at the full council's next meeting on 2 March. A new management committee would meet every two weeks, starting in August 1983 and comprising the current chairman, vice-chairman, immediate past chairman and six other members elected from the Council to serve on a two-year basis.

At the Annual General Meeting in June the following men were handed the task of running the game, although the Council still had powers of ratification: Bob Ashby (Featherstone), Jack Bateman (Swinton), Phil Brunt (Castleford), Harry Ditchfield (Widnes), Jack Grindrod (Rochdale), Reg Parker (Blackpool), Brian Pitchford (Warrington), Joe Seddon (St Helens), David Wigham (Whitehaven).

The RFL had also capitulated in the battle to end the international transfer ban. The newly formed Professional Players Association had shown its teeth with legal threats if its members were stopped from moving to Australia. While the decision would officially be ratified at an international board meeting in September, English clubs were effectively allowed to sign top stars four months earlier when the RFL indicated it would propose ending the ban.

As the RFL held up its end of the bargain, the new British management team of Oldham coach Myler and Hull board member Gemmell kick-started the countdown to the 1984 Ashes series by unveiling a 47-man summer training squad. With 14 months to go before the trip to Australia, each player was given a weight training schedule prepared by McKenzie to follow individually before three summer camps. The players were also expected to complete at least three five-mile runs ahead of the first get-together on 4 June.

Among the plethora of new faces was Bradford's Ellery Hanley, who had just exploded into the wider public consciousness with his televised length-of-the-field try in a Challenge Cup semi-final against Featherstone at Headingley. Castleford's rapidly improving prop Kevin Ward was also called up, as were Widnes's teenage winger Joe Lydon and Oldham's talented young second-rower Andy Goodway. The latter two had both just made their Great Britain debuts in Carcassonne where Len Casey captained a side that ran out 20-5 winners. Both had scored tries, as did Brian Noble and the recalled John Joyner. There had also been first-time international starts for Oldham loose forward Terry Flanagan and the coach's nephew Tony Myler from Widnes.

There were accusations of nepotism aimed at coach Myler. Eight training squad members came from his previous club, Widnes, and four were from his current employers, Oldham, who had as many representatives as champions Hull.

There was no space for the up-and-coming Bob Eccles or the two men who had combined so well to set up Britain's only try the previous autumn – David Stephenson and Mick Crane. There was also no Henderson Gill. In fact there was just one Wigan player included, the young Colts product Dennis Ramsdale, even though the Central Park outfit finished third in 1982/83.

Also surprisingly excluded were Hull KR's Chris Burton, Leigh's Ian Potter and Bradford's Alan Rathbone, who had just played in France and in the return fixture in Hull on 6 March. In that game Myler's men had won 17-5 with tries from Warrington's highly-rated teenage centre Ronnie Duane, Andy Gregory and Peter Smith. Critically, just one change had been made from the match in Carcassonne with Mumby replacing Burke at full-back. This was a stark contrast to the revolving door policy of the previous autumn. The full summer training list read as follows:

- Bradford: Ellery Hanley, Keith Mumby, Brian Noble.
- Castleford: Kevin Beardmore, Keith England, Gary Hyde, John Joyner, Kevin Ward.
- Featherstone: David Hobbs, Peter Smith, John Gilbert
- Hull: Lee Crooks, Steve Evans, Trevor Skerrett, David Topliss
- Hull KR: Garry Clark, George Fairbairn, Phil Hogan, Mike Smith, David Watkinson
- Hunslet: Graham King

- Keighley: David Moll
- Leeds: Andy Smith
- Leigh: Des Drummond, John Woods
- Oldham: Ray Ashton, Terry Flanagan, Andy Goodway, Mick Worrall
- St Helens: Chris Arkwright, Roy Haggerty, Neil Holding, Gary Moorby
- Salford: Ron Smith
- Warrington: Ron Duane, John Fieldhouse
- Widnes: Mick Adams, Mick Burke, Andy Gregory, David Hulme, Joe Lydon, Tony Myler, Keiron O'Loughlin, Mike O'Neill
- Wigan: Dennis Ramsdale
- Workington: Howard Burns, Ian Hartley.

While Stephenson and Gill had both had problems in regularly attending the previous year's summer camps organised by John Whiteley, they weren't the only ones.

Players failing to show would become something of an issue this time around too. At the final training session on 17 July six players did not bother to turn up without giving notice.

'I don't think they [the absent six] wanted to take the final tests today because they possibly have not maintained the strict training programme which Rod McKenzie outlined for them,' said Gemmell.

Players were tested on running stamina (12 minutes), sprint speed (40 metres), flexibility, muscular endurance (leg lifts) and had one-minutes tests for pull-ups, sit-up and dips. Lydon proved quickest over 40 metres although Drummond came top over 30 metres.

McKenzie was reportedly impressed with the early signs, although running endurance proved to be a concern. He wanted all the players to go for one long-distance jog every week.

'After all, it is running stamina which allows a player to perform as well at the end of the game as at the beginning,' said McKenzie.

The 1983/84 season kicked off with teams now gaining four points for a try and handing the ball over to their opponents after the sixth tackle, but that was the least of coach Myler's worries as he attempted to arrange a trial match at Swinton on 6 September. With only two more Tests, left to play – both against France – before he would pick his squad for the 1984 Ashes trip, these types of matches took on greater significance. The Oldham coach had tried to fix up an extra fixture with New Zealand in April but both Hull clubs refused to let their Kiwis play at such a critical point in the season, with the title on the line.

At Swinton, not many of the squad shared their coach's view and on the day a large number cried off claiming to be injured. Gemmell and his coach had to find extra players, which meant St Helens winger Barry Ledger plus Eccles and Crane were among the 26 who were split into two teams as follows: Greens: Mumby, Hyde, Hanley, Mike Smith, Ledger, Holding, Ashton, Skerrett, Noble, Goodway, Moorby, Hartley, Crane; Reds: Lydon, Clark, Joyner, O'Loughlin, Ramsdale, Topliss, Burns, Eccles, Watkinson, England, Hobbs, Haggarty, Flanagan.

Myler wasn't the only person having problems. In Australia, 1983 would prove something of a sharp contrast to the brilliance of the Invincibles the previous year.

Western Suburbs, Cronulla and Newtown were all suffering serious financial problems which ultimately proved the death knell for the latter, while a TV investigation alleged corruption within the News South Wales Rugby League Association (NSWRL). Reporter Chris Masters claimed that officials had siphoned funds from particular clubs and international matches by under-reporting attendances. ARL and NSWRL chairman Kevin Humphreys resigned from both positions. As a result of the programme, a Royal Commission (the Street Royal Commission) was formed. Its findings resulted in New South Wales chief magistrate Murray Farquhar being sent to prison. Humphreys was fined $4,000 and was placed on a 'two-year good behaviour bond'. He would later make a public apology.

Meanwhile, the reign of Arthur Beetson, who replaced Stanton as coach in 1983, was brought to a shuddering halt after the Kangaroos lost their first match in five years. Tries from centre James Leuluai, winger Joe Ropati and second-rower Graeme West helped New Zealand to a 19-12 win at Lang Park in Brisbane in July.

With Queensland having taken the State of Origin series the selectors flooded the Test side with Maroons. Full-back Colin Scott, centre Gene Miles, props Brad Tessmann and Dave Brown, and second-rowers Wally Fullerton-Smith and Paul Vautin were all given the nod. New South Wales had just four players in the line-up and controversies over the balance of representation between the two states rumbled on into the following year's Ashes, which would again pitch Stanton, who returned as coach in 1984, against the British.

One player who suffered more than most from the Queensland/New South Wales power struggle was Peter Sterling. Despite his brilliant efforts in England the Parramatta player did not represent his country for almost four years (1983–86), although this was partially due to his decision to move to Hull and a perceived lack of commitment to the cause down under.

However, he would have another opportunity to cement his place among the pantheon of greats.

'I don't think I have ever seen a player contribute more to a team performance than he did,' was Malcolm Reilly's assessment. 'He was a coach's dream.'

His team-mate Brett Kenny said: 'The thing I always remember about him was he was always involved in everything. Whether at

Parramatta or Test level, you couldn't keep him out the game. As Ron Massey (Parramatta's assistant coach) said: "When Peter Sterling walks onto a football pitch he lights it up. Everyone just looks." That's what he did with Parramatta at the highest level of football ... at Test level.'

John Monie, who replaced Gibson as coach of Parramatta in 1984, offered the best insight into what made Sterling so special.

'In 1986 I realised for the first time what was happening with Sterling. A coach's view of the game is completely different to 95 per cent of players' perspectives. We coaches sit up above the game and look down on the whole thing.

'It's like looking at a chessboard. We can see when players should do things and when players shouldn't do things. What started to happen with myself and Sterling in 1986 was I could sit in the grandstand, mentally alert and physically fresh and Sterling could be playing the game that I was watching. And when I saw something happen that maybe we had talked about at training – where I said, "If you see this situation you should react by doing this" – there he was out there on the field doing it, just as I saw it.

'We went over these situations at training – that's coaching, putting players in situations where they're under a bit of pressure and they react the way a coach wants them to react. In 1986 Sterling began to do things that I saw in my mind that I'd expect a player to do. As a coach that doesn't happen very often. Maybe players are a second behind us or maybe a play behind us. But Sterling ... when the situation happened – bang. He did the right thing, and I'd never seen a person who could react to a coach's mind. He's a player who does it at the same time you think it.'

Sterling's signing by the Boulevard club was the first big move by one of the Invincibles, although a second player would follow in the most remarkable of circumstances.

In November 1983 struggling Wakefield announced the ten-week signing of Wally Lewis. Barry Hough, a Trinity supporter, offered the half-back star £600 per match but Lewis jokingly said he would want double and was amazed when his eye-watering terms were agreed to.

Lewis was paid ten times more than his team-mates and it did prove a problem as not many of them were prepared to shake his hand when he arrived at Belle Vue in early December. However, his debut drew a crowd of 7,972, nearly four times their average gate. In one match the gate receipts funded more than half his salary, although the club's hope that he would help them escape relegation was in vain.

While Lewis's arrival drew quite a fanfare of publicity, the return of Phil Larder after his fact-finding mission to Australia and the United States proved less newsworthy. On 7 December Larder presented his findings to the RFL's full council having met with Bettinson's coaching sub-committee a week earlier. He had spent time with Jack Gibson at Parramatta, Frank Stanton at Balmain and Bobby Fulton at Manly. In the USA he stayed with the LA Rams and experienced a feeling of deja vu: Larder was amazed to discover the training methods at the Rams were almost identical to those at Parramatta. It turned out that Gibson was a regular visitor to California.

The director of coaching explained that developing strength was the key aspect underpinning all his findings, as that was the main difference between British rugby league players and NFL regulars.

He also identified four key proposals he believed needed implementing by the game's decision makers:

- Having an employee of the league studying American sports marketing techniques;

- Seriously considering reducing the number of fixtures played and significantly reducing the length of the season;
- Seriously considering summer rugby;
- Holding conferences for club secretaries and staff which should include instruction in marketing techniques and public relations

He wanted to see all British coaches work their way through his new National Coaching Scheme. After all, if they didn't possess the knowledge that everyone in the game now seemed to consider was crucial, how could they possibly pass it onto players?

Only one club voted against the proposal that all coaching members at professional clubs, including A teams and colts, should be qualified to Rugby League Certificate Grade One level by September 1986. There were four levels of the certificate and it was hoped that coaches at both amateur and professional levels would take the course. But there was a problem: few of the British game's most senior coaches were happy and two hastily arranged exemptions were added on condition that those coaches attend one of the day courses. Those exempt were:

i) Coaches who had held a first-team post at a professional club for a minimum of five years;

ii) Anyone who had coached an international side.

The exemptions did little to appease the men coaching the Division One and Two clubs and the RFL went on a PR offensive after a national newspaper article picked up on the story and explained how the likes of Arthur Bunting, Peter Fox and Alex Murphy would be 'going back to school'.

Larder said: 'There is no way that I am going to tell professional coaches how to coach. That would be ridiculous. If the professional coaches have got this impression from reports then concern would be understandable.'

Media chief Howes outlined how it would all work in a lengthy newspaper article, explaining that even for experienced coaches it would be a useful exercise because they could learn from the rapid leaps forward taken in sports science.

The newly appointed Keighley boss Geoff Peggs and Leeds coach Maurice Bamford had already taken Larder's new course ahead of the RFL edict and the latter agreed to attend the first of the one-day seminars in Bradford. Many of those in attendance clearly did not want to be there. Dewsbury's Jack Addy was among them and it took an intervention by Peter Fox to calm everybody down.

'Maurice did the introduction,' recalls Larder. 'I was walking around thinking about the next session and they are all having a go at Maurice. Then Peter said "Listen, guys, I think this course is going to be brilliant for us. Listen to what Phil and Maurice are going to say. We might learn something. And if I learn more than you my team's going to beat yours the next time we play." And Peter just got them all onside.'

The next session was held at Warrington for the Lancashire coaches and this time Larder was prepared. Ahead of the meeting he contacted Wigan boss Alex Murphy and the two men did a deal to make sure he was on board. However, things did not start well, with Bamford crying off at the last minute. In addition, there was no sign of Larder's secret weapon five minutes before the start time and the atmosphere was not good. A couple of the attendees had brought the aforementioned national newspaper article with them and were positively bristling.

'It is starting at 9am and it gets to two minutes to nine and I think "bollocks" because Murphy is not there,' recalls Larder. 'So I get up to the front and start introducing myself and I am very nervous. Anyway, just at this point I hear this car coming and look through the window and it's Murph in his bright red Wigan car and he comes bounding in wearing his Wigan tracksuit. He stands up and says, "I am really looking forward to this course. We should listen to Phil and take on board what he says. We'll have a chat and then have a little game of touch and pass and I'll still show you I'm better than all of you." It was a fabulous course.'

By the end of 1984 the number of qualified coaches coming out of the scheme passed the 1,000 mark with the rate at 60 per month. Larder also built up a network of regional heads to expand the scheme.

While the director of coaching made considerable progress on one front, Myler was not so fortunate. The problem of club co-operation had become a serious issue by the time he named a 21-man squad for the forthcoming matches against France on 29 January (away) and on 17 February (home).

With regular and worthwhile meet-ups becoming increasingly difficult in the run-up to Christmas, because clubs were reluctant to release their stars, Myler added a number of players who had not featured in his summer training squad. They included Oldham centre Des Foy, Barrow scrum-half David Cairns and Leeds prop Keith Rayne.

With the coach set to unveil a 41-man training squad on 1 February, from which he would pick his squad for Australia, the Test in Avignon at the end of January would effectively act as a trial for those hoping to force their way into his thinking. Those who made it had an extra incentive courtesy of self-made Halifax-born millionaire David Brook: via his Harrogate-based company Modern Maintenance Products, he had pledged £100,000 to the tour. Each Test victory would mean an extra £5,000 for the squad, a figure matched by the RFL. That was on top of the long-standing agreement which meant that players shared 35 per cent of tour profits.

In Avignon, 20-year-old Foy claimed a try on his debut. Rovers teenager Garry Clark also made his bow and fellow youngster

Duane played, meaning the backs division was rich in promise if nothing else.

Hull KR's prolific loose forward David Hall claimed a first GB start in a side captained by Keith Mumby but the 12-0 victory was overshadowed by a terrible leg break for Hull KR hooker David Watkinson, which ruled him out for the rest of the tour and the remainder of the season.

After they returned from France, Myler's new 41-man training squad was unveiled. The plan was to meet regularly in Huddersfield where Rod McKenzie would monitor fitness levels. The squad's make-up reflected the dominance in the domestic set-up of the Hull clubs with Rovers duo George Fairbairn and Chris Burton back in favour and their clubmate Hall called up. Two 18-year-olds from Hull were included – try machine Garry Schofield and prop forward Andy Dannatt – plus there were recalls for Widnes's fit-again winger John Basnett, Bradford back-rower Dick Jasiewicz and Widnes forward Fred Whitfield, who was one of ten players from Myler's former club.

However, the Great Britain coach would fall out with his ex-employers after they refused to let any of their players, bar Basnett, train with the national set-up ahead of the Test with France at Headingley. The management's no-train-no-play policy forced a number of changes, with Schofield making his debut aged 18 years and seven months. It would also lead to the resignation of Widnes coach Harry Dawson the following month. Vince Karalius took over.

At Headingley all the points in a dour 10-0 win came via the boot of David Hobbs. French winger Didier Bernard came closest to scoring a try in the dying stages, dropping a pass with the line at his mercy. With just 7,646 watching on a Friday night it was not the end Myler would have wanted. He and Gemmell had just over two months to work out who would make the final cut. With 30 in his squad there was at least room for manoeuvre. It would be the biggest squad to leave British shores.

Expansion was a theme of the time. In the run-up to the Test team announcement, the RFL had a big decision to make. The admission of Mansfield Marksmen and Sheffield Eagles meant there would be 36 professional teams from the start of the 1984/85 season and a 20-team second division which made it impossible for every team to play each other home and away.

At a meeting of the RFL Council on 18 April, a range of restructuring ideas were debated. There were plenty who favoured the creation of three divisions; others were prepared for something even more radical. Bramley's Ronnie Teeman, who had been part of the group that had rescued the club at the end of the previous year, proposed dividing clubs into six groups of six. Clubs would play each other home and away (ten matches) and there would be extra games against clubs of similar ability from other groups. The top 16 would then play a Premiership-style knockout to decide the overall champions. Unsurprisingly, it did not get much support.

However, the solution was almost as complicated in that there would be no change to the structure other than a new and convoluted fixture schedule for the second division, which meant they did not play everyone home and away.

Life was also getting complicated for Myler and Gemmell. Their plan started to unravel just days after their largely youthful party was unveiled. Central to their plans was Hull KR's Len Casey, who was one of three over-30s named. The others were captain Trevor Skerrett and Mick Adams from Oldham. There was a surprise call-up for 29-year-old Leigh centre Steve Donlan.

Casey had been sent off in Hull's fractious 38-16 victory in the Humberside derby at Craven Park in April. He made matters worse by barging touch-judge Keith Worrall and was banned for six months. The RFL insisted he be withdrawn from the Ashes party but Casey attempted to have the decision overturned in the High Court, only for the judge to rule against him.

There would be more bad news when Skerrett was ruled out with cartilage trouble while Hall, John Woods and Steve Evans also withdrew. The tone of the trip was set by a dizzying array of comings and goings in the week before the departure for Darwin on 13 May. In fact, the final make-up was not settled until 24 hours before the party left.

Myler said: 'At least I will have players around me who are keen to go and will have no worries about leaving the country for three months.'

Late inclusion Chris Arkwright, the St Helens utility player, was one caught up in the messy final preparations. Five days before departure he was withdrawn on the advice of the RFL doctor after his knee swelled up following the Premiership semi-final against Hull KR. Two days later he saw two St Helens specialists who passed him fit. It was no secret that he had a troublesome right knee but with the huge squad he would not be expected to play twice a week and had been managing to play regularly for Saints.

Gemmell said: 'You must prove your fitness before leaving for down under.' The problem for the Great Britain management was Tony Myler went away having had a knee cartilage operation just five weeks earlier and clearly was not match fit. In came the likes of Brian Case of Wigan and St Helens loose forward Harry Pinner, while Hull KR's young forward Wayne Proctor came from nowhere to make the plane. Noble, aged just 23, would be captain.

It left the travelling party as follows:

Manager: Dick Gemmell

Coach: Frank Myler.

Business manager: Roland Davis

Fitness director: Rod McKenzie

Physio: Ron Barritt

Backs: Ray Ashton (Oldham), Mick Burke (Widnes), Garry Clark (Hull KR), Steve Donlan (Leigh), Des Drummond (Leigh), Ronnie Duane (Warrington), Des Foy (Oldham), Andy Gregory (Widnes), Ellery Hanley (Bradford), Neil Holding (St Helens), John Joyner (Castleford), Joe Lydon (Widnes), Keith Mumby (Bradford), Tony Myler (Widnes), Garry Schofield (Hull), Mike Smith (Hull KR).

Forwards: Mick Adams (Widnes), Kevin Beardmore (Castleford), Chris Burton (Hull KR), Brian Case (Wigan), Lee Crooks (Hull), Terry Flanagan (Oldham), Andy Goodway (Oldham), David Hobbs (Featherstone), Brian Noble (Bradford), Mike O'Neill (Widnes), Harry Pinner (St Helens), Wayne Proctor (Hull KR), Keith Rayne (Leeds), Mick Worrall (Oldham).

Noble struck a defiant tone in a newspaper column on the eve of departure.

'Knowing all the players selected in the team, I can sense the spirit is right,' he wrote. 'The major thing about these 1984 Lions is that pulling on a Great Britain shirt really means something to us … we have the right type of players to go out there and give everything. If we lose, it won't be for any lack of effort or commitment.

'I think that is an important factor. When I made my Test debut against the Australians in 1982 I could sense some of our players going into the match thinking they were going to be beaten – it wasn't easy for a young bloke, trying to psyche myself up for a big game, to appreciate. I don't think any of the lads in this tour team will think that way – we want to give it our best shot.

'Another big motivating factor for us is hearing all the critics writing us off. Obviously, those people who understand the game a little deeper recognise the gap in standards between top Sydney football and what we have here in Britain. But they also realise that Test matches, like cup finals, are one-off affairs and can be great levellers when the underdogs go into the game fully committed, fit and motivated. I am sure we will.

'What a lot of people don't realise is that gaining tour selection is the culmination of a lot of hard work by players. I've been working for four solid years to achieve this, doing my own conditioning and body work. I know the top Australian players have been doing this for several years. It's up to us to have the same dedication to match them.'

It was not a view shared by others who had been through the experience before. The great Leeds winger John Atkinson, writing in the *Cumberland News*, predicted Great Britain would lose every Test.

Another to have his say in the media ahead of the main action was Andy Gregory, a man with a growing reputation for ruffling feathers. In an interview with Australian journalist George Dunkersley, the Widnes scrum-half boasted that he was the best half-back in the world, saying, he despised one of the other halves in the tour party: 'He's a bloke I don't like at all and he's not having my Test place.'

Gregory would not play in any of the three Tests in Australia on a trip that highlighted the importance of meticulous planning. Being fit was one thing but if you ignored all the other strands of what made a successful tour then you were going to have problems. Hosting regular management meetings might have been a good start but the importance of good communications was largely overlooked.

After the second Test in Brisbane, which sealed the series victory for Stanton's side, manager Dick Gemmell sent back an interim tour report in which he heaped praise on Rod McKenzie.

In one segment he wrote: 'The players have enormous respect for him and follow his training instructions to the letter. He even tells them what food to eat and when to eat it, controlling their diet to produce the right balance before a game.'

While McKenzie was playing his part when the sessions happened, they didn't always take place as planned.

One example came early in the tour when the British squad were kicked off a public park pitch because a group of bank employees wanted to play touch football. And then when they were finally directed to another training pitch a mile away it turned out to be the size of a tennis court.

Quite how Gemmell could outline how diets were being controlled is a mystery as the players were largely left to fend for themselves after training finished. The squad rarely sat down together for evening meals and when they stayed in a luxury Sydney hotel their meal allowances were not sufficiently plush, which meant they had to find nearby takeaways and cafes to make their money go far enough to feed themselves.

There was talk of a curfew after they lost 18-16 to Toowoomba but finding a player who remembers one is difficult. More than one squad member, when not picked for a particular game, decided to take their bat home and 'disappeared' for a few days. On their return there was no punishment, so instead of being sent back to the UK in disgrace, those pleasing themselves were picked for subsequent matches.

While Myler certainly experienced a lot of bad luck as his side lost every one of the six Tests down under (they made history by being the first British side to lose to New Zealand 3-0), he did not inspire confidence ahead of the first Test in Sydney on 9 June by forgetting Neil Holding's name when telling the squad the line-up. The fact that he was reading out the list from the back of a cigarette packet meant he probably didn't have space for all the names.

At Myler's press conference to announce his first Test team he left journalists bemused by reading out 18 names in a random order. There was some method to his apparent madness with a number of starters carrying niggles. He later confused the situation by claiming to know his 15 but added that he did not want to name them until he had 'finalised the team tomorrow'.

The following day Myler admitted he had been unaware that Donlan had been struggling with a back injury for a week.

'Donlan told me today that he couldn't play,' said Myler. 'I didn't even know he was injured.'

After much to-ing and fro-ing, once the Lions team was finally unveiled back-rower Goodway was forced into the front row because of an injury to Rayne. Hanley was on the wing, full-back Mumby was in the centres and, most surprisingly, centre Foy was at No 6. The Oldham youngster had only played the position a handful of times but overall there was plenty of pace in the side and Goodway was probably the quickest prop Britain had ever had.

Foy's selection was all the more confusing because star centre Lydon, fresh from two 70-metre tries in the Challenge Cup Final, was on the bench and because Hanley had played the previous Test against France at stand-off.

However, the young Oldham player was full of confidence and looking forward to facing up to the challenge of going head-to-head with Wally Lewis.

'I just want to do well,' said Foy on the eve of battle. 'Wally Lewis is a good player but they are all good players.'

Myler added: 'Foy has pace, can tackle and expressed a keenness to play opposite Lewis.'

Under Stanton, Australia had won 14 straight games and everyone expected him to make it 15 but the Balmain boss was refusing to concede anything.

'They [GB] use the ball well and are all very skilled. Frank Myler is a shrewd operator. He seems to have done a good job with a young side.'

The biggest danger for Stanton was making sure his team played for him. The side was packed with Queenslanders who had just helped the Maroons win the first State of Origin match in Brisbane. Boustead, Vautin, Lewis, Miles and Meninga had all scored tries in a 29-12 victory over Stanton's New South Wales side. The 'We Did It For Artie' narrative was ramped up by the press and, with the dumping of Beetson as national coach still fresh in the memory, Stanton returned to international duties with the interstate rivalry at fever pitch.

Ahead of the series Beetson had said: 'The only fair way to select the Australian coach is on the results of the interstate series. If Queensland get beaten fair and square then I won't be whingeing.'

Stanton replied: 'I don't necessarily agree with what Beetson is saying. It's a fact of life some years that some teams are stronger than others – and the coach can't change that.'

To add to the mix Stanton's abrupt and disciplined style was in complete contrast to Beetson's more laid-back approach but, critically, Stanton had the support of new ARL President Ken Arthurson and he had a record of delivering Test match victories.

In the first Test nine Queenslanders, led by captain Lewis, took to a bone-hard field which was not fit for international sport. The SCG's multi-use had caught up with it. The Socceroos had played there just a few days earlier and the soccer markings had not been covered up particularly well.

The opening exchanges became memorable for an all-in brawl triggered by Lee Crooks, who wanted to remind Price about their exchange from two years earlier.

Crooks said: 'We were packing down for the first scrum. I said to Ray: "Remember 82?" He said: "No." And I said: "Well you will in a minute." He's packed down and I have gone straight through the scrum and smacked him in the face. Anyway, we have won the scrum and our lads have gone after the ball so it's me and a load of Australians and it was mayhem.'

Post-battle the Lions more than held their own but another bit of bad luck created an opportunity for Australia and Lewis took full advantage. An injury to in-form scrum-half Neil Holding after 15 minutes left the Lions down to 12 men and, with Lydon preparing to take the field as injured Andy Gregory gave his Widnes team-mate a series of instructions, the Australia captain linked superbly with Wayne Pearce before diving between the sticks. The conversion made it 8-0.

Earlier, Mick Burke had missed a golden chance to give his team the lead after Australia had been penalised. Winger Ross Conlon was more accurate just a few minutes later.

With Lydon playing scrum-half for the first time in his life Britain did well to regroup and hold their own until half-time. Burke's first successful kick on 35 minutes meant the teams turned around at 8-2.

As the second half wore on, Myler's troops found it harder and harder to find a way around Australia's iron-clad defence. With Price crossing on 53 minutes, after a long ball out from Pearce had a created an overlap, it was critical that the tourists scored next. However, what followed was another midfield bust-up, with Crooks once again trading blows with Dave Brown after Noble and Greg Dowling had started it all off. Goodway tried to help his front-row partner reassemble his shoulder pads before he was sent to the sinbin for ten minutes. Dowling was also ordered to cool off.

The good news for Great Britain was they were still getting the rub of the penalty count and from the next penalty Lydon injected some pace into the play, drew his man and fed Drummond. The Leigh winger stepped inside four would-be tacklers in a scintillating run and produced a brilliant pass out of the tackle for 18-year-old Schofield to score between the posts. He became the youngest Ashes try-scorer, beating the record of Boustead (19 years and 70 days). The previous youngest British scorer was Alex Murphy (19 years and 74 days). Burke's kick made it 12-8 and it was game on but hopes of a famous victory were killed off as Boustead tiptoed his way down the line after Brett Kenny had broken the line. Then, with the light fading, Murray took advantage of a moment's indecision to touch down, breaking the double tackle of Foy and Lydon.

In the final few seconds Conescu went on a dart and was floored by an appalling forearm smash to the jaw by Hobbs. The Aussie hooker lost some teeth and the Britain substitute was sent off. It left a sour taste in the mouth for many watching and the Featherstone man was taken to task by the local media.

'I am obviously sorry about what happened to the hooker,' said Hobbs. 'It wasn't intentional. All I can say is that it is not my style of play. It was just a split-second thing.'

However the indiscretions in the first Test were made to look like a Women's Institute afternoon tea party compared to the events at the SCG the following weekend, when Queensland and New South Wales met for their second encounter of the year. As fireworks exploded in the sky, a brutal mass brawl erupted after just the second tackle of the match. It was triggered by the flurry of blows rained on Gene Miles by Balmain prop Steve Roach. Manly centre Chris Close also lost control after a bout of fisticuffs with Ray Price but was eventually floored after exchanging blows with the towering Roach.

Once the dust settled a dour battle ensued – it was 0-0 at half-time – and Queensland ran out 14-2 winners to secure another series victory.

Ahead of the second Test in Brisbane, Myler and Gemmell had a big decision to make at stand-off. They were keen to get Tony Myler on the park but he had only played one full game against Central Queensland and was struggling with a damaged thigh muscle.

Frank Myler said: 'I have got to be prepared to take a gamble and also to give Tony every chance of making it.'

Another player they wanted to be fit was Holding, who had not appeared since straining knee ligaments in the first Test. On standby was the fit-again Gregory.

Both Holding and Myler were risked, while Rayne came back in allowing Goodway to revert back to his preferred second-row spot. Worrall moved to loose forward, which meant Adams started on the bench alongside Gregory. Lydon was injured.

For the home side Grothe came in for Conlon on the wing and Price was replaced by Vautin, another Queenslander. Pearce moved to the lock position. It would be another bruising encounter with many, especially in the home camp, making it clear they thought the tourists had gone too far this time. Lewis appeared to have been targeted although Chris Burton remained adamant that no special plans were made for the Australia captain.

'I know it looks like it but we were not sent out with instructions to get Lewis,' recalled Burton.

In between the rough stuff Australia turned around 6-0 up with Grothe the beneficiary of a stunning offload from Miles for the game's opening score.

A remarkable effort from Pearce gave the home side breathing space as he burst through two tackles and displayed customary strength and determination to see off the despairing efforts of Burke and Drummond to dive over.

Some fabulous interplay from Drummond, Adams and Schofield during a 70-metres surge upfield resulted in the latter diving in at the corner to give Britain late hope.

However, there would be no dramatic late fightback, because Meninga had the final say, barging his way over from close range.

This time it was just 18-6 but it meant the Ashes were gone for at least two more years.

Britain's tactics in Brisbane caused an extraordinary response. Manly coach Bob Fulton even suggested that the Lions should be sent home.

'I love a good, hard rugged game of football but you can leave me out of all the elbowing and kneeing that went on. It was obvious from the start what they were going to do. It's a disgrace that they were allowed to get away with it.'

Fulton, coach of the crocked Vautin, also declared that Adams had been chosen for some 'special treatment' in the impending third Test and would be better off retiring from rugby league.

'Britain should do their team and Adams a favour by leaving him out of Saturday's Test. He should mark down an inglorious performance in Brisbane last week as his last appearance.'

Myler wasn't taking that lying down.

'It's those sort of statements that start a war. I think it's total trash and needs treating with contempt.'

Adams added: 'I won't be losing any sleep about it but at the same time talk like that incites players. As far as I am concerned the business in the Brisbane Test was a pure accident.'

Myler told Australian journalists he had told his team to 'cut out the rough stuff' but also that he wanted to hear something similar from Stanton.

'I don't want to see a repeat of the incidents in the first two Tests,' said the Great Britain coach. 'But we have been painted as the sole villains. It's pie in the sky stuff. The Aussies have to share the blame and the whole matter of one or two isolated incidents has been blown way out of proportion.'

Stanton responded by saying: 'We have attempted to play our football in the right spirit through the first two Tests. We will continue to do that at the SCG on Saturday. I just hope that the British players practise what they preach.'

Such was the pre-match build-up that ARL president Arthurson called both camps together to tell them that foul play would not be tolerated.

'There seems to be a feeling that the Australians have a right to get even for the Paul Vautin incident,' said Arthurson. 'They have no such right.'

While discipline was clearly a big deal, of more concern to the management was a serious flu bug affecting a number of players, including Myler, Worrall, Crooks, Burton, Pinner, Noble and Goodway.

There was some good news in that Schofield had shaken off a hip problem, although Hanley had a problem with his foot and a special pair of boots to support his instep was brought in. It meant that for the third successive Test the backs would remain unchanged. In the pack Hobbs, Case and Adams would replace the stricken Crooks, Rayne and Worrall.

The match followed a similar vein to the others. There was just one point in it at half-time with Hanley touching down for the visitors. But, once again, Britain just could not find a way to threaten for long enough as Grothe, Conescu and Jack all touched down to help secure a 20-7 win and a third successive 3-0 series whitewash.

When the Lions flew to New Zealand they did so without McKenzie, whose attention to detail would be sorely missed. There was also the problem of injured players not being flown home. It meant that by the time they played the final Test in Auckland they only had 17 fit to play. In between times, training sessions were cancelled ad hoc and on more than one occasion the players turned up to find the balls had been forgotten. With a fit and hungry New Zealand to ope with, it was not a huge surprise that they struggled.

The Kiwis had become a slick, well-oiled machine under Graham Lowe and the core of their side had been relatively unchanged for three years. Gary Kemble, Dean Bell, James Leuluai, Fred Ah Kuoi, Dane O'Hara, and both the Tamati and the Sorensen brothers played in all three Tests, which were won 12-0, 28-12 and 32-16.

One of those who had been a very interested spectator throughout the Lions tour was the recently-retired coach Gibson, who had been co-commentating on the Tests for TV.

In a newspaper column he wrote: 'From my vantage point Great Britain must pay specific attention to three areas. First, their dummy-half defence is brittle and I was of the opinion that Australia made more yards in this area than any other.

'Secondly, when a forward was the first receiver from the dummy half position he rarely had a backup runner within passing distance. And they continually tried to break Australia's forward defensive line one out. This manoeuvre failed on every occasion and allowed the runner to be gang tackled.

'Finally they must realise that tackling legs instead of heads will never leave them short on players and penalties and respect. Maybe most of all, you win football games.

'The British players will take back home more than memories from this tour. The experiences they have been exposed to on the football field will reap benefits further down the line. Their youthfulness will enable them to remember and re-enact some of the positive factors that have eluded them this series.

'When they get back home their clubs will be the beneficiaries but on the other hand some club officials with the Great Britain team could take only problems with them.

'In their anxiety to recruit and sign up players from Sydney and Brisbane for the English competition, there will be plenty of mistakes. It seems nearly all the leading clubs from Britain have some sort of representative in Australia. Their aims are all the same – they are hell bent on getting signatures on contracts.

'There will be success stories but also plenty of failures. The money they are prepared to offer will attract plenty of takers. Spending cash on one-year contracts has more problems than happy endings. For my money there would be far higher dividends if they recruited coaches.'

Ironically one of the headline-grabbing coaching changes of the summer involved Myler returning to Oldham as a full-time general manager. The announcement was made while he was in Australia and on his return he resigned as Great Britain coach. Meanwhile, manager Gemmell made his own little piece of history by failing to produce a tour report and he returned to Australia to start a new life.

Gibson was certainly right about the invasion of players for the start of the 1984 season. St Helens, thanks to the efforts of Ray French, managed to secure Meninga and the less-well-known Phil Veivers from Southern Suburbs, who would go on to become a great servant at Knowsley Road.

Parramatta's Muggleton joined Sterling at Hull and those two clubs announced a formal partnership.

Coach Arthur Bunting said: 'I know Parramatta desperately want Garry Schofield and when Peter Sterling was here he was keen for players like Shaun Patrick and Gary Divorty to go to Sydney. There are others who would benefit and I want them to go – in fact I think it is essential.'

Parramatta wingers Eric Grothe and Neil Hunt would join Leeds while Wigan brought the delights of Brett Kenny and Eastern Suburbs' prolific winger John Ferguson to Central Park. At Hull KR the less-heralded Gavin Miller arrived from Easts, a signing that proved to be an absolute masterstroke.

Not all clubs got it right, as Gibson also foretold. Queensland winger Steve Stacey disappeared from Salford in November after playing just seven games. He left a note to say he was returning to Australia. He did not tell coach Kevin Ashcroft he was leaving. It left chairman John Wilkinson having to sort the matter out with the help of solicitors.

The most remarkable influx was at Halifax. Chairman David Brook, whose company had sponsored Great Britain during the 1984 Ashes tour, used his time well down under.

Brook avoided the 'big names' to a large extent and signed eight Aussies, including 1982 tourist Chris Anderson. Joining him at Thrum Hall were young and up-and-coming stars such as Queensland-based prop Martin Bella, Canterbury back-rower Paul Langmack and his team-mate Michael Hagan, the 20-year-old half-back. Anderson, who was still only 32, replaced Colin Dixon as coach, which caused a great deal of unrest in the town and among the existing squad, as the popular Welshman had just led the side to promotion. Captain John Carroll asked to go on the transfer list and there were accusations that British players were being overlooked. The exciting influx of talent certainly had an effect on the gates at Thrum Hall, however. In the early stages of the season they more than doubled.

Other clubs also feeling a significant bounce were unbeaten Saints (gates up 30 per cent after six games), Wigan (up 15 per cent after five) and Hull KR (up 12 per cent after six). In fact, by the end of November two-thirds of the 36 professional clubs were reporting increases. Considering this was in the midst of the miners' strike and at a time when hooliganism was in its pomp, it was an encouraging development.

The RFL's search for a replacement for Myler began in earnest in early October with the nine-man board considering the respective merits of Peter Fox (Bradford), Malcolm Reilly (Castleford), Roger

Millward (Hull KR), Allan Agar (Featherstone) and Maurice Bamford (Leeds).

To the surprise of many in the game Bamford and Fox made the final two. The Bradford legend had performed the role before and his 'old school' reputation and outspoken nature made him a potentially difficult choice. His challenger had spent most of his coaching career in the amateur game and was at Oulton Raiders when he joined Leeds in November 1983.

In contrast, Millward had led Hull KR to unparalleled success in his first four years at Craven Park and was considered ahead of his time in terms of training methods, while Reilly had brought so much of what he had learned in Australia to bear at Wheldon Road since coming home – they built a gym at the ground, for example – and by 1984 Castleford were once again a force to be reckoned with. Reilly's methods were credited with helping to transform the careers of prop Kevin Ward and hooker Kevin Beardmore.

Bamford was named coach in late October by the odd vote in nine. His enthusiasm and passion for coaching had clearly struck a chord. He would eventually be full-time, leaving Leeds in May 1985 and being replaced by Fox. He would also oversee the newly-formed U-21s side, which replaced the U-24s, and become a development officer for Leeds City Council. Concentrating on youth would be an early theme of his tenure. He enlisted the help of Larder as his assistant.

'We've got a lot of young players in the game at the moment,' said the 48-year-old. 'In fact, I believe we've never been as well off for them as we are now. Up to now this young talent of ours has not been given a fair crack of the whip. We've been picking the tried and tested for too long. The time has now come for a reappraisal. We should be choosing the 20-year-olds who will still be young when the Australians come over in the winter of 1986.'

Bamford followed in his predecessors' footsteps by indicating that he wanted regular weekly sessions with the top players although he admitted that arranging those sessions might be a be problem. He would again be reliant on the goodwill of players and clubs, including his own. The plan was for him to stay on at Leeds until the end of the season and then concentrate on GB.

The national team were not due to play again until their France doubleheader in March and by then Great Britain would finally have a new manager to replace Gemmell. The contenders were Bob Ashby (Featherstone), Maurice Lindsay (Wigan), Phil Brunt (Castleford), Reg Parker (Blackpool) and Les Bettinson (Salford), the latter winning the day.

Bettinson was a Cumbrian who became a stalwart at the Willows, playing 330 times for Salford. He then coached the club to two titles in 1974 and 1976 before joining the board a year later.

The new manager's first job was to field questions from an eager press pack in the wake of Bamford's first Great Britain selection. There were ten new caps in the 15 players named; missing were Andy Gregory, Myler, Crooks, Burke, Schofield and Lydon.

Bamford said he wanted to foster a new team spirit. Taking a pride in the shirt would be a big theme of his stint but some of his selections were completely out of left field. Whitehaven's 20-year-old centre Vince Gribbin was plucked out of Division Two to partner Leeds' talented young star David Creasser. Gill was back in from the cold, as was the unflinching but unpredictable Rathbone. Hull's talented teenage pair of Gary Divorty and Andy Dannatt got the nod, Wigan's brilliant 18-year-old full-back Shaun Edwards was thrown in, while Leeds prop Roy Dickinson was one of only two over-25s in the side. The other was hooker Watkinson. It proved to be a dream start as 20-year-old Deryck Fox, another new face, led the way with two tries during a 50-4 romp at Headingley.

Bamford had promised that all 16 new faces in his 26-man squad would see action which meant another raft of alterations for the return match in Perpignan on 17 March. In came

Leigh full-back Chris Johnson, Warrington winger Phil Ford, Wigan front rowers Nick Kiss and Shaun Wane, while Hull KR scrum-half Paul Harkin and Leeds prop Roy Powell were on the bench.

However, this time things did not go so well with France establishing an 18-point half-time lead after two of their tries resulted from interception passes. The good news was the two-try debut of Ford, although Britain succumbed 24-16.

The Great Britain coach would have just one more trial match against a French Presidents XIII in Limoux in July before the Kiwis came calling and he planned to watch their matches against the Kangaroos in Auckland in preparation. On his return he would oversee summer training for a squad of 29. Eight other players were forced to decline the invitation to the training, four of whom had taken opportunities to play in the Sydney Premiership. Schofield linked up with Frank Stanton at Balmain (he found the training hard according to the former Kangaroos supremo), Crooks went to Western Suburbs, Goodway to Manly and the recalled Brian Noble opted to test himself at Cronulla.

A host of other English players headed south for the summer. It was testament to the rising stock of the British game which got another boost with the return of the War of the Roses. This new version of an old idea would see the Great Britain coach pick the teams but only players from Yorkshire and Lancashire could represent their counties of origin. It mirrored the Queensland v New South Wales series and the hope was that it would develop into a major event at the start of each season. Fox would take charge of the white rose boys and standing in the red corner would be his old foe Alex Murphy.

However, what certainly did elevate British rugby league to another level was the 1985 Challenge Cup Final in May. More than any other single game it did more to raise the profile of the sport, drawing 99,801 rugby league fans to London on a glorious summer's day.

Millions watched a remarkable 80 minutes of wonderful entertainment as a Brett Kenny-inspired Wigan held off a remarkable fightback from a Peter Sterling-inspired Hull to claim a 28-24 win. Three tries in 12 minutes brought Arthur Bunting's side back from the brink with James Leuluai famously instrumental. The victory would prove to be a springboard for Wigan. In contrast, it was the beginning of the end of the glory days for the Airlie Birds. At the timeit seemed impossible that is how it would transpire.

Wigan, who had been revived by a group of four local businessmen, started the 1985/86 season with Goodway, Ella and Dowling added to the squad at considerable expense. They also, reportedly, spent £300,000 on improving facilities; vice-chairman Maurice Lindsay was definitely thinking big.

'By the time it [Central Park] is finished we will be way ahead of many second division soccer clubs and starting to rival the likes of Manchester United for facilities,' said Lindsay. 'Rugby is increasingly becoming a family game and we believe it will take over from soccer as the main sport in the next ten years.'

While Lindsay's assertion seems ludicrous more than 30 years later, at the time it did not. Attendances across the four professional divisions were still dropping in soccer – they would not bottom out until 1986. In addition, hooliganism was still an enormous problem and the Heysel Stadium disaster meant the English game had been ostracised by the rest of Europe. With the Bradford City fire also happening in May of that year, the 1984/85 soccer season ended in terrible fashion, although for the first time in its history Division One games were now being shown live on TV. In August 1984 ITV started its new venture with Chelsea v Everton on a Friday night. Nobody knew it then but Pandora's Box had been opened.

In contrast, rugby league was attracting enormous TV audiences. More than nine million watched the series between Great Britain and New Zealand, and the biggest attendance for a Test between the two countries for 25 years (22,209) watched the decider at Elland Road.

The millions tuning in to the Saturday afternoon viewing enjoyed a different kind of tension from that they had enjoyed at Wembley six months earlier. Against the Kiwis substitute Lee Crooks had held his nerve to kick a touchline penalty two minutes from time to make it 6-6 and leave the series at 1-1.

Britain went into the three-Test adventure with a new captain, Harry Pinner, and a new mascot. Sully the lion became a familiar sight over the next few years. He was named after former Great Britain winger Clive Sullivan, who had just died from cancer. Final preparations involving the 26 players had gone well at Lilleshall and the 15 selected for the opener on 19 October travelled to Headingley watching a video montage of themselves doing good things on a rugby pitch. It was a trick that Larder had picked up on his travels; preparing the side mentally was something that the management was finally taking seriously.

Bamford, for all his talk of 'choosing 20-year-olds', brought back many of the 1984 tourists, although there were debuts for Widnes prop John Fieldhouse and Wigan second-rower Ian Potter, who was finally given his chance. There was also a surprise call-up for Saints stand-off Chris Arkwright, who was not in the original squad. He was selected after Hull KR's Chris Burton became unavailable because of suspension.

The Kiwis won their fourth successive match against Britain in thrilling style. In the dying moments Dane O'Hara, Gary Prohm and Kurt Sorensen combined to send Leuluai in for a try, although there was considerable consternation in the home camp at the validity of the final pass which looked to have gone forward. Olsen

Filipaina made it 24-22. A few minutes earlier some masterful work from Hanley created the opening for Lydon, who put Great Britain ahead for the first time since Andy Goodway's try had given his side the lead early on. It had been a ding-dong affair from the start. After Britain had taken the lead, the Kiwis claimed three tries in quick succession. But three goals kept their half-time lead down to 14-12. Lydon and Burke had shared the kicking duties.

Two weeks later Central Park was the venue for a must-win encounter for the host nation. With Crooks out with a thigh problem Bamford recalled 36-year-old Leeds prop Jeff Grayshon, who had not played for his country for three years.

Critically, New Zealand would be without their talismanic captain Mark Graham. He was a big miss as the home side levelled the series on the back of a remarkable effort from Schofield, who became the first Brit since Billy Boston (1964) to score four tries in a Test.

The decider also acted as the first World Cup match, with the format having been revived. The five Test-playing nations would play each other home and away over the next three years with the finale taking place in October 1988 down under. With the top two in the standings making the final, the Great Britain/New Zealand matches were always going to be pivotal, which may have added to the tension evident on the day.

Crooks kicked his side back from the brink after the visitors led 6-0 at half-time. The Hull man had come off the bench after Grayshon was retained but got his chance with Goodway off injured after just 25 minutes following a disgraceful assault by Sorensen. The big forward was sinbinned and tensions simmered throughout until a huge brawl broke out late in the second half. The police had to be called to help break up the players. It was not the ideal end, especially with so many people watching from their front rooms.

A fight of another kind was brewing at the RFL. Rugby league was alive with whispers of secret meetings involving leading clubs and in February 1986 the story broke. Ten clubs, led by Maurice Lindsay's Wigan and Hull (Roy Waudby), were threatening to break away if radical changes were not made. They were especially unhappy about the 15 per cent levy paid by top division clubs and the three up, three down promotion/relegation system. Lindsay was clearly a man prepared to ruffle feathers to get his way. Just a few weeks earlier he had incurred the wrath of the wider sporting community by unveiling the signing of two Springbok rugby union internationals. Winger Ray Mordt and loose forward Rob Louw had arrived from apartheid South Africa in defiance of a wider sporting ban.

Wigan clearly needed more money to fund their extraordinary transfer policy. Just days before the Super League story broke they announced the £100,000 signing of Lydon from cash-strapped Widnes having already spent £80,000 (plus two players) on Hanley from Bradford the previous September. Widnes secretary Ron Close said: 'There would have been no future without selling Joe, and Wigan's offer was too attractive to turn down.' Lydon's departure was the last straw for coach Eric Hughes, who resigned.

However, Lindsay's dreams of forcing the issue would largely be dashed at a tension-fuelled six-hour meeting of the Council at which second division clubs, led by Rochdale's Joe Grindrod, argued their case. In a classic case of who blinks first brinksmanship, a list of reforms was produced that included cutting the levy to 8 per cent and reducing the top flight to 14 in time for the 1987/88 campaign. There was no change to promotion and relegation. The Wigan supremo would have to wait ten years for his Super League dream to become reality and the irony that his club suffered most from its introduction would not be lost on many in the game. The salary cap and falling gates ended Wigan's stranglehold on the domestic game.

Things were not going much better for Lindsay's side on the pitch. Despite all that money being spent a terrible start to the 1985/86 season left Wigan too much ground to make up on surprise long-time leaders Halifax, who hung on to claim first spot in controversial circumstances.

There were calls to replay Halifax's final fixture against Featherstone following allegations that it had ended two minutes early with the score 13-13. One point was good enough for Chris Anderson's side to secure top spot while a single point was also sufficient for Rovers to relegate York, who still had one more match to play. Timekeeper Andrew Hardcastle was adamant that there was no evidence of wrongdoing.

Halifax's rise to prominence was reflected in the selection of their second-rower Neil James, who was on the bench for the France showdown in Avignon on 16 February. This game would be Britain's second World Cup match. James was among a number of recently arrived British players at Thrum Hall who Anderson knitted together with his band of Australians to great effect.

For that France game Bamford retained veteran Grayshon, although he suffered a late problem and had to pull out, allowing Wane to win his second cap. Gill, fully recovered from a leg break, came back on the wing for Lydon. Goodway was unavailable for personal reasons, which meant Crooks returned.

In France, the home side fought back from 10-2 down to take a share of the spoils, which rocked Bamford's plans. He had wanted to blood some more new faces when the teams met again at Wigan on 1 March but the 10-10 scoreline caused a rethink.

'What I want to avoid at Wigan is a further denting of confidence, not only for the team but for the spectators,' said the GB coach. 'We need to go out and not only win, but win well at Wigan and it would not be fair to give new lads this kind of pressure in their first Test.'

Bamford did try some new faces at Central Park: James was promoted to the starting line-up and Castleford centre Tony Marchant, Hull KR winger David Laws and Leeds back-rower Kevin Rayne all made their debuts. He also wanted to play Grayshon but the Leeds man just could not shake off a twisted ankle. The 17-man squad also included Hunslet's highly regarded half-back Graham King but the selection of an experienced scrum-half, playing in the lower reaches of Division Two, raised more eyebrows.

The side, lacking the injured Pinner and Hanley, did little to suggest they would worry the Australians the following autumn in running out 24-10 winners although there were some incisive bursts from James and his try was richly deserved. The handling ability of Crooks was also to the fore.

It left Bamford, Larder and Bettinson with plenty to consider. Three trial matches in late August against a Humberside XIII, Wigan and St Helens were arranged, followed by a four-day camp at Lilleshall in early September. It was better than nothing but in contrast Don Furner's Kangaroos played three Tests against New Zealand in July and then would stop of at Papua New Guinea ahead of arriving in Manchester in early October.

The manner in which Australia comprehensively dispatched New Zealand was an ominous early sign. They then ran in 12 tries as PNG were battered 62-12, even though two of the most feared Invincibles controversially did not make the plane: despite his remarkable efforts to make the trip Pearce was left out on 'fitness' grounds. Grothe also stayed at home in slightly strange circumstances.

In the third Test against New Zealand, Pearce tore cruciate ligaments in his left knee but somehow managed to recover in time. Having been given the all clear to play by his specialist at the end of September, he led his international team-mates on a

10k run the day before his official ARL fitness test. However, the Australian team doctor Bill Monaghan deemed him not fit.

Pearce said: 'Both my specialist and myself are satisfied that I have made a complete recovery. But I just have to accept what's happened.'

Grothe was less willing to take it on the chin. Having helped Parramatta to Grand Final glory he experienced swelling on his knee but after a week's rest was expected to be fine. But Monaghan said no at the second time of asking.

'This is what angers me most,' said Grothe, who even had his official tour pictures taken. 'The way it was done. For me it was train or else. Where were the rest of the blokes?'

'Shearer's bloody lucky to get a tour,' said the now-retired but still vocal Ray Price. 'Go to any pub or club in town and they'll tell you that clubs like Manly and Canterbury are getting more than a little extra help from influential people.'

The former Aussie loose forward was referring to Manly winger Dale Shearer, who had a long-standing groin issue, as did Canterbury's Steve Folkes. Greg Alexander, the Penrith half-back, was a late replacement for Grothe.

With Pearce and Grothe out, only five of the Invincibles returned to Britain – Lewis (c) Sterling (vc), Kenny, Meninga and Miles. The 1986 tour would prove the perfect platform for the Australia captain to re-emphasise his standing within the game as its undisputed king. To watch Lewis in full flow was to see that balding head motionless in deep thought while the legs pumped furiously. A team-mate of the great Hungarian soccer player Ferenc Puskas once said that if there were 1,000 ways to score a goal then Puskas would find the 1,001st. Lewis was the rugby league equivalent. His extraordinary ability to do things that nobody could see coming was without parallel. He saw and executed passes that were bordering on obscene and he did it in a way that unites all truly great sportsmen. He made the sublime look easy.

More than 30,000 packed Central Park as Lewis captained the Kangaroos to an opening 26-18 victory over a powerful Wigan side now coached by Phil owe and lacking talismanic try machine Ellery Hanley. Fresh from scoring 55 tries, the Leeds-born star would go on to register a staggering 63 tries in 1986/87.

'Ellery was a freak,' recalls team-mate Crooks. 'He could run faster going backwards than most of us running normally.'

Larder, who would help England win the rugby union World Cup in 2003 and who was part of the 2001 British Lions management team, described Hanley as the best player he ever worked with. Better than Johnny Wilkinson, Jason Robinson, Brian O'Driscoll ... the lot.

The prospect of a Lewis v Hanley duel was certainly mouth-watering. The Wigan player's absence against France earlier in the year was clearly felt and his fitness remained an issue in the run-up to the first Test at Old Trafford. A knee problem was hindering his ability to perform at the very top of his game. Pinner, the Britain captain of 1985, was certainly out of the reckoning, though. A mysterious problem affecting his ankle had meant he was unavailable to train with the squad at Lilleshall.

Bamford and co were leaving no stone unturned in their attempts to ensure ideal preparation and even employed former American football kicker Dave Alred to help pass on a few tips to the likes of Lydon and Crooks. The training squad was also swelling in size. By the end of September it was up to 35 with the additions of Gill, Featherstone duo Peter Smith and Paul Lyman and Bradford's Keith Mumby. The four additions had all performed well in Yorkshire's defeat of Lancashire in the War of the Roses match.

Bamford unveiled his 15-man squad for the first Test on 12 October. Watkinson would take over the captaincy and pack down alongside Ward, who was playing his second Test at the age of 29. Lydon was named full-back and Marchant made his debut on the wing. There were many calls for Andy Gregory to return to scrum-half but Fox, so effective for Yorkshire a month earlier, got the nod.

The scale of the task facing Great Britain was reinforced by the Kangaroos' efforts in their three other warm-up matches before the first Test. The midweek team, nicknamed 'F Troop', destroyed Hull KR 46-10 and Cumbria 48-12 while a Leeds side that included four Australians, were beaten 40-0.

Furner had so many options in the back division he was able to leave Meninga on the bench along with Terry Lamb, scorer of five tries against Hull KR. Such was the Canterbury stand-off's form, his non-selection for the starting line-up proved the biggest source of debate in the run-up to the clash. The problem for Lamb was that he was trying to depose Lewis.

Hanley weighed in at an award lunch, suggesting that Lamb was the better. 'Lewis cannot make a break against our defence,' said the British lynchpin. 'He will use the pass or the kick and they are the only options he has.'

On the eve of the Test former Australia full-back, Graham Eadie, writing in a newspaper column, delivered a scathing assessment of the home side's chances.

'The Great Britain coach, Maurice Bamford, is making the same mistake that all others have by ignoring youth and sticking with old failed players. He has a squad of 50 [sic] and has left the door open to add more players. It is impossible to get a team to function properly when you have so many in a squad.

'A couple of the back rowers have impressed but I don't think they will have it up front where Australia is very strong. I can see an overall difference of about 50 points between Australia and Great Britain over the three Tests.'

French referee Monsieur Rascagneres, in his distinctive orange shirt, was also back in Ashes action four years on from his memorable officiating debut, and when Lydon set the record 50,000 crowd at Old Trafford alight with a brilliant effort to reduce the arrears to 16-10 early in the second half anything seemed possible.

But the raucous British fans had barely calmed down when one step and a shuffle from Lewis quelled their optimism and he set up Miles for a try under the posts.

By the time Schofield crossed for Britain's third try just seconds before the final hooter, Furner's side were away and clear.

Faced with coming to terms with a 38-16 defeat, coach Bamford took the unusual step of telling his dejected players he would pick the same team for the second Test. The following month he penned an article to explain why.

'Test matches between Great Britain and Australia over the last 16 years – since 1970 – have been something of an uphill struggle for us. Any coach will tell you that confidence in one's self and one's team-mates is vitally important.

'The first thing I had to do immediately after the game was rebuild the shattered confidence of that team. Before the Test every member of the squad had been confident they could win. I had to shake the team out of their disappointment. The only thing I could say was "same team for the second Test".

'That proved I had confidence in them and hopefully that their own confident attitude before the Test had been rebuilt enough for them to say, "We're going to have another chance at Elland Road."'

For the Great Britain coach events in Leeds two weeks later would prove something of a nadir. On more than one occasion the crowd chanted 'what a load of rubbish' as his team were surgically dismantled 34-4. Bamford's boys did not deserve such disrespect; their opponents treated the crowd to some exquisite handling that would not have looked out of place in top-class basketball. Time and again the Kangaroos kept the ball alive in remarkable fashion. Such was their dominance they could have doubled the six tries they registered and it would not have been unfair. That was all after the home side more than held their own for the first 20 minutes, during which there were some encouraging moments for new boy Barry Ledger on the wing. Hanley was absent because of his troublesome knee so Marchant moved into the centres allowing the St Helens debutant to play in his favoured position.

ARL president Ken Arthurson said: 'This is the hottest side I've ever seen. The 1982 Roos were a wonderful team but many of them were near the end of their careers and took little rests in games.'

While the Aussie press were purring about their stellar side, the Great Britain coach took the defeats hard. He had invested so much into the project and he and Larder had overseen so many positive changes it was difficult to reconcile the fact that Great Britain seemed just as far away from the Kangaroos as they had done four years earlier.

Five changes were made for Central Park, which also acted as GB's third World Cup fixture. With Britain having failed to win their previous two games the prospect of not making the final was now a real possibility. It was later conceded by manager Bettinson that some of the changes were made because they had to be seen to be trying something new to help restore the public's confidence. They decided to pick a few in-form players. With Pinner's ankle finally responding to treatment, the St Helens loose forward was brought back in, as was Andy Gregory, riding high with rampant Wigan. His team-mate David Stephenson was recalled after four years in the wilderness, Widnes winger John Basnett won his second and final cap two years after his last and Chris Burton came into the second row. The Australian press suggested that the appearance of the Hull KR second-rower indicated that their beleaguered hosts might try a more disruptive game plan.

It did not look good in the early stages as the Kangaroos surged into a 12-0 lead after 15 minutes, but then the home side settled down and started to play. By half-time the lead had been halved with Pinner and Myler linking up superbly to put Schofield through a gap.

Myler was again involved as Britain levelled matters. This time Stephenson supplied the final ball for the Hull youngster to claim his second try of the afternoon.

The sin-binning of Burton for a high tackle on Lewis changed the momentum, although Australia's penalty try on 57 minutes was tinged with controversy. Basnett had tackled Shearer without the ball but there was still a long a way to go for the Australia winger.

A goal and a drop-goal kept the home side in it but then Lewis did what Lewis does and that was that. He made a mesmeric run down the line and touched down 11 minutes from time, securing a 24-15 win.

Furner's squad became the unbeatables and Lewis was adamant they were better than the Invincibles. Even Meninga and Sterling, who had less reason to be biased, gave Furner's side the nod due to the better standard of opposition, although Hull's 1982 side might have begged to differ.

Afterwards Bamford said it was the first time his team had stuck to his game plan. It would also be the last time they would do so. The following month he stepped down as coach citing his desire not to tour in 1988. His wife had health concerns and it was accepted that leaving now would give his replacement the time to plan. Bamford would return to coach Leeds after Fox was ousted from the Headingley hotseat.

For GB, this time around, there would be no official selection procedure to find a replacement. After a couple of informal chats,

38-year-old Malcolm Reilly became national coach in December 1986 with Larder as his assistant and Bettinson remaining as manager. After 11 years in charge at Castleford Reilly would take on the GB role full-time once the season finished in May.

Reilly's legendary status would ensure he got the respect of the players. As a player he was something of a phenomenon, having only turned to rugby league aged 19 when the soccer match he was due to play was cancelled because of bad weather. Two years later he won the Lance Todd Trophy at Wembley. He was not bombastic in nature and concentrated on issuing concise, calm instructions. His dedication to fitness meant that even as he closed in on 40 he could do anything he asked his players to do. Players would run through a brick wall for Reilly because they knew that if it came down to a fight between a brick wall and their coach, there was only going to be one winner. He also took 'being competitive' to new levels. Stories of him demanding to arm wrestle his players have become the stuff of legend although when he met his match in the form of Halifax prop Paul Dixon he just could not let it go.

'I was just going to bed and Mal demanded a rematch,' recalls Dixon. 'He did eventually beat me with my right hand but he couldn't beat me with my left.'

It is remarkable to consider, decades after the event, that a man of Reilly's playing ability made just nine appearances for Great Britain over a five-month spell in 1970. His move to Manly a year later meant the RFL would not allow his selection and then on his return in late 1975 he became player-coach at Wheldon Road. There were murmurings of a recall thereafter but nothing more happened. The man himself was never told why he wasn't recalled to the international set-up although the story goes that his time in Australia was considered too much of an act of rugby league treason.

Reilly's strategy was to build an Ashes side around a handful of players he knew he could trust. He started with Ellery Hanley and Kevin Ward. Added to the list later were Andy Gregory, Shaun Edwards, Kevin Beardmore and Garry Schofield, and Martin Offiah in time. Before Reilly could concentrate on the 1988 trip, he would have just six opportunities to try out different options – two games against PNG and four against France.

The first came just a month after his appointment, at home against France on 24 January 1987. The game would also act as Britain's fourth World Cup pool game. Injuries to Ward, Basnett and Myler meant there had to be opportunities for others to stake a claim. There was also an problem with Andy Gregory so his clubmate Edwards partnered new captain Hanley in the halves. There were debuts for Warrington duo Mike Gregory (loose forward) and Mark Forster (winger) plus St Helens experienced second-rower Roy Haggerty, while Castleford prop Keith England made the bench.

Gregory caught the eye as the French were thrashed 52-4. He crossed twice, as did Edwards and Hanley.

For the return in Carcassonne two weeks later Chris Burton was added to the second row in place of Goodway, and England was given a start in place of Crooks. Andy Gregory, now at peace with Wigan, was back in the No 7 jersey so Edwards moved to stand-off, Hanley to centre and Stephenson dropped to the bench where he was joined by Dixon.

However, the match nearly never took place. Upheaval within the French RFL – their Australian coach Tas Baitieri was sacked and their president suspended – led to the players refusing to play. They only agreed to leave their dressing rooms after a rallying call from Baitieri. Financial problems would mean France could not tour down under later that summer so Australia, New Zealand and PNG were all awarded two World Cup points.

With French pride on the line, Reilly's players were subjected to some of the worst thuggery seen on a pitch in recent times. Mike

Gregory had his nose and cheekbone broken by a punch from prop Rabot, and Schofield was kicked on the floor. The Great Britain coach called his hosts 'animals'. His side ran out 20-10 winners after trailing at half-time.

With no more international action until 24 October when the touring Kumuls would play their first Test on British soil, Reilly, Larder and Bettinson began to plan for the following year's Ashes series. One of their first jobs was to find a replacement for fitness consultant McKenzie. The Carnegie College lecturer had overseen the previous summer's training squads and coined the phrase 'wheelbarrow players'. There were still too many professionals 'who will not train unless they are pushed'. McKenzie cited examples of amateur swimmers and runners who did not need financial incentives to push themselves. Someone who knew all about that was Yorkshire-based athletics coach Wilf Paish, the man behind the success of Tessa Sanderson, Peter Elliott and others.

The GB management turned to Paish for advice, although with Reilly in charge there would be no place to hide for those not physically right. At the end of the 1986/87 season the Great Britain coach outlined his demands. Those wishing to play for him were expected to raise their games ahead of testing at Carnegie College in August. Before that there would be two two-day summer training camps for 36 players.

Unlike his predecessors Reilly would complete all the tests himself. This would prove something of a masterstroke. In the 12-minute run both Reilly and Larder were among the quickest and in the gym the coach really came into his own, stunning his players by lifting more weight than any of them. There's nothing like being shown up by the 'old man' of the party to incentivise a group of alpha males to do better. Courtesy of the diligent Larder, every player now had a comprehensive personal profile. The good news for Britain was a number of their top stars were clearly benefitting from the gradual move towards full-time professionalism. The likes of Edwards and Hanley consistently produced some of the best Test results under Reilly and Wigan's drive for dominance would ultimately benefit the national side.

By the time of the Papua New Guinea encounter, Reilly was restless. He found it hard to adjust to the lack of regular contact with players now that he was full-time with the RFL but such was his will to win that his attention to detail became obsessive. The new season could not come quickly enough, which meant that at least he could watch domestic matches. He was certainly a very interested spectator when Fox again got one over his old foe Murphy as Yorkshire, with Ward and Hanley to the fore, retained the War of the Roses trophy with a 16-10 win at Central Park.

Many of Reilly's Ashes squad would come from Wigan's title-winning team of 1986/87. Graham Lowe's side finished 15 points clear of St Helens and Warrington and won 28 of their 30 league fixtures. It made sense to choose tried and tested club combinations with so little match time before the first Ashes Test on 11 June. That belief was reinforced by Wigan's defeat of Australian champions Manly 8-2 in the first World Club Championship final in front of a 36,895 crowd at Central Park. Their side comprised 13 Englishmen, and not since 1978 had a British club side beaten a team from Australia.

'Wigan matched Manly in every aspect on that field,' said coach Lowe. 'We were more disciplined, which is so vital in tight matches, as my players have learned. Physically we more than matched them, our commitment was absolutely spot on. We had the mental toughness to win the game, our defensive commitment was magnificent and we lifted away a barrier by defeating them.'

Against PNG the Central Park outfit provided eight of the team, the most from any one club in 37 years. In came full-back Steve Hampson and experienced prop Brian Case. Injuries afforded an opportunity for St Helens hooker Paul Groves and Leeds' dynamic back-rower Paul Medley to stake a claim. The latter did so in great style during a 42-0 victory. Beardmore's battle to stay clear of problems was a long-term concern, however.

The following month Reilly raised eyebrows with an interview he did with the Australian media. He said: 'With players like Brett Kenny, Wally Lewis and Peter Sterling dictating in the middle of the park, even Benny Hill could have coached a winning side. I don't mean to sound disrespectful to the coaches involved but the Kangaroos did have a huge advantage in playing strength.'

The Great Britain management spent the run-up to Christmas working out 16 of their 28-man Ashes squad. The remainder were identified in the first four months of 1988. For Larder there was still the day-to-day job of building his network of development officers to ramp up the output of coaching courses and clinics at all levels of the game. But he was unable to fix the problem caused by the rift between BARLA and the RFL, which meant the country's best juniors could often be compromised because BARLA and the RFL/Schools wanted them for their respective age-group sides. The development system lacked co-ordination.

'The New Zealanders, through their junior Kiwi team, allow their best young players to be in one side regardless of their ethnic background or whether they are professional or not. At present they take their U-19s players in two four-day training camps each year but they soon hope to move the system into U-17s and U-15s. This is frightening because it will mean young players will be introduced to intensive weights and power-producing methods, like heavyweight training, from the moment they leave puberty.

'Having such camps enables the national coaching officials to keep a close eye on each young player's development while advising them on physical conditioning, diet and individual skills. We are trying to do the same thing here in the UK. We believe that our players are better than in New Zealand but we can't hit the right section of kids because the system is split.'

However, as the one man who had been on the inside since 1982 and therefore able to see how much progress had been made, Larder was genuinely hopeful of causing an upset down under.

'I truly believe, and I told Australian coaching director Peter Corcoran so recently, that our next set of professional tourists are going down under with a real chance of winning. This is the first time I have felt like this since I took this job on several years ago and I'll be very disappointed if we don't reach the World Cup final.'

Unless they could beat Australia in the third Test and then beat the Kiwis in a one-off Test eight days later they would fail to reach the final. It was certainly a tall order. Before all that were two dates with France, who had restored some order thanks to their new coach Jacques Jorda. On 24 January the teams met in Avignon when 29-year-old Des Drummond was on the wing. He was enjoying a new lease of life at Warrington. Paul Loughlin, the stylish centre from St Helens, was also in, as was Oldham's Scottish-born prop Hugh Waddell, who had caught the eye as the high-flying Division Two outfit reached the semi-finals of the John Player Trophy. Waddell had started playing professional rugby league after spotting an advert asking for rugby league players while on holiday in Blackpool, having been turned down by Keighley who were worried about him travelling to and from his home in Burton upon Trent. St Helens back-rower Andy Platt was also recalled, Beardmore was fit enough to wear the No 9 shirt and Widnes winger Martin Offiah was deemed good enough after just half a season in the game. While the London-born union convert was definitely quick and could score tries by the bucketload, many pundits believed his slightly unorthodox defensive methods would be cruelly exposed by the Kangaroos.

The Test in Avignon was in the balance until Schofield, in characteristic style, grabbed a French pass and went in for an interception try; the visitors eventually claimed a 28-14 win.

Two weeks later at Headingley, Castleford winger David Plange was handed an opportunity, with Offiah making way. In the forwards, arm-wrestle king Dixon's better defensive qualities meant he was tried in the second row ahead of Medley.

Gregory and Hanley both touched down inside five minutes but the visitors did not capitulate and Great Britain took the spoils 30-12 thanks to further efforts from Hanley, Plange and Schofield.

On 5 April 24 names were unveiled for the trip with three others to be selected from a group of nine. The squad was announced this way because several key men had injury doubts. Chief among these was Crooks, who was working his way back after a shoulder injury. There were also concerns about the robustness of Drummond's troublesome knee.

Critics highlighted the absence of Widnes players among the party. Offiah and David Hulme were the only representatives from the soon-to-be league champions and the problems started to mount up as Hampson, who was expected to play in the Tests, broke his arm. Another certainty for the Tests was Goodway but he then withdrew because he was planning to open a restaurant and wanted to be in the UK to oversee the final preparations.

With just three Premiership matches left – the squad would fly out to PNG the day after the final – the management decided to gamble on Crooks, Drummond and Waddell, while Haggerty replaced Goodway. Halifax's Ian Wilkinson was also drafted in. His ability to play in a number of positions worked in his favour.

But their plans were again disrupted when Lydon and Drummond were withdrawn at the behest of the RFL. Both players had been involved in clashes with spectators in the latter part of the season and it was alleged that Drummond had been racially abused at Widnes during their Premiership semi-final. Lydon's incident happened on April 1 when Wigan took on St Helens.

Both players were said to be devastated at the harshness of the punishment which lead to a call-up for Leeds centre Carl Gibson. Widnes flier Darren Wright would also fly out after the squad reached Australia.

On the eve of departure Reilly said: 'I'm happy with the squad that we've chosen and, barring further injuries, it's one that can go from strength to strength out there. We have some fabulous backs. It's up to us to get a pack together that can compete at this level.'

The final 26-man squad read as follows:

Manager: Les Bettison

Coach: Mal Reilly

Assistant coach: Phil Larder

Business manager/PR: David Howes

Forwards: Kevin Beardmore (Castleford), Brian Case (Wigan), Lee Crooks (Leeds), Paul Dixon (Halifax), Karl Fairbank (Bradford), Mike Gregory (Warrington), Paul Groves (St Helens), Roy Haggerty (St Helens), Paul Medley (Leeds), Andy Platt (St Helens), Roy Powell (Leeds), Hugh Waddell (Oldham), Kevin Ward (Castleford).

Backs: Shaun Edwards (Wigan), Mike Ford (Oldham), Phil Ford (Bradford), Carl Gibson (Leeds), Henderson Gill (Wigan), Andy Gregory (Wigan), Ellery Hanley (Wigan), David Hulme (Widnes), Paul Loughlin (St Helens), Martin Offiah (Widnes), Garry Schofield (Leeds), David Stephenson (Leeds), Ian Wilkinson (Leeds).

In Papua, the heat was stifling and staying hydrated was a big concern, especially for the coach. And when Edwards limped off the pitch at Port Moresby after just seven minutes he must have wished they could have gone straight to Australia. It was an injury that would require surgery. The tourists won that game 42-22.

After one more club game, the Lions headed south and arrived to find a country in the grip of national fervour; the bicentennial celebrations were in full swing. In January 1788 11 ships had arrived in what would become Sydney harbour but this party from Britain was somewhat smaller. With the State of Origin under way there were concerns that the Lions were not big news. But after years of easy victories the problem was that they were a hard sell which would be reflected in the attendances for the Test matches.

While Edwards was laid up his British colleagues were adjusting to life under Sergeant Reilly. As a player Reilly had embraced the physical challenge set by John Whiteley on the 1970 tour and 18 years later he was hellbent on making sure his charges were in the best physical shape of their lives. If any of the squad were considering complaining at the harshness of the regime it would not be long before their coach would give them a quick reminder that, at the age of 40, he could still outlast them regardless of the challenge.

Following an easy win in Cairns, the tour started in earnest with a trip to Newcastle Knights. Unlike previous sojourns the RFL wanted a much tougher lead-up to the first Test, which obviously constituted a gamble. A couple of bad defeats might have dampened spirits and that is exactly how it played out.

A 28-12 victory in Newcastle was followed by a 36-12 reverse to Northern Division in Tamworth. Then, in their final warm-up, Britain were humiliated 30-0 by Premiership champions Manly.

But the British management had taken a gamble by not playing many of their star men because they felt the risk of injury was too great. It meant that Hanley, both Gregorys, Ward, Beardmore, Dixon, Platt and Schofield received extra training instead of playing.

With Crooks having pulled a thigh muscle Reilly would have to name a pack light on international experience. His response was to push Dixon into the front row.

'We can match them man-for-man along the line,' he said. 'Ellery Hanley for Bob Lindner. Andy Platt is every bit as good as Paul Vautin. Andy Gregory is an outstanding player. Kevin Ward outplayed the Canberra forward [Sam Backo] in the Grand Final. It all depends on how we combine,' he said. But Reilly was less complimentary about the British game as a whole.

'The development of the game at home is a problem. There is a scheme agreed on but it's ten years too bloody late. It's one of the reasons I've relinquished [the position as GB coach] for Leeds. There can be no improvement in international games until development of the domestic game improves. Realistically, that will take six to ten years.

'[In England] I've got to teach basic skills to players already in the first team. Correct attitudes are not being developed towards the game. Schools of excellence have to be set up.'

Reilly's assertions about Ward and Hanley certainly appeared to be valid as his side performed heroically to establish a 6-0 lead at half-time in Sydney. The Castleford prop scattered Kangaroos to all parts while Hanley showed his class to claim the first try, brushing off Sterling and then just having the pace to see off Lindner's challenge.

In the second half Don Furner's men rallied impressively with Sam Backo crossing six minutes in. With Sterling getting a grip on proceedings, centre Peter Jackson's two tries in 11 minutes decided the contest and Australia won it 17-6.

'The courage and commitment were there but big improvements can be made,' said Reilly. 'Our organised defence will have to be worked on. We were split wide out. We allowed them too much possession and made elementary mistakes instead of putting pressure on. If we can organise ourselves around a sound kicking game we have a good chance. I'm not bothered who Australia pick for the second Test or what changes they make. We have better players.'

Reilly always demonstrated great clarity of thought and calmness under pressure but even he must have been bemoaning his luck when Schofield broke his jaw in the next tour match against a Combined Brisbane XIII. Schofield flew home with Medley, who had a serious neck injury, and with the Central Queensland game on 17 June imminent, the Lions were down to 15 fit players.

The Widnes duo of Andy Currier and Paul Hulme were hastily flown out to bolster the ranks.

Another player with a big problem was Platt, who battled on despite having a flaked bone in his wrist. The good news was that the bone was not weight-bearing. However, he required a constant supply of painkilling injections. The Saints back-rower was named in the XIII for the second Test at Lang Park. Hanley was moved back into the centres to replace Stephenson and played alongside in-form Phil Ford, who moved off the wing. This freed up a spot for Henderson Gill. In the forwards Mike Gregory replaced his captain at loose forward, Dixon moved back into his favoured second-row position and Powell came off the bench and into the front row.

For Australias, Pearce returned to the No 13 jersey in place of Linder, although the absence of local favourite Allan Langer was quite a problem for the scoreboard operator who flashed up 'Bullfrog – shame our favourite No 7 isn't here'. Bullfrog was a reference to team manager Peter Moore.

Pearce's presence proved important while Lewis upped his game to inspire the hosts to a 34-14 Ashes-securing success. The Kangaroos captain had demanded and delivered a fast start – they were 14-4 up after 20 minutes – and was also upset at the number of high tackles dished out by the tourists, who were clearly growing frustrated that they were not doing themselves justice.

'They would do better in Test matches if they tried to tackle around the legs and not knock our heads off,' Lewis told reporters in the dressing room. 'We had to take it on the nose all night and still come up with a win without retaliating.'

'There was high tackling on both sides,' was Reilly's response. 'If that's what the Australians are saying it sounds like whingeing. Our blokes copped plenty too. And the Australians, I can tell you, were guilty of a lot of provocation.'

Some years later the Great Britain coach admitted he had got his side too worked up and the rush of early penalties meant they conceded too much of the early momentum.

Waiting for The Lions in Sydney was ARL chairman Arthurson, who just like four years earlier, called a peace summit of sorts ahead of the third Test. It didn't help the atmosphere when papers such as the *Sydney Daily Mirror* splashed the headline: 'Bloody revenge – We'll Smash the Poms to Pieces Next Time'. At that time in Australia there was a particularly unhealthy tabloid battle, so certain editors were encouraged to up the sensationalist ante.

With Furner coaching a Presidents XIII to a 24-16 victory in the final warm-up game ahead of the third Test, the scene was set for the Kangaroos to win their fifth straight series 3-0. Such was the certainty among home fans that with less than a week to go before kick-off only 4,000 tickets were sold. In the end just under 16,000 would attend.

Meanwhile the bookmakers were giving Great Britain a 25-point start, which seemed reasonably fair with Dixon, Platt and Beardmore now on the sidelines. It meant Widnes half-back Paul Hulme made his Test debut at hooker, a position he had never played before. Key forward Ward was struggling with a very sore ankle but played, as did centre Stephenson, who took to the field with a shoulder problem. Winger Ford filled in at full-back and prop Powell was a late replacement for the injured Richie Eyres, who had played just once after flying in with John Joyner to bulk up the numbers. In the front row Waddell made his debut. Even before he had gained international recognition the Oldham player had had a dream that he played just one Test which Great Britain won. What transpired on that famous night in Sydney was certainly the stuff that dreams are made of.

While Mike Gregory's now famous run to the line sealed the victory, the chance was created by his namesake Andy. The scrum-half played the game of his life to inspire the Lions and his over-the-top pass to Martin Offiah after 16 minutes got the ball rolling. Another brilliant pass out of the tackle from Ward had created the opportunity.

At the quarter point the Wigan playmaker teased the Australia defence again before delivering a pass inside to Ford, who weaved his way to the line to double Britain's advantage when there appeared little danger of him doing so. It was 10-0 and remained so until the interval.

And when the little No 7's grubber kick fell nicely for Henderson Gill to make it 16-6 early in the second half a win looked on the cards. It was a critical score after Lewis had got his side off the mark just a couple of minutes earlier.

Backo reduced the arrears by barging over to score for the third successive Test but then it was Loughlin's turn to take centre stage with a quite brilliant line break which took the long-striding St Helens centre past three defenders. He released Gill on his outside but there was still 40 metres to go. The Wigan winger outpaced Garry Jack; cue dancing in the stands and on the pitch.

Fittingly, it was Andy Gregory who would set up Britain's final score. With seven minutes left he took the ball on his own

10-metre line and, showing remarkable acceleration, embarrassed two Kangaroos, who ended up tackling each other. With Martin Offiah steaming up on the outside but being pulled back by Lewis, there was a moment's worry that Mike Gregory would not have the legs to keep Pearce at bay. But from 40 metres out it was obvious he did. They had won for the first time on Australian soil for 14 years and a run of 15 successive defeats at the hands of the Kangaroos had been ended in spectacular fashion.

In a newspaper article, Lewis wrote: 'They were a different team yesterday. Maybe the new players had something to do with that but I am sure all of them would agree the bloke who deserves most of the credit is Malcolm Reilly.

'Malcolm has copped more flak this tour as coach than he ever did as a player but he kept plugging away and has pulled off one of the great form reversals of all time. All of our blokes would prefer to forget the game but it's not the end of the world. A few good things came out of the series for Australia, such as the emergence of Peter Jackson and Sam Backo. We have to look hard now at some of our weaknesses but there is still plenty there to build on.'

The victory meant that if Reilly's men could beat New Zealand in Christchurch on 17 July they would return in October to take on Australia in the World Cup final.

It wasn't to be, though. In awful conditions the new-look Kiwis edged it 12-10 with substitute Gary Freeman scoring two first-half-tries. The loss of Hanley with 15 minutes to go had a detrimental effect and the Lions could not quite claw back the gap. It was a bitter blow after the highs of Sydney but all those in the 1988 squad needed to consider the bigger picture. The most important gap had been closed.

Chapter Eleven

The Postscript

O N 4 December 1994 the era of the Invincibles came to an end.

In a town known for its bullfighting festival, one of rugby league's greatest matadors said farewell. Just 5,000 were there to see Mal Meninga play his final match for Australia in Béziers, although fittingly he bagged a try and so did a lot of his team-mates. France were crushed 74-0.

Before that moment, though, the giant centre from Queensland would offer a constant reminder that, although British rugby had rediscovered its mojo, becoming top dog was another matter. Twice in three years (1990 and 1992) Meninga was on hand to keep Malcolm Reilly's boys at bay.

The early 90s were undeniably the high point for the Ashes in the modern era with a string of titanic battles. Reilly kept driving on his countrymen and they kept getting closer and closer.

In 1990 Meninga's late try at Old Trafford kept his side in the series and he led them to a 14-0 win at Elland Road in the third Test.

Two years later the tourists levelled the series with a stunning 33-10 win when all six forwards came from Wigan and Schofield and Edwards pulling the strings at half-back. But once again the Australia captain did for them in the decider in Brisbane. That game was the final pool game of the 1992 World Cup and just over three months later there would be a rematch at Wembley when Reilly was able to name what is widely regarded as the finest British side since 1970: Lydon, Hunte, Connolly, Schofield, Offiah, Edwards, Fox, Ward, Dermott, Platt, Betts, Clarke, Hanley.

Yet again it just wasn't quite enough. More than 70,000 British fans held their collective breath as an epic struggle was played out. The match was decided by Steve Renouf's try in the second half. One missed tackle by substitute John Devereux one too many in this most compelling of battles. It was wonderful theatre and an Ashes battle, as it was designed to be, on a knife edge.

In 1994, Meninga again led Australia back from 1-0 down in the Ashes thanks to a stellar supporting cast which included Laurie Daley, Ricky Stuart, Bradley Clyde and Brad Fittler. If anyone expected the Kangaroos to take their foot off the gas, they just did not understand Australian rugby league. It is, after all, the Australian national sport and was always going to attract more than its fair share of top athletes. In the UK, soccer's pre-eminence and financial muscle means that those talented in both sports are likely to choose the round-ball game. Ryan Giggs was one who had that decision to make but how was he ever going to turn down Sir Alex Ferguson?

Meninga's influence would continue to be felt in retirement. He supported Rupert Murdoch's Super League in the two-year battle with Kerry Packer-backed competition, which would eventually lead to the creation of the NRL in 1997. The same year Meninga took over as coach of Canberra Raiders, who he had served with such distinction as a player.

That was also the year in which his fellow Invincible John Muggleton switched codes after four years as assistant with North

Sydney Bears. The former Parramatta forward would lead his own revolution. He was the first defensive coach to be appointed by an international rugby union team and all that he had learned under Gibson and Monie was brought to bear as the Wallabies won the 1999 World Cup without conceding a try in the knockout stages.

Muggleton's influence was universally recognised. Meanwhile, Larder had already joined Clive Woodward's England set-up. In 2001 he was also part of Graham Henry's British Lions management team and, on his return from the tour of Australia, was bombarded with requests to recommend defensive coaches with a rugby league background. This led to Mike Ford going to Ireland, Clive Griffiths to Wales and Dave Ellis to France.

When Henry went back to New Zealand in 2004 he became head coach but his remit included overseeing defence. He used the 'iron curtain' system Larder had introduced him to three years earlier. As Richie McCaw lifted the World Cup for New Zealand in 2011 – it was Henry's last act as coach – he did so having co-ordinated a defensive pattern that had its roots in all Larder had gleaned from Gibson and Stanton. It was a fitting tribute to a small group of men who were decades ahead of their time.

But the influence and fallout from the Invincibles' era was much more than that. More than anything the team's legacy is British rugby league. The game would, of course, have evolved in the 80s and 90s even if the Invincibles had never existed. They just made sure it developed in a very specific direction and at a much quicker pace. The end of the committee systems, coaches picking their teams, the flood of foreign players, the influx of foreign coaches, changes in training systems and professionalism all happened in the way it did because of the 1982 Kangaroos.

But the greatest compliment I can pay them is to point out that when you revisit all that grainy footage of Frank Stanton's side you could be watching an expansive, stellar modern-day outfit.

Unlike every other sport I can think of, nothing has been lost in the intervening decades.

Their brilliance shines now with just as much clarity as it did then.

And so it will forever.

Match Statistics

5 October 1982
Hull KR 10, Australia 30
Australia: 1 Brentnall, 2 Grothe, 3 Meninga, 4 Rogers, 5 Ribot (Lewis), 6 Kenny, 7 Sterling, 8 Young, 9 Krilich, 10 Morris (Muggleton), 11 Boyd, 12 Reddy, 13 Price.
Tries: Sterling (2), Young, Rogers, Lewis, Meninga. Goals: Meninga (6)
Hull KR: 1 Fairbairn, 2 Hubbard, 3 M. Smith, 4 Robinson, 5 Clark, 6 Hartley, 7 Walsh, 8 Holdstock (Lowe), 9 Watkinson, 10 Crooks, 11 Burton, 12 Kelly, 13 Prohm.
Tries: Hartley, Prohm. Goals: Fairbairn (2)
Referee: Fred Lindop (Wakefield)
Attendance: 10,742.

13 October
Wigan 9, Australia 13
Australia: 1 Schubert, 2 Anderson (Rogers), 3 Ella, 4 Miles, 5 Boustead, 6 Lewis, 7 Mortimer, 8 McKinnon, 9 Brown, 10 Hancock, 11 McCabe, 12 Muggleton (Price), 13 Pearce.
Tries: McCabe, Muggleton, Boustead. Goals: Ella (2)
Wigan: 1 Williams, 2 Ramsdale, 3 Stephenson, 4 Whitfield, 5 Hill, 6 Foy (Fairhurst), 7 Stephens, 8 Bamber (Campbell), 9 Kiss, 10 Shaw, 11 Juliff, 12 Scott, 13 Pendlebury.
Tries: Gill. Goals: Whitfield (3)
Referee: Gerry Kershaw (York)
Attendance: 12,158.

15 October
Barrow 2, Australia 29
Australia: 1 Schubert, 2 Anderson, 3 Ella, 4 Miles, 5 Ribot, 6 Lewis, 7 Murray, 8 Hancock (Brown), 9 Conescu, 10 Morris, 11 Boyd (Rogers),

12 Reddy, 13 Pearce.
Tries: Schubert (2), Conescu, Pearce, Murray, Ella, Rogers. Goals: Lewis (3), Rogers
Barrow: 1 Tickle, 2 Bentley, 3 O'Regan, 4 McConnell, 5 James, 6 Mason, 7 Cairns, 8 Gee, 9 Wall, 10 Flynn, 11 Gillespie (Herbert), 12 Szymala, 13 Hadley.
Goal: Tickle
Referee: Derek Fox (Wakefield)
Attendance: 6,282.

17 October
St Helens 0, Australia 32
Australia: 1 Brentnall, 2 Boustead, 3 Meninga, 4 Rogers, 5 Grothe, 6 Kenny, 7 Sterling, 8 Young, 9 Krilich, 10 Boyd (Lewis), 11 Pearce, 12 Muggleton, 13 Price (Morris).
Tries: Boustead (2), Grothe (2), Boyd (2), Rogers, Sterling. Goals: Meninga (4)
St Helens: 1 Griffiths (Smith), 2 Ledger, 3 Arkwright, 4 Fairclough, 5 Litherland, 6 Peters, 7 Holding, 8 James, 9 Glover, 10 Gelling (Brownhill), 11 Mathias, 12 Forber, 13 Platt.
Referee: Robin Whitfield (Widnes)
Attendance: 8,190.

20 October
Leeds 4, Australia 31
Australia: 1 Brentnall, 2 Boustead, 3 Meninga, 4 Rogers, 5 Grothe, 6 Kenny, 7 Sterling (Ella), 8 Young, 9 Krilich, 10 Boyd (Morris), 11 McCabe, 12 Muggleton, 13 Pearce.
Tries: Meninga (2), Ella (2), Rogers, Boustead, Grothe. Goals: Meninga (5)
Leeds: 1 Hague, 2 Alan Smith (Massa), 3 Wilkinson, 4 Dyl, 5 Andrew Smith, 6 Holmes, 7 Conway, 8 Dickinson, 9 Ward, 10 Burke, 11 Rayne (Sykes), 12 W. Heron, 13 D. Heron.
Goals: Conway (2)
Referee: Billy Thompson (Huddersfield)
Attendance: 11,570.

24 October (Ninian Park, Cardiff)
Wales 7, Australia 37
Australia: 1 Ella (Boustead), 2 Anderson, 3 Lewis, 4 Miles, 5 Ribot, 6 Murray, 7 Mortimer, 8 McKinnon, 9 Brown, 10 Morris (Conescu), 11 McCabe, 12 Reddy, 13 Schubert.
Tries: Ella (4), Ribot (2), Murray, McKinnon, Lewis. Goals: Lewis (4), McKinnon

Wales: Hopkins (Workington), Camilieri (Widnes), Fenwick (Cardiff City), Bevan (Warrington), Prendiville (Hull), Hallett (Cardiff City), Williams (Cardiff City), Shaw (Wigan), Parry (Blackpool), David (Cardiff City), Herman (Fulham), Juliff (Wigan), Ringer (Cardiff City). Substitution: McJennett (Salford) for David.
Tries: Williams. Goals: Hopkins, Fenwick
Referee: Gerry Kershaw (York)
Attendance: 5,617.

30 October
FIRST TEST (Boothferry Park, Hull)
Great Britain 4, Australia 40
Great Britain: 1 Fairbairn, 2 Drummond, 3 Hughes, 4 Dyl, 5 Evans, 6 Woods, 7 Nash, 8 Grayshon, 9 Ward, 10 Skerrett, 11 Gorley, 12 Crooks (Heron), 13 Norton.
Goals: Crooks (2)
Australia: 1 Brentnall, 2 Boustead, 3 Meninga, 4 Rogers, 5 Grothe, 6 Kenny, 7 Sterling, 8 Young, 9 Krilich, 10 Boyd, 11 Pearce, 12 Reddy, 13 Price.
Tries: Boustead, Boyd, Grothe, Kenny, Meninga, Pearce, Price, Reddy.
Goals: Meninga (8)
Referee: Julien Rascagneres (France)
Attendance: 26,771
Gate receipts: £65,254.

3 November
Leigh 4, Australia 44
Australia: 1 Ella, 2 Anderson, 3 Meninga, 4 Miles, 5 Ribot, 6 Lewis, 7 Mortimer, 8 McKinnon, 9 Brown, 10 Morris, 11 McCabe, 12 Muggleton, 13 Schubert.
Tries: McCabe (3), Ribot (3), Anderson (3), Muggleton (2), Lewis. Goals: Meninga (3), Lewis
Leigh: 1 Hogan (Tomlinson), 2 Drummond, 3 Henderson, 4 Donlan, 5 Worgan, 6 Woods, 7 Green, 8 Wilkinson, 9 Tabern, 10 Pyke, 11 Chisnall (Hunter), 12 Clarkson, 13 Potter.
Goals: Potter (2)
Referee: Trevor Court (Leeds)
Attendance: 7,680.

7 November
Bradford 6, Australia 13
Australia: 1 Brentnall, 2 Anderson, 3 Miles, 4 Rogers, 5 Grothe, 6 Kenny, 7 Murray, 8 Young, 9 Conescu (Brown), 10 Hancock, 11 Reddy, 12 McCabe, 13 Price.

Tries: McCabe, Brentnall, Miles. Goals: Rogers (2)
Bradford: 1 Green, 2 Barends, 3 Mumby, 4 Davies, 5 Pullen, 6 Kells (Carroll), 7 Alan Redfearn, 8 Grayshon, 9 Noble, 10 Van Bellen, 11 Idle, 12 Jasiewicz (Parrott), 13 Rathbone.
Goals: Mumby (3)
Referee: Mick Beaumont (Huddersfield)
Attendance: 10,506.

9 November (Brunton Park, Carlisle)
Cumbria 2, Australia 41
Australia: 1, Brentnall, 2 Boustead, 3 Meninga, 4 Ella, 5 Ribot, 6 Lewis, 7 Sterling (Rogers), 8 McKinnon, 9 Krilich (Price), 10 Hancock, 11 Muggleton, 12 Schubert, 13 Pearce.
Tries: Ribot (2), Meninga, Ella, Boustead, Sterling, McKinnon, Pearce, Rogers. Goals: Meninga (7)
Cumbria: Hopkins (Workington), Mackie (Whitehaven), D. Bell (Carlisle), McConnell (Barrow), Moore (Barrow), Mason (Barrow), Cairns (Barrow), Herbert (Barrow), McCurrie (Oldham), Flynn (Barrow) W. Pattinson (Workington), P. Gorley (St Helens), Hadley (Barrow). Subs: Beck (Workington) for Mason, Hartley (Workington) for Pattinson.
Goal: Hopkins
Referee: Stan Wall (Leigh)
Attendance: 5,748.

14 November
Fulham 5, Australia 22
Australia: 1 Ella, 2 Anderson, 3 Miles, 4 Lewis, 5, Ribot, 6 Murray, 7 Mortimer, 8 McKinnon, 9 Brown (Conescu), 10 Boyd, 11 McCabe, 12 Muggleton, 13 Schubert.
Tries: Murray, Ella, McCabe, Muggleton, McKinnon, Ribot. Goals: Lewis, Ella
Fulham: 1 Eckersley, 2 Cambriani, 3 Allen, 4 Diamond, 5 M'Barki, 6 Crossley, 7 Bowden, 8 Beverley, 9 Dalgreen, 10 Gourley, 11 Herdman, 12 Souto, 13 Doherty (Tuffs).
Tries: M'Barki. Goals: Diamond
Referee: Billy Thompson
Attendance: 10,432.

16 November
Hull 7, Australia 13
Australia: 1 Brentnall, 2 Boustead, 3 Meninga, 4 Rogers, 5 Grothe, 6 Kenny, 7 Sterling, 8 Young, 9 Krilich, 10 Boyd, 11 Pearce, 12 Reddy, 13 Price.

Tries: Grothe (2), Boustead. Goals: Meninga (2)
Hull: 1 Kemble, 2 O'Hara, 3 Evans, 4 Leuluai (Banks), 5 Prendiville, 6 Topliss, 7 Dean, 8 Harrison (Sutton), 9 Bridges, 10 Rose, 11 Proctor, 12 Crooks, 13 Crane.
Tries: Topliss. Goals: Crooks (2)
Referee: John Holdsworth (Leeds)
Attendance: 16,049.

20 November
SECOND TEST (Central Park, Wigan)
Great Britain 6, Australia 27
Great Britain: 1 Mumby, 2 Drummond, 3 Smith, 4 Stephenson, 5 Gill, 6 Woods (Holmes), 7 Kelly, 8 Grayshon, 9 Dalgreen, 10 Skerrett, 11 Eccles, 12 Burton (Rathbone), 13 Heron.
Goals: Mumby (3)
Australia: 1 Brentnall, 2 Boustead, 3 Meninga, 4 Rogers, 5 Grothe (Lewis), 6 Kenny, 7 Sterling, 8 Young, 9 Krilich, 10 Boyd, 11 Pearce, 12 Reddy (Brown), 13 Price.
Tries: Price, Sterling, Grothe, Meninga, Rogers. Goals: Meninga (6)
Referee: Julien Rascagneres (France)
Attendance: 23,216.

23 November
Widnes 6, Australia 19
Australia: 1 Ella, 2 Anderson, 3 Meninga, 4 Rogers, 5 Ribot, 6 Lewis (Murray), 7 Mortimer, 8 Young (Muggleton), 9 Brown, 10 Morris, 11 Boyd, 12 McCabe, 13 Schubert.
Tries: Mortimer (2), McCabe, Ribot, Rogers. Goals: Meninga (2)
Widnes: 1 Burke, 2 Basnett, 3 Lydon (J. Myler), 4 O'Loughlin, 5 Camilieri, 6 Gregory, 7 Hulme, 8 Tamati, 9 Elwell, 10 S. O'Neill, 11 Newton, 12 Prescott, 13 A Myler.
Referee: John McDonald (Wigan)
Attendance: 9,790.

28 November
THIRD TEST (Headingley, Leeds)
Great Britain 8, Australia 32
Great Britain: 1 Fairbain, 2 Drummond, 3 Stephenson, 4 M. Smith, 5 Evans, 6 Topliss, 7 Gregory, 8 O'Neill (Courtney), 9 Noble, 10 Rose, 11 P. Smith, 12 Crooks, 13 Crane.
Try: Evans. Goals: Crooks (2). Drop goal: Crooks
Australia: 1 Brentnall, 2 Boustead, 3 Meninga, 4 Rogers, 5 Ribot (Lewis),

6 Kenny, 7 Sterling, 8 Boyd (Brown), 9 Krilich, 10 Morris, 11 McCabe, 12 Reddy, 13 Pearce.
Tries: Price, Sterling, Grothe, Meninga, Rogers. Goals: Meninga (6)
Referee: Julien Rascagneres (France)
Attendance: 17,318
Receipts: £41,150.

Australian appearances in Great Britain

	Apps	Tries	Goals	Pts
Anderson	7	3	-	9
Boustead	8(1)	8	-	24
Boyd	10	3	-	9
Brentnall	9	1	-	3
Brown	5(4)	1	-	-
Conescu	2(3)	1	-	3
Ella	7(1)	9	3	33
Grothe	7	7	-	21
Hancock	4	-	-	-
Kenny	8	2	-	6
Krilich	8	1	-	3
Lewis	7(5)	3	9	27
McCabe	8	7	-	21
McKinnon	5	3	1	11
Meninga	10	6	50	118
Miles	6	1	-	3
Morris	6(2)	-	-	-
Mortimer	5	2	-	6
Muggleton	6(2)	4	-	12
Murray	4(1)	3	-	9
Pearce	9	4	-	12
Price	6(2)	2	-	6
Reddy	8	1	-	3
Rogers	9(3)	8	3	30
Ribot	8	10	-	30
Schubert	7	2	-	6
Sterling	8	5	-	15
Young	8	1	-	3